THE TIBETAN TANTRA

FRONTISPIECE

Rare Tibetan tanka, now one of the last of its kind, acquired near the Indo-Tibetan Border by the editor in 1956.

ESOTERIC TEACHINGS OF THE TIBETAN TANTRA

INCLUDING
SEVEN INITIATION RITUALS
AND THE SIX YOGAS OF NĀROPĀ
IN TSONG-KHA-PA'S COMMENTARY,
TRANSLATED BY CHANG CHEN CHI,
FORMER LECTURER AT
THE KONG-KA LAMASERY,
MEINYA, EAST TIBET

Edited by

C.A. MUSES, M.A., Ph.D.

SAMUEL WEISER, INC.
York Beach, Maine

First published in hardcover 1961 by
The Falcon's Wing Press

Copyright © C.A. Muses, 1961

First paperback edition 1982 by
Samuel Weiser, Inc.
P.O. Box 612
York Beach, Maine 03910

ISBN 0-87728-307-9

Printed in the U.S.A.

CONTENTS

CONTENTS *(Concluded)*

PLATES: *Frontispiece* (in color)   III: (Part I, ch. 7)
           I: (Part I, ch. 2)   IV: (Part II, ch. 1)
          II: (Part I, ch. 6)   V: (Part II, ch. 5)

Introduction

Steady and increasing demand for authentic teachings of the now virtually lost culture of Tibet has led to this second and revised edition, timely because of the growing interest in these matters, and with good reason: the fundamental esoteric basis of all religions has to do with higher, nonordinary states of consciousness leading to beatitudes and powers of our hidden potential as gods in embryo—not a mere figure of speech.

The editor is grateful still to the translator he chose to do this important rendition some years ago when Professor Chen Chi Chang had just begun to work on his English translation of Milarepa's songs. Professor Chang is well versed in the reading of the cursive Tibetan script of the editor's rare and richly illustrated Nyingma initiation manuscript (much of which is still untranslated) and, moreover, has a first-hand grasp of Tibetan Buddhist terminology gained during his experience at the Kong-ka lamasery in East Tibet before its conquest by Maoist armies in the 1950s.

The rendition is on the whole literal; yet the translator, a devout Buddhist, sometimes tended to interpretations that the editor felt required some broadening and deepening, especially for the non-doctrinaire and open-minded reader. Such indications have been provided in editorial notes and there is no need for further detail here. The second half of this volume is a translation of a penetrating work of the great Gelug-Kajü* commentator Tsong-khapa (born in 1355) from an original in the Library of Congress.

Buddhism in Western translations and in assorted missionary movements from the Orient has suffered from two principal defects. First, it has been offered too often to "unawakened Westerners" much as the Christian missionaries offered Christianity to "unawakened savages." Intolerant and patronizing proselytism is always an intellectual and spiritual affront to human dignity, especially that sort which says, "Only we have the truth. You must come to our institute or join our circle of disciples to

---

*The Kajü or Kargyu (Tibetan spelling *bka'-brgyud*) sect—"The Lineage of the Proclamation"—was founded by Gampopa about 1100 C.E. An offshot was the Gelug (Tibetan *dGe-lugs*) sect founded by Tsongkhapa c. 1400.

learn it." But truth is the monopoly of no person or group of people. It permeates all religions in their inner, noetic aspect. As Ramakrishna demonstrated by his own experience, the bliss attained by sincere following of Buddhist, Christian, Hindu, or Sufi teachings is indeed the same bliss. There are many doors to the room of that blessed state and it is time for men to stop squabbling *outside* the doors as to the merits of a particular door, but rather to walk into the room itself and begin to live anew.

The second obstruction to the full benefit of esoteric or tantric Buddhist teachings in the West has been the misguided attempts of merely book-learned scholars to dominate the field and portray it in over-intellectualized and too narrowly dogmatic terms. The essence of tantric and esoteric Buddhism lies in the heart and not in the wordy mind. Nor does it lie in the exaggerated detail of some of its visual imagery. True meditation and contemplation do not consist in imagery but in a serene, primarily *affective* and *non*imagistic state in which noetic power flows and is distributed to the entire being.

Some years ago in *East-West Fire: Schopenhauer's Optimism and the Lankavatara Sutra* (John Watkins, London, 1955) I pointed out that nirvāṇa is no snuffing out but is simply the attaining of an awareness far beyond an ordinary ken, like the apparent blackness of light when it is going away from us and we view it from behind. Those left behind the one who has reached the reality of nirvāṇa see it as emptiness and nothingness, but the one who has attained it knows it as a pleroma, an all-embracing fullness. Let the world of samsāra or ordinary consciousness be symbolized as "1", the nirvāṇa process as zero, and their interaction by the horizontal bar of relationship or division. Then we have $\frac{1}{0} = \infty$ which is true mathematically. For those who wish this written technically, we have $\lim_{n \to 0} 1/n = \infty$. Thus the interpenetration of samsāra by nirvāṇa leads to an infinity of self-realization.

In all this the heart is paramount and, by an esoteric Tibetan pun, the sound *nyingma* can mean "ancient" or "heart" although the two words are spelled differently as "pair" and "pear." Thus the "old teaching" of the finest Nyingma lamaseries was also "the heart teaching." Here "heart" means not only "core-teaching" but love-centered teaching. For love is the master-power in humanity, causing all true intelligence (as opposed to pedantry) and accelerated evolution of the human into the blossoming of nascent divinity as, in Buddhist terms, the ten bodhisattvic stages are passed through until the eleventh stage of full enlightenment. Here is the deepest meaning of the eleven-headed Avalokiteśvara or Chenrezi, the Infinitely Merciful One. It is the attainment of Wise and Powerful Love, culminating in a psychoenergetic "body of light," the vajra or diamond body "that rises phoenix-like from the ashes of the final illusion," as written in our commentary on the Lankavatara Sutra.*

In these considerations also lies the true meaning of the most secret tantric path, in Tibet called the Vajrayāna or Thunderbolt Vehicle. It is secret only because most do not have enough of the intelligent love-will to find and pursue it. For those who place such a level of high desire *first*, however, the precious means (upaya) will mysteriously arise in their lifetimes, and they will be able to tread this path of Love-Will-Wisdom, of Heart, Hand and Head harmoniously joined. But heart or love must rule the other two or wisdom will become unwise and the love-will will deteriorate again into self-will. As we wrote some years ago:

> Set not the Heart on any thing
> Let not the subject rule the King
> Set not the Heart on anything
> But let the Heart grow, laugh and sing.

This is the true tantra, a joining of the vajra-power of Love with the skillful means (upāya) that acts like a fruitful womb to make the intent and inmost spirit of that love manifest to all.

All of us have this divine lineage (gotra) within us. We must simply desire to realize it enough to put it first in our value systems. Then it germinates and blossoms. Reflecting the skillful means (in Hindu tantra called shakti, the realizing, manifesting power) and the semen-like, seeding vajra power (of Shākta or Śiva in Hindu terms) a man and a woman who are a rightly matched pair (yogi-yogini or shakta-shakti) may develop toward nirvāṇa more quickly than either alone. Sometimes such delicately matched pairing is not found by a given person in a given life; then other, though somewhat slower paths remain.

---

*East-West Fire, Watkins, London, 1955, p. 49.

The tantra is not, as often said by oriental writers, primarily for male development using the woman as a mere prop in a rather selfish enterprise. Rather, both partners near divinity through becoming closer in their relationship and they regard each other ever more preciously. Also, there is no contradiction in concept between Hindu and Buddhist tantra as, at times, it has been misleadingly or erroneously said.* On the contrary, since it is based on the very constitution of man and woman both physical and psychical, the true tantric teaching is one and the same process of conjugate metamorphosis, whether expressed in terms that are Babylonian (Ishtar-Tammuz), Buddhist (Prajñā-Vajra), Christian (Sophia-Christos), Egyptian (Isis-Osiris), or Kabbalistic (Shekinah-Ruach).

The merely book-learned who do not know the tantra by experience and devoted contemplation, seek to separate with words instead of livingly describe, and so the blind attempt to lead the blind. But those whose hearts will not let them sell their divine birthright for a mess of word-pottage are the true Children of Horus who can soar, falcon-like (paraphrasing the ancient Pyramid Texts) into the shining skies of the immortals and dwell like the imperishable stars that shall never again set below the horizon of life-in-death. Life unalloyed then is theirs—and a far-reaching

---

*Indeed, the origin of the latter is the former. Well summarizing the situation in her essay on Tantric Buddhist Art (China Institute in America, N.Y., 1974, p. 7), Eleanor Olson wrote that "the roots of Tantric Buddhism are in ancient pre-Buddhist India." They are deeper yet.

In fact, Tantric practice and doctrine stems from the most ancient yoga, dating back to the deific trimūrti figurine, seated in yoga posture, unearthed at digs in the old Indus Valley civilization that was contemporary with Sumer and the beginnings of the Egyptian Old Kingdom. These doctrines and practices, so closely associated with the later Śiva, also find parallels in the ancient Hittite worship centered around a chief god (Teshub) and goddess having respectively bull and lion vehicles.

Finally, as Shashibhusan Dasgupta well notes (*Obscure Religious Cults*, Delhi, 1976, p.116): "The psycho-physiological yogic processes, frequently referred to in the lyrical songs of the Vaiṣṇava Sahajiyās and also the innumerable short and long texts, embodying the doctrines of the cult, are fundamentally the same as are found in the Hindu Tantras as well as in the Buddhist Tantras and the Buddhist songs and Dohās. There are sometimes discrepancies only in details and differences more often pertaining to terminology and phraseology than to conception." Thus Tantra lies deeper doctrinally and is older in time than either Buddhism or Hinduism.

opportunity to help others along whatever way best suits personality make-up and surrounding conditions.

One of the several highlights of this book is the chapter of initiations containing the prophecy of Mi-Gyur-Dorje, a young lama of the seventeenth or eighteenth century. This remarkable prophecy clearly depicts the contemporary age, including the final break-up of Tibet by China. The story of how it came to be included in this book is not without interest.

We had gone over a wide selection of texts in the manuscript and had most of them translated. One day, while idly reading through the Tibetan, my attention was riveted by certain strange phrases in a portion of the manuscript we had not before noticed. Soon it came to the point where I knew this material was vital and I rushed over with it to Chen Chi, who could read it more thoroughly than I, and asked him to lend his opinion. Not long after, he came running to my study and excitedly, happily exclaimed, "It's an important and rare prophecy. We *must* include it!" So we did.

And now our joint blessings on the nameless Way to all who read this book. May the wind of the inner doctrine that underlies the core of every sincere religion be ever at your back, urging you forward in self-realization. May your Love blossom into the profound intelligence that is Wisdom and into the wonderful deeds that are the ultimate Magic. May you find mutually accelerating partners at each stage of growth.

And remember,

> The ageless melody, unheard,
> heals...
> The healing vision, unseen,
> leads...
> The true leaders, unknown,
> rescue.

May you find! For we are embarked on a momentous decade and the time draws nigh, but Love can absorb all shocks and become even greater thereby. Only Love is wise and strong enough for this. Seek, then, to radiate it uncaring as the sun whether your light and warmth be returned or no, so your darkened earth-body shall become an enduring radiant body—as different from what you now are as caterpillar from butterfly.

Finally there remain only some words of good will and caution. We begin by drawing attention to the initial quotation in this book from the *Shes-rab sdong-bu* ("Wisdom Tree") of Nāgārjuna: "Although a man may be book-learned, if he does not apply in his behaviour what he knows, he is as the blind man who even with a lamp in his hand cannot see the road." Thus, Tibetan wisdom itself overthrows what may be called the pedantic illusion which has beset the West. Typically representing it are the types who, in effect, preach the fallacy that by textual and/or linguistic erudition the secrets of the operative meaning of the tantra (Hindu or Tibetan) are gained. Neither is that meaning gained by garish dislays of ecclesiastical pomp or titles, Western or Eastern.

Nothing could be wider of the mark. It is only through practice in actual relationships between the aspirants—the yogi and yogini, shakta and shakti, vajra and prajñā—that the effective knowledge, the distilled wisdom of truly loving experience, is gained. Note that we do *not* (as do some unfortunately male-centered writers and later corrupted texts) speak of "the yogi and his shakti" or of his seeking "a suitable prajñā," as if the female partner were simply a necessary object or device for the principal benefit of the male's development. On the contrary, she is as much a person as he is and her development is of equal and *complementary* importance.

The previous fallacy is often compounded with a pedantic insistence (mostly on the part of those wishing to de-emphasize the dependence of Tibetan on Hindu tantra) upon the "separateness" or "substantive difference" between Buddhist and Hindu tantra and hence yoga. Aside from the fact that Hindu tantra stresses the fierce forms (Kali/Durga-like) of the Goddess rather than the gentle forms (Parvati/Tara) stressed in Tibetan Buddhist tantra, there is no fundamental doctrinal difference in the actual esoteric sexual practice which is the heart of all tantra.

Concomitantly, Hindu tantra stresses the mild and passive form of the god (the passive, supportive, poison-absorbing Śiva) rather than his active, and even fierce, form as the Thunderbolt Power (vajra- and yang-like) and powerful skillful means (upaya). But the Hindu (non-Buddhist) and Tibetan (Buddhist) tantra *both* include fierce and gentle forms of *both* God and Goddess.

Finally, the sexual imagery of the most ancient and authentic tantra is not mere effete allegory but is quite pragmatically operational and effective, being guided by the all-powerful love-energy field generated between rightly matched partners. And the oldest doctrine did not teach the slavish fear of sperm-ejaculation any more than a woman should be afraid of losing ova monthly. *Thig-le* in esoteric Tibetan can refer to basic sexual energy or kundalini rather than merely to male semen. That energy is noetic, i.e. stemming from the nature of consciousness and its transformations; the physical results are simply *effects*.

It is noetic energy that the practical tantra builds, focuses and equilibrates, leading to its blossoming in terms of a higher energy body actually transcending physical death and rising above its ordinary foetal-like condition that characterizes the bardo state of most between incarnations. Thus tantra providing the most direct and powerful key for circumventing such hold-over states and achieving the fullest possible acceleration of higher human evolution, whether during states preceding or following upon the dissolution of the physical body.

I have a postscript for you. There is an old Mongolian proverb that used to be far more spoken—and lived—on the vast Central Asian steppes than it is now. The words are:

> *Tegüncilen kü cinar-tur*
> *adsu setkil ügei samadhi.*

Actually this is a free Mongolian translation from the Sanskrit treatise *Tathābhāvā citta samādhi*. More importantly, it means:

> The samādhi (bliss or deep serenity) which
> persists in you without any intellectual activity
> and throughout all daily changes of consciousness—
> that indeed is the true samādhi
> or result of meditation.

This was considered the most sacred samādhi by the wisest Mongolian lamas. They chose well.

C. Musès, M.A., Ph.D.
Santa Barbara, California
September 1981

Although a man may be book-learned,
  If he does not apply in his behaviour
    what he knows,
He is as the blind man
  who even with a lamp in his hand
Cannot see the road.

Stanza 169 of the
Shes-rab sdong-bu ("Tree of Wisdom")
of Nāgārjuna, *ca.* 100 B.C.

PART I

SEVEN INITIATION RITUALS
OF THE
TIBETAN TANTRA

CHAPTER ONE

THE INITIATION RITUAL
OF THE FIERCE GURU

From the Treasury of Consciousness[1] of the Heavenly Dharma, and among the profound Teachings of the Whisper Succession, this is the Initiation of the Fierce Guru, the most secret of the secret, the Four Inner Teachings condensed in one initiation ritual.

All the practice of the Initiation of the Fierce Guru (Padmasambhava) can be summarized into three performances.

(The preparations for the initiation by the guru:)
Instantaneously one's self becomes the Fierce Guru,
Red in color, with one face and two arms.
In his right hand, he holds a vajra,
And in his left, he holds a scorpion[2].
At the five parts of his body[3] stand the five deities in
    armor.
Upon the crown of his head there is a Garuda bird, the
    king of all creatures.
His right arm embraces the Great Red Mother,
And he sits on the cushion of the Sun-Lotus, which is
    covered with the corpse of a demon.
From the three places[4] of the Father and Mother Buddha
Shine forth infinite rays of light,
After they have shone on all sentient beings and blessed
    them,
They invite the Wisdom Buddha to come down from
    above,

And all merge with him; thus the guru attains the Initiation.

Oṃ Ah Tsiga Nitsi Namobigawadi Hūṃ Au Hūṃ Pai!*

The Front Arising Buddha [so named because arising through the power of the Ritual Vase in front of the candidate], the Fierce Guru, red in color,

Has one face and two arms.

In his right hand is the vajra, in his left the scorpion.

All the wrathful adornments are complete on him.

At the five places are fixed five Skull-Rosary Holders of the Fierce Buddha[5];

And in his heart-center stand the five gods with armor bright.

On the top of his head stands a Garuda bird, the king of all creatures.

In his arms, he holds the Red Mother.

He is the only director of the four inheritances[6], the wrathful one.

In all the corners and directions stand the ten wrathful ones.

In the four directions are manifest the Four Great Kings.

In his heart-center appears a thunderbolt-grasping Buddha,

Also holding the Heavenly-Iron-Made wheel of many spokes.

From the center of the wheel shines the red word *Hūm*.

The main incantation encircles the *Hūm* word.

The seeds of the retinue deities, together with the red *Hūm* word,

---

* "In the name of the Lord." This expression, in varying states of orthographical corruption, occurs throughout the mantric liturgies of the MS. *Ed.*

Radiate the great beams of light which invite the initiation Buddhas to descend.

For this one should render offerings, obeisance, and praise.

Om Ah Tsi Ne Tsi Name Babawadi Hūm Ah Pai, Ba-tsa Hūm Yauga Hūm!

(And then repeat the foregoing prayer once more.)

The Front Arising Buddha... [A gap in the manuscript here.]

All the grace and blessing of the Buddhas are embodied in the Front Vase [which helps concentrate the power of the Gtor-ma as a Leyden-jar type of receptacle].

Om Ah Hūm Ahtsi Gani Gana moBagawadi Hūm Pai.

Au Hūm Pai

The Gtor-ma instantaneously becomes the Fierce Guru,
With three faces and six arms.

The right face is white, the left blue.

Beneath is the curved knife, the skull and blood.

The vajra and the scorpion are in the two lower arms;
In his hands, he also holds the sword and the stick.

His body glows red as the burning flame.

The Six Ornaments adorn him.

He stretches one foot and bends the other;
The two feet are spread wide apart.

The five Lotus-born deities remain at the five places.

His left arm hugs the Blue Mother-Buddha.

From her heart the seed-word radiates beams of light,
Through which the Wisdom Buddha is invited to descend.

Om Ah Hūm Hre Ahtsi Nitsi Ganamobagawadi Hūm Hūm Pai Ah Hūm Hūm Pai. Ba-tsa Hūm Yagha Hūm Ragsha Hūm.

(Toward the Front Vase and Gtor-ma one should practice the initiation incantation, repeating as aforesaid. Perform the eight offerings[7].)

Oṃ Ah Hūṃ Guru Dasasariwa Ra Ahmarda Banemta Gagta Kahe Ah Gm...

Hūṃ! Subdue all beings in the Three Kingdoms.

He is the Vajra, Victor over female demons, the Bhagavad,

Standing in a black-red blazing flame.

He has three eyes, wide open, angry!

His two feet, far apart as in running, trample the corpse of the female demon;

To the scorpion holder, the Fierce Guru, I render obeisance and praise.

(Then the disciples perform the Cleansing Ritual[8] and the Mandala Offering.)

Now, I am going to relate to you a brief history of this initiation. In the Pure Land of *Aog-*min resided the Buddha All-Perfect[9] with the five Divisional Buddhas and infinite Bodhisattvas encircling him. Before Bodhisattva Avalokiteshvara, Buddha All-Perfect urged Buddha Amida to preach the *Tantra of the Fierce Guru,* called the *Origin of the Light,* and to preach also the *Tantra of Expelling the Spirit of the Prideful One.* Immediately all the devils of disease, non-men demons, and MaSran demons became fiercely angry. They raised the Eight-Divisional Demonic Forces as a sweeping storm. Thereupon Bodhisattva Avalokiteshvara went before the Lotus-Born Guru (Padmasambhava) and urged him, saying:

"This is the time to subdue the Eight Divisions of Demons in this world. This is the time for you the Fierce Guru to display your miracle powers."

Thereupon the Lotus-Born transformed himself into the body of the Fierce Guru. (He cried:)

"*Shri!* This is the roaring voice of the Great Powerful One!

I now conquer you, the Eight-Divisional Demons!" [i.e. the demons of the eight divisions of space.]

(By his saying this all demons were conquered.)

"After the subjugation – *Samaya Hūṃ Pai!*"

(Thus the demons were commanded to observe the precepts.)

"I am the combined body of all Buddhas, the Wrathful One!

Who else is more powerful than I?

All the potentialities of the Tathagatas converge in me.

I am the most powerful of the forceful ones.

What I desire is the hearts of the Eight-Divisional Demons!

What I like to eat and drink is their flesh and blood!"

With fiery anger he wrenched out the hearts of all the Eight-Divisional Demons, and crushed them on the plain. Afterward he revived them and said:

"When hungry I am the being who eats the flesh of the male demons. When thirsty, I drink the blood of the she-demons. When active, I tear the double-sexed demons to pieces."

After saying this, he ate all the hearts of the Eight Divisional Demons who had committed sinful deeds. At the time of eclipse, he collected all the sinful flesh and blood of the demons into a huge heap as a sacrificial food to benefit the scorpions[10] and ate them all. Thereupon, the Eight-Divisional Demons called for help and begged for forgiveness. Then he agreed that at every eclipse time he would provide blood and flesh to the Eight-Divisional demons in the Three Regions, and thereby prohibited them from killing sentient beings. In order to prevent them from further slaughter, he gave them the Krum Ga [11], the Chief Mandala's food [Note the personification of the mandala]. Whoever among the demons should break the rules, he declared, would be punished and offered as sacrificial food to the numerous scorpions.

Thereupon, all demons assembled together to witness the flesh-adornment. Those who had broken the rules were sent as sacrificial food to the scorpions. The offenders all cried and begged for mercy, but to no avail. They became frenzied and howled loudly; but they had no choice but to walk toward their destiny. The Eight-Divisional Demons then brought the moonlight, presented it to the fire by holding Dagiratsa fast, and then offered it to the Krum-Ga Principal Mandala as sacrificial food to the assembly [12].

At the Four Relative Times [13], the Eight-Divisional Demons all assembled together by order of the Wrathful One. The Wrathful One then asked:

"Who has committed sinful deeds? Who has afflicted the sentient beings? Who has troubled the servants of Buddhist temples? Who has offended the precepts? Who has violated my rules?"

He then looked at the faces of the demons; those who had cheated him, he tore apart. He uttered the Main Incantation [14] of Hayagriva [15] and wielded his mental power of Thunderbolt Holder (Vajrahetu) to cut the demons into pieces and to put all the demons who had damaged the Buddhist religion into the Fire Sacrifice as an offering to be burned. The troublemakers and those who had impeded the cause of Dharma – these he made living sacrificial food

for the scorpions. As for all those who afflicted the servants
of the temple, he used his Wheel to cut them up and his
weapons to chop them into pieces. All the sinful demons
who had harmed sentient beings became food for the scorpions. Thus he subdued all the Eight Divisions of Demons.
He bound them to the precepts, admonished them not to
harm any Buddhist and not to incite any kind of trouble.
He also ordered them to assist the servants of the temples:
on the tenth of every month, they should come before the
Fierce Guru and attend the Congregation of the Sacred
Offering [16], help to set in motion the Wheel of Dharma;
and for the benefit of sentient beings they should fight
against those demons who make harm.

The Fierce Guru then said:

"Oh! you pitiful demons! Now, I safeguard you.

Though you are the lokas of Ghost,

Eventually you will all become the Great Blissful Body;

You will all become the perfect Buddha."

This is stated in the *Tantra of the Blood-Drinking Wrathful One, Drag-b'o-g'rag-atung-rol-b'ah-rgyud.* Though there
are many different Treasures [sacred or revealed books]
and lineages of the teaching of the Fierce Guru, this one
belongs to the Whisper Succession of the Heavenly
Dharma Treasury.

As said in the *Sutra of the Fountain of the Noble Dharma:*

"The Bodhisattvas, the perfect Bodhisattvas, are able to
procure abundant hidden teachings from the walls, woods,
caves, and from Heaven Circles, even at a time when Buddha is no longer in the world."

The Incarnation of Buddha [in the Tibetan youth] Mi-
gyur-rdo-rje was a demon-subduer; this was prophesied in
many Treasury Dharmas. When he was thirteen years old,

in the Black month of the Fowl year, he saw the Fierce Guru appear in the forest many times. The Fierce Guru himself conferred the Tantra instructions and practice, together with the various teachings necessary to the Incarnation of Buddha. Therefore this teaching has the advantage of being a near-succession one [17] and of possessing an unusual benevolent power (grace). In comparison with other teachings, the teaching of the Fierce Guru is an easier and faster way to attain the Siddhis (yogic accomplishments) and Signs [18], as said in the *Tantra of the Fierce Act* (*Drag-b'o-prang-lashi-rgyud*):

"This teaching is greater than others; the Accomplishments and Signs are also greater. If one practices this teaching for seven days, no doubt he will attain both the Common and Superior Accomplishments [19]."

If one recites ten thousand times the Main Incantations' Inner Narration, he will be immune from sickness; if one recites it only one hundred times, he will subdue the Ghost [20]; if one recites it two hundred thousand times, he will become a gem-like *Brgyal-bseng,* enlightened Master. For those well-gifted ones, only one hundred recitations will bring all the Eight Kinds of Demons to bow before them; they shall wear the war dress and subjugate all evils; they shall have faith and practice devotions continually. These various accomplishments are pledged as stated in the aforementioned Tantra.

It is also stated in this same Tantra:

"One who practices this teaching shall attain both Common and Super-Accomplishments. He shall become a Gem-like person as Padmasambhava."

In the Fierce Instruction, Padmasambhava said:

"If one continously recites the incantation, his sins will

gradually be cleansed and his obstacles removed; he shall never separate from his Guru; the Buddhas in the Three Times will assemble around him like the gathering clouds; the devas and angels will all circle around him. His power will be great enough to spellbind the ghosts and demons; the Eight Kinds of Demons will serve him as slaves; the ocean-like Guards of Dharma (Samaya-Holders) will give him the knowledge of things to come, and also will instruct him and preach to him. They will also tell him both the good and bad outcomes. All the ghosts and spirits will become his messengers. He can destroy his enemies and conquer hindrances if he wishes. With one thought he can subjugate heretics. His accomplishments are beyond measure and words. In the future life he will be born in the Pure Land of *Ao*-rgyng (the Pure Land of Padmasambhava). The Father and Mother Guru will protect him as their own son. The merits of this teaching are indeed inconceivable. As from all directions the clouds gather, the rain of accomplishments will fall upon him. Is there any teaching more profound than this? To subjugate the enemy, this is the sharpest; to annihilate obstacles, this is the quickest. It is the nearest way to accomplishments; the precepts are easier. The preparations for offering are simple, the power is great, and the merits are many.

"If one possesses this treasure, the devas and ghosts will offer him their lives and hearts. He will influence and charm people; his merits [21] will become great; prosperity and good omens always follow him; all his wishes will be granted; the signs of Siddhis and performance [22] will come fast; his power will be as great as Herugas [23], great enough to subdue the male and female spirits. The accomplishment is easier and the incantation more effective. There is no question about the profoundness of this teaching; even those evil-possessed monks who practice this teaching will [overcome themselves and attain the accomplishment of Mahamudra[24]. Such a profound teaching one can hardly find anywhere else. If you do not believe what I say, you may look for yourself.

"Hard it is to find an easy yet powerful teaching like this! Hard it is to find an immaculate teaching like this! Hard it is to find a teaching without a defect; one which can bestow the transcendental accomplishments and bring forth the great powers. This teaching is the treasury of both the mundane and transcendental accomplishments; it is a teaching for those easy-going, leisure-pursuing seekers who are lovers of pleasure. It is a teaching and practice for lustful seekers; and also for those who have compassion and yearnings for serving sentient beings; for those who want to practice Dharma as well as for those who want power. It is a helpful teaching for lustful and fame-desiring monks to practice; it is also a teaching for faithful and sincere disciples; for congregation-attendants; for unrestrained and passionate yogis to practice; a helpful teaching for credulous and enemy-despising yogis to practice; and also for those people you should consider as brothers in Dharma, the protectors of the Treasury.

"Yet you should spread this teaching with great caution. It should be kept secret from both sinful and Dam Med[25] persons; from sophisticated and foulmouthed persons. This teaching should not be given to skeptical and defamatory persons; it should not be bestowed upon heretical and insincere persons. It should not be given to the thief of Dharma or to those disciples who do not observe the precepts. Keeping this sacred teaching from such persons is a rule you should observe. You should not be idle but should cooperate with your brothers in the Vajrayana[26]." So the Guru says.

Now, to obtain this profound and solemn initiation, you disciples should follow me in reciting the following prayers three times:

"I concentrate my mind and sincerely pray to the Three Pillars[27] and all Buddhas. I pray to the Fierce Guru with his retinues. I pray that you grant me the profound initiation."

Now follow me in reciting the Take-in-Refuge Prayer together with the Vows of Bodhisattva in front of the Fierce Guru and all Buddhas.

"I take refuge in the Three Precious Ones;
I confess all my sins and evil deeds.
I offer my sympathetic joy for all virtues of sentient beings.
I pray the Buddhas and Bodhisattvas to protect me and remember me.
From now until the day of my attainment of Buddha-hood,
I submit myself completely to the care of the Buddhas and Bodhisattvas.
For the sake of benefiting self and others,
I now take the Vow of Bodhisattva.
As a servant I render my service to all sentient beings;
For the good of all beings I hope the day of Enlightenment will come soon!"

(Recite this prayer three times and use the holy grass of the vase to bless the disciples.)

Now you should visualize the Wisdom Buddha and follow my instruction:

Instantaneously the disciples all become the Fierce Guru:

Three faces, six arms; the right face is white, the left blue.
The first two arms hold the curved knife and the human
    skull full of blood;
Below them, the second pair of arms hold the Vajra and
    the scorpion;
The last two arms hold the sword and the rod.
His body is red in color, burning like fire:
Adorned with all the fierce elements he stands,
One foot stretching, the other curved.
In the Beyond-Measure Palace on his head
Sits a white Padmasambhava with one face, and two
    hands holding the iron shackles,
Also adorned with various silk ornaments.
In the center of the Golden Circle in the throat
Sits a red Padmasambhava with one face, and two hands
    holding the iron chain.
In the center of the Weapon Circle in the heart
Sits a purple-brown Padmasambhava with one face, and
    two hands holding a wheel,
With adornments over his body.
In the six-edged center of the Dharma-producing Chakra
    in the navel
Sits a yellow Padmasambhava with one face, his two
    hands holding a rope.
In the center of the black triangle in the secret parts
Sits a green Padmasambhava with one face, and two
    hands holding a curved knife.
His left arm embraces the Mother, green in color with
One face, her two arms holding the curved knife with
    all fierce adornments.
From her heart the seed-word *(Śri)* radiates a great
    light;

The light passes through the southwest direction of
    Rgya-yab-gling (the Pure Land)
And falls upon the body of Padmasambhava, touching
    his heart.
Instantaneously, from the heart of Padmasambhava
    springs a Fierce Guru
With myriads of Outer, Inner, Secret, and Most Secret
    Buddhas [28] around him;
With great roars and sounds of thunder, they all descend
    here,
And, entering your body, they dissolve in you.
Thus should you visualize. Now blow the trumpet and
    play all musical instruments. [Pray thus:]
    play all musical instruments.
"*Hūṃ!* The Outer, Inner, Secret, Most Fierce Gurus,
Pray come down and bless us!
Pray grant the highest Initiation to us, your faithful and
    well-destined disciples;
Pray dispel the evil-persuaders and smash the hindrances
    to longevity.
Oṃ Ah Hūṃ Guru Gorda Sarva Samaya Oṃ Ba-tsa Ah
    We Sha Ya Ah Ah!" (Recite many times.)
"*Di Tsha Ban Tsar!*" (Recite to retain the Buddhas.)
Thus by the grace of the initiation, a pure foundation
(for further advancement) is laid. Now, in order to attain
further initiations, follow me and recite the following
prayers:
"I sincerely pray to the Three Pillars and all Buddhas,
I sincerely pray to the Fierce Guru and his retinues,
I beseech you to grant me the Outer, Inner, Secret, and
    Most Secret Initiations."
In response to this prayer, the Buddhas in front of you

all send forth from their bodies the Outer, Inner, Secret, and Most Secret Fierce Gurus in large and small forms, and they all enter into you and unite with you. Thus should you visualize:

Hūm! This is the Outer Practice, the Outer Fierce Guru: He Has three faces and six arms.

I now put his image on you, on the disciple's head; Thus the initiation of the Fierce Guru is attained by you. *Om Ah Hūm Guru Gorda Ga Ya Ah Bi Di Tsa Hūm!*

Hūm! This is the Inner Practice, the Inner Guru: He has three faces and four arms.

I now put his image on your, the disciple's, head; Thus the initiation of the Fierce Guru is attained by you. *Om Ah Hūm Guru Gorda Ga Ya Ah Bi Di Tsa Hūm!*

Hūm! This is the Most Secret Practice, the Most Secret Fierce Guru:

His two arms embrace the *Yum* [consort], red in color. I now put this image on your, the disciple's, head; Thus the initiation of the Fierce Guru is attained by you. *Om Ah Guru Gorda Ga Ya Ah Bi Di Tsa Hūm!*

(Thereupon throw the flowers.)

Hūm! The conqueror of the Three Kingdoms[29] and demons, the Lord of all Vajras!

He is reddish-black, with his three fierce eyes wide open. He tramples upon the body of a demon with his two feet. May the Fierce Guru and all Buddhas grant us the Blessing!

After attaining the Outer, Inner, Secret, and Most Secret Initiations [the four lower tantric initiations], one should ask for the Initiation of Vase. The disciples are to recite the following prayers:

"I pray the Three Pillars and all Deities;

I pray the Fierce Guru and his retinues;
With sincerity and great yearning
I beg you to grant me the Initiation of Vase."
(The initiating guru holds the Vase in his hand.)
This Vase, in its outer symbolic aspect, is made of invaluable gems; in its inner aspect it symbolizes the Beyond-Measure Palace made of *Gnam-lchags*[30]; it is infinitely spacious. In this Beyond-Measure Palace sit numerous Outer, Inner, Secret, and Most Secret Fierce Buddhas. From their bodies flow out the streams of nectar which enter your body through the Divine Gate of the head. The Great Bliss-Wheel (Chakra) of the Head, the Dharma-Wheel of the Heart, the Transformation-Wheel of the Navel [related respectively to the Sambhogyakaya, Dharmakaya, and Nirmanakaya, higher bodies of the buddha-state], and all parts of the body from the crown of the head down to the soles of the feet are full of the blessing nectar. You should regard it thus [as the initiating guru holding the ritual Vase speaks]:

Hūm! This is the *Gnam-lchags* made in the Beyond-Measure Palace
Where the Fierce Guru abides.
I now enact this for you, and place them [these streams
of nectar] on your head.
The Initiation of the Fierce Guru is thus given to you!
Oṃ Ah Guru Gorda Guba Ahbi Ditsa Hūṃ!

Oh! by the force of this initiation, your four hindrances[31] are cleared and Four Initiations obtained; you also have attained the capability of practicing the Four Paths, the capacity of realizing the Four Bodies[32]... The nectar continues to flow and enter your body, until the nectar is so overflowing that it gushes out of your head and becomes an image of Buddha Amida, which remains on the top of your head as an adornment.

(Sprinkle the holy water over the disciples, and throw the flowers.)

Hūṃ! The Lord who conquers the Three Kingdoms...

He is reddish-black...

He tramps upon the body of a demon...

May the Fierce Guru and all Buddhas grant us the blessing!

(Recite the prayer of benediction as before.)

Now follow me in reciting the prayers for the Initiation of Symbols.

(The guru holds the Thunderbolt in his hand.)

This is the Nine-Spoked Thunderbolt of the Fierce Guru, made of *Gnamlchags,* and with the Buddhas on its prongs.

Hūṃ Gu Rum Gu Phi!

This Thunderbolt has nine perfections; the fire of wisdom burns within it. By obtaining the Initiation of this Vajra, the eight-four-thousand kleśas will all be destroyed. No one will be able to harm you if you attain this Initiation. You will achieve the stability (of meditation). You shall therefore contemplate the Vajra Principle; the transcendental Wisdom of the Voidness.

Hūṃ! This is the Symbol of the Hand of the Fierce Guru,

The Gnam-lchags-made Thunderbolt!

I now place it on your head;

Thus, you are given the Initiation of the Fierce Guru.

Oṃ Ah Hūṃ Guru Gorda Ba-tsa Ah Bi Ditsa Hūṃ!

(Thereupon the Guru holds the sword.)

Now, I shall grant you the Initiation of the Symbol of the Wisdom-Sword[33] of the Fierce Guru. This Wisdom

Sword can cut the inner Clinging of Ego and also cut off
the gates of Saṃsara. You should therefore be granted the
Initiation of the Wisdom Sword.

Hūṃ! This is the Hand Symbol of the Fierce Guru,
The blazing Sword of Wisdom.
I now place it on your head;
Thus, to you is given the initiation of the Fierce Guru.
Oṃ Ah Guru Gorda Dani Ahbi Ditsa Hūṃ!
(Thereupon, the Guru holds the Curved Knife.)

Now another Hand Symbol of the Fierce Guru, the
Gnam-lchags-made Curved Knife. This, the wild thunderbolt, symbolizes the Five Wisdoms[34] of Buddha. It has a
five-ribbed thunderbolt handle. Because the nature of being
is away from playwords[35] the center part of the knife is
broad; to elucidate the sole oneness (of the absolute truth)
it has one sharp blade. By merely attaining the Initiation
of this Symbol, one is able to realize the nature of being
which is away from playwords; thus he attains the Five
Wisdoms of Buddha and is able to annihilate the eighty-
four thousand kleśas. Thus should you think.

Hūṃ! This is the Hand Symbol of the Fierce Guru,
The Thunderbolt curved-knife.
I now place it on your head;
Thus, to you is given the Initiation of the Fierce Guru.
Oṃ Ah Guru Gorda Gida Ahbi Ditsa Hūṃ!
(Thereupon the Guru holds the scorpion [usually only
a picture] in his hand.)

Now, another Hand Symbol of the Fierce Guru, the
transformed Gnam-lchags-made scorpion. It has nine
heads, nine mouths, nine eyes, nine stings. The right sting
touches the top of the universe, the left one touches the
bottom of the earth. The body flames with the fire of hell.

By merely touching the scorpion to your head, all the sins,
obstacles, mishaps, and demon-enemies of your body,
mouth, and mind are all hungrily swallowed by this scorpion. From now on, all the demons and enemies who attempt to afflict you will only re-afflict themselves. They
will all be subdued by you. Thus should you think.

Hūṃ! This is the Hand Symbol of the Fierce Guru,
The heaven-made scorpion with nine heads,
I now place it on your head;
Thus to you is given the Initiation of the Fierce Guru.
Oṃ Ah Guru Gorda Racha Ah Bi Ditsa Hūṃ!
(Thereupon the Guru holds the human skull in his
   hand.)

This is another symbol of the Fierce Guru, the Wis-
dom-Ga-ba-la (human skull) with the adorned metal cover
(adornment) on it. This skull is filled with the cardinal
heart-blood of the just-slaughtered Four Demons. By
attaining this Initiation of Skull, you will be able to realize
the truth of the Wisdom of Non-Existence; the Five Poisons [36] will naturally be dissolved into the universal essence
(Dharmadatu); the blood-ocean of Saṃsara will thus be
dried up. You should now think of these merits.

Hūṃ! This is the hand-symbol of the Fierce Guru,
The heaven-made Human Skull.
I now pray to the Fierce Guru and his retinues and all
   deities,
With my deepest sincerity and concentration I pray thee:
Grant me now the *Inner Initiation.*

Moved by your sincere prayers, the Father and Mother
Fierce Guru bring forth a sound of agreement, by which
all the Buddhas and the Three Pillars are invited to descend here. They all enter into your mouth and become

the nectar-like Bodhi Heart [37] (absorbed in you). By embracing this Ga-ba-la [skull] and touching it with your head you cause the nectar to flow out from it; the stream of nectar enters into your body from the divine head-opening [38] until the nectar fills every part of your body. By the power of this nectar, a burning-like blissful feeling and warmth is generated within you; thus the Initiation of Wisdom [39] is attained by you. You should meditate on this teaching. Thus you will attain also the Precious Initiation of Longevity. (Thereupon, the Guru holds the Nectar [in the skull] in his hand.)

Hūm! This is the Non-Outflow [40] nectar!

I now place it on your head;

Thus the Initiation of the Fierce Guru is given to you.

Hoping that with little effort you will attain the

Three Bodies of Buddha.

Om Ah Guru Gorda Ahmer Daga Ya Waga Tsi Tsa Sarva Ahbi Ditsa Hūm!

(Throw the flowers.)

Hūm! The Lord who conquers the Three Kingdoms —

He is reddish black —

He tramps upon the body of a demon —

May the Fierce Guru and all Buddhas grant us the blessing.

(*Recite the prayer of benediction as before.*)

Now, although the main section of the Initiation is completed, a Gtor-ma initiation still is to be given; because it is said that if the Initiation of the Gtor-ma is not received, there will be delay and difficulties in attaining the Mundane [or lesser] Siddhis.

Though you have attained the main Initiation, however, if you do not have the Initiation of the Gtor-ma, the mundane accomplishment will be delayed, therefore we should perform the Initiation of the Gtor-ma.

This Gtor-ma is identical with the Fierce Guru and all Outer, Inner, and Secret Buddhas. They all assemble here like the gathering storms, with great power and roaring sounds. By dint of my sincere prayer they all vaporize (melt into light) and enter into the body through the divine Head-opening. The Fierce Guru's body, mouth, and mind become one with yours. In this mood, you should repose your mind in the non-active and relaxed state. (This is the essence of the Teaching of Mahamudra.)

I pray the Dharmakaya Buddha Amida, the Sambhogakaya the All-Merciful One, the Nirmanakaya Padmasambhava. I pray the Outer, Inner, Secret, and Most Sacred Fierce Mother and Father Gurus. I pray the Sow-Mother of the Three Lineages; I pray the Fierce Manjuśri, the great Yama, the Lord of the Fierce Hayagriva, the Powerful Vajrapani, the transformation body of the Mother of Music: the Fierce Black Mother, the Accomplishments-bestower, the Burning Fierce Afflicter white and black, the dragon subduer Great Eagle, the Fierce Vajra, the Fierce Jewels, the Fierce Lotus, the Fierce Accomplishments, the upper Fierce Hūṃ Gara, the east Fierce Victors, the southeast Fierce Blue Club Holder, the north Fierce Yama, the southwest Fierce Fire Refuge, the west Fierce King Hayagriva, the northwest Fierce Inconquerable, the north Fierce Demon Holder, the northeast Fierce Three Kingdom Winner, the lower Great-Power-Fierce One, the Four Great Guards of the Gate, the Illumination Holder Fierce Gurus and all Deities — to all of you I pray. I pray you to bestow the initiations to these disciples and to grant them your grace. I pray you to protect them from the det-

riment of Chal Sen, Dam Si, and Eight-Divisional Demons;
also protect them from injury, nervous malady, madness,
ulcers, and all illness and diseases. I pray you to expel the
damaging power of wicked ghosts, the inducements of the
Misleader, and possible harms done by evil spirits. I pray
you to protect these disciples' body, mouth, and mind;
grant them shelter, and hide them.

*Oṃ Ah Hūṃ Shri Ahtsiga Netsiga Namo Baghawade Hūṃ
Hūṃ Pai Ah Hūṃ Hūṃ Pai Ba-tsa Hūṃ Hūṃ Pai Ba-tsa
Hūṃ Yaga Hūṃ Ragsha Hūṃ Oṃ Ahtsiga Nitsiga Namo
Bagawade Hūṃ Ah Pai Ba-tsa Hūṃ Yacha Hūṃ Racha Hūṃ
Oṃ Ahrtsiga Netsiga Namo Bhagawade Hūṃ Ah Hūṃ Pai
Gaya Waga Tsida Ba-tsa Racha, Racha!*

(Throw the flowers.)

Hūṃ! May all the Gurus and all the Buddhas in the past,
   present, and future

Grant us the blessing and prosperity through their body,
   mouth, and mind.

May all the accomplishments be granted to us.

May all the tutelary deities fulfill all our wishes.

May all Mother Guards destroy all malicious enemies.

May the Ocean-like Oath-Holders bestow happiness and
   prosperity.

These are the Outer, Inner, Secret, and Most Secret Initiations of the Fierce Guru given one by one in a concise
manner. This initiation is a profound yet symbolic one.
Though it is not very clear in the distinction of the Four
Successive Initiations, it has the implied meaning of the
Four Initiations. Therefore you may consider that by it
you have obtained all of the four initiations[41].

The teaching of the Fierce Guru in other sects than this
one is generally perilous, for, if one does not practice the

Peaceful Incantation of Padmasambhava for a long period, or does not recite it in a great amount, one will be liable to excite the enmities and troubles and see many frightening visions. However, this teaching is different. Because the Outer Practice and Secret Practice of this teaching are amalgamated with each other, it is safe yet powerful; even beginners can practice it.

As for the advantages of reciting the invocation of the Fierce Guru, the Guru Padmasambhava himself said: "If one wants to receive the special grace from Buddha and achieve the accomplishments fast, he should then practice the meditation of the Fierce Guru. I have all the merits that the Buddhas have. The outer and inner incantations of the Fierce Buddha, the blessing and siddhi of all male and female Sky-Travelers[42], the jewel-like virtues and benefits are all found in me. If one merely practices my meditation and prays to me, he will see all Buddhas and Bodhisattvas; he will achieve all the Outer and Inner accomplishments of Tantra; he will be able to give the blessing of initiation and accomplishments to others; the female Guards will gather around him; all the protectors of Dharma will serve him as ushers; his orders will be obeyed; his instructions will be carried out by the Guards. Solely by practicing this teaching and meditating on me one will attain all the merits and accomplishments. By prayer and meditation on me, one will achieve his wishes."

This is the essence of meditation practice,
This is the teaching of the Fierce Guru.
It is blessed by all the Buddhas,
And blessed by all Outer and Inner Deities of Mandalas.
It is the concentration of the powers of all Buddhas.
If one recites the incantation one hundred times,

He will be cleared of the evil sins and hindrances.
If one recites the incantation one thousand times,
He will be delivered from the outer and inner obstacles.
If one recites the incantation ten thousand times,
He will dominate the Eight-Divisional Demons.
If one recites the incantation one hundred thousand
    times,
He will attain the transcendental accomplishment.
By merely hearing the name of the Fierce Guru and
    thinking of it,
He will be protected from the evil spirits.
You should recite the incantation and practice this med-
    itation. Now follow me in reciting the following prayer:
Whatever the admonishments our master has given to
    us,
We will follow and obey and practice.
From this moment on, please, always remember us!
I offer you my whole being and all my possessions,
Pray have pity on me and consider me as your disciple!
Pray be my shelter and refuge at all times!
At the ending of this Initiation ceremony, the disciples
should offer the Mandala [and say]:
Samaya Cha Cha Cha Chawa Gudaya!
The foregoing initiation practice was given by the in-
carnation lama, Mi-rgyur-rdo-rje, the Immutable Vajra.
When he was thirteen years old, on the tenth day of the
Black Month of the Fowl Year, he actually appeared (be-
fore the eyes of the people) as the Fierce Guru Padma-
sambhava himself, with all adornments and dressings. The
Outer, Inner, Secret, and Most Secret Initiations are usually
to be given separately and practiced separately; however,
it is said, in some special occasion the Guru may put all four

initiations into a condensed one. This teaching is revealed from the treasury after a well-prepared sacrificial ceremony.

If* there is any mistake or error in this work, I beg the forgiveness and pardon from the Guards and Deities. By the merits of carrying out this work, I hope that the tradition of the Treasury Finding will be growing, that the Treasury Finders will have no obstacles, and that all sentient beings will gain great benefits and happiness.

* From now to the end of this concluding section it is the original compiler and amanuensis of the teachings of Mi-rgyur-rdo-rje who speaks to us personally. See pp. 9-10. *Ed.*

NOTES

1 The treasures of Wisdom recorded in universal consciousness, to which access can be had by enlightened beings such as the original author of these texts, Mi-rgyur-rdor-rje. — *Ed.*

2 The scorpion represents both sin and the demonic forces which tried to prevent Padmasambhava from introducing the teachings of the true Dharma into Tibet. As the Fierce Guru grasping the scorpion, Padmasambhava manifests his power and triumph over both the immoral and irrational forces of the universe.

3 The five Chakras or psychic centers in the human body.

4 The psychic centers in the forehead, throat, and heart.

5 Another name for the Fierce Guru.

6 The reference is not clear but probably refers to the four lineages of Buddhism: the Sravakayana, teachings for Gotama Buddha's direct disciples; Pratekayana, for those who realize the truths of Buddhism intuitively through their own efforts; Bodhisattva teachings, for those aspiring to Buddhahood; Tantricism, for those following the esoteric doctrines.

7 Eight Offerings: incense for burning; powdered incense for rubbing the body; lights (candles); fruits; flowers; food; music; and water.

8 Cleansing Ritual: a special incantation which is used to purify the mandala.

9 Buddha All-Perfect; a reference to the Adi Buddha who, according to a tradition of the Red School, was the first human being to become enlightened (here, tradition diverges from the orthodox view of the Adi Buddha).

10 Scorpions; swallowers of evil.

11 Krum-ka: transcendental sacrificial food.

12 This is an enigmatic statement; the text is not explicit.

13 The four seasons comprise the greater circle or wheel of time, while the divisions of sunrise, noon, sunset, and midnight form the lesser wheel. The meaning and observances connected with these times is highly important in the practice of Tantricism.

14 Before beginning any Tantric practice, it is customary to recite incantations to dispel any untoward influences.

15 The Tibetan transliterates the Sanskrit *v* as *w*, since the Tibetan alphabet does not possess a *v*. We have reinserted v as the correct spelling of this important name. *Ed.*]

16 Congregation of the Sacred Offering: the 10th of the month, according to the lunar calendar, is considered a particularly auspicious time for those practicing Tantric yoga to congregate, make offerings to the angels and deities, and receive the grace-waves necessary for success in their practices.

17 An important Tantric tradition is that an esoteric teaching should have a "warm" or "close" succession to be most effective. If the teaching is handled too long by humans it becomes "cold" losing its initial strength to transmit power. This particular initiation ritual was revealed to the incarnation lama, Mi-rgyur-rdo-rje. A close disciple of his recorded it sometime later.

18 Evidence of mystical development.

19 Common = worldly; Superior = transcendental. See footnote 28, Chapter IV.

20 According to Tibetan rtaditions, ghosts and demons manifest through the negative (Yin) aspect of universal forces while human beings belong to the positive (Yang) aspect of such forces. For this reason, ghosts and demons are much more likely to be seen in Tibet and other little-populated regions where their manifestation is not blotted out by the positive auras from large aggregations of human beings.

21 All virtues and fortunes.

22 Miracle powers.

23 Tantric Buddhas.

24 Mahamudra (The great Symbol): A Tibetan teaching, analogous to Chinese Zen, which seeks enlightenment directly through realization of the "pure essence of mind." [A more correct meaning, without the intellectualistic flavor of "mind" would be given by "pure essence of consciousness."]

25 Oath-breakers.

26 The Tantric (esoteric) Brotherhood, analagous to the Sangha (exoteric) Brotherhood of general Buddhism.

27 Tibetan *Rtsa-wa-gsums;* can be translated as *Three Pillars* or *Three Foundations.* (1) Foundation of Blessing, from one's

personal Guru. (2) Foundation of Accomplishment, from practicing the yoga of a tutelary deity. (3) Foundation of Career, through appeals for guardianship and protection in wordly affairs from special "guardian deities" such as Mahakala.

28 The Buddhas of the four types of initiation.

29 Three Kingdoms: World of Desire, World of Form, World of the Formless.

30 Gnam-lchags; "falling from heaven" or "heaven-made." According to tradition certain ritual objects made of heavenly material are allowed to fall upon the earth, where they are discovered and venerated. The Vajra or thunderbolt of the Fierce Guru, referred to subsequently in the text, is one of these objects.

31 Sometimes called the four devils: illness; interruptions; kleśas; death.

32 The Trikaya body of Buddha plus the Dharmadhatu (universal body).

33 The sword, representing the sharp cutting power of discrimination, is always of Wisdom in the hands of Manjuśri.

34 Four of these Wisdom Accomplishments of the Buddha are: Wisdom of Performance, of Observation, of Equanimity, of the Great Dharmadhatu Mirror. This fourth one has some bearing also on the Tantric.

35 *Playwords:* the affirmative, arbitrary, limited notions of human beings which might be represented as a long, sharp-pointed knife. In contradistinction to these concepts, the all-inclusive enlightened view of reality is symbolized by a knife whose blade is broad and well-rounded (curved).

36 The Five Poisons: the five kleśas.

37 Tantricists borrow and adopt exoteric Buddhist terminology for their own purposes. Originally Bodhi-heart referred to a special quality of devoutness; here, however, in connection with the nectar, it means fluid or secretion — source of energy and compassion.

38 Crown of head.

39 The third type of initiation; the first two being Initiation of

Vase and Inner (Secret) Initiation. The fourth initiation is that of Mahamudra.

40 The universal process in Saṃsara is a process of reciprocal interchange of energies in which nothing in the universe can maintain its energy very long but must lose it or have it renewed. In the world of Saṃsara everything "leaks" — is filled only to become empty again; there exists not stability or true "conservation of energy."

41 The translator is very skeptical and critical about this statement, unless the teaching of the third and fourth initiations are given separately in a secret manner.

42 *Sky Travelers:* Tib. Db'a-wo or Mka-*agro*. [Usually Mka-*agro*-ma. This term refers to goddesses or accomplished yogis who without effort can traditionally traverse whole mountain ranges and travel in both the physical skies and the heights of consciousness. *Ed.*]

CHAPTER TWO

From the Treasury of Consciousness This Is

THE INITIATION RITUAL
OF THE
FIERCE GURU WITH PHURBA[1]

Before the execution of the Initiation Ritual of the Fierce Guru with Phurba, the preparation of Vase, Gtor-ma, etc., should all be arranged as instructed in the foregoing ritual.

The Taking-in-Refuge Prayers and the Arising of Bodhi Heart should be practiced first, and so forth. [*Note:* The reference here is to standard ritual.] And instantaneously one should think that the Samaya Buddha is identified with the Wisdom Buddha. The Visualization process is thus completed.

Oṃ Ah Hūṃ! Welcome the Wisdom Buddhas!

The Initiation Buddhas all hold the Vase of Wisdom in their hands.

In their hearts stands the *Hūṃ* word.

Encircling the *Hūṃ* is the garland of mantras.

The garland of mantras evolves swiftly,

Glowing with infinite beams of light,

Which shine forth to the Pure Land of the Golden Mountain[2],

Attracting numerous Fierce Gurus to come down here.

They all coalesce with the Samaya Buddhas.

Oṃ Atsiga Nitsiga Namo Bhagavade Ba-tsa Gili Gilaya Hūṃ Pai!

(Thus, the phurba practice of the Fierce Guru is completed. *Samaya, Chia Chia Chia!*)

The instruction of the ritual, incantation, and visualization are given as follows:

"Think yourself become the Fierce Guru;

From out of his body fire blazes.

Think that this flame consumes all the devils and demons...

You should think that all manifestations and forms are the body of the Fierce Guru.

You should think that all sounds are the Fierce Incantation of Buddha.

You should thus think that no demon or devil can possibly harm you[3]."

Recite the chief incantation; then recite the following incantation:

Ba-tsa Merda Ba-tsa Sumerda Ba-tsa Hora Merda Ba-tsa Hūm Merda Ba-tsa Racha Merda Ba-tsa Ma Merda Ba-tsa Gha Merda Ba-tsa Yam Merda Ba-tsa De Merda Ba-tsa Merda Merda Ye Merda Svaha!

(Samaya Chia Chia Chia. Ka Tam Gu Haya Chia Mum Gana Ta!)

After this initiation ritual (for the guru), the offerings and apology practice should be performed according to one's capability.

After this, the Eight Offerings should be served. The prayer to Padmasambhava should be recited. Then the disciples should gather and offer the Mandala.

(The Guru addresses the disciples.)

Padmasambhava himself said,

"I, the Lotus-Born of *Ao-rgyng*[4],

Preach the Dharma of the Nine Vehicles[5].

In the East and in the West,
I also spread the Teaching of Knowledge and the
    Teaching of Practice.
In the Snow Country of Tibet,
I promulgate Dharma and fulfill the wishes of Buddha's
    sons.
I display my power and perform miracles
And help all the faithful ones by leading them to the
    path.
The inimical devils and demons are all subdued by me
And restrained under oath.
I am Dharmakaya, the All-Perfect Buddha.
My real being is absorbed in the plane of Universal
    Quintessence.
I am Sambhogakaya, the body of the Fierce and Peace-
    ful Buddhas[6];
My consciousness manifests in the form of Buddha's
    body and Wisdom.
I am Nirmanakaya, the Lord of the Esoteric Doctrine.
I am the Treasury of Tantras and Instructions.
Guru Gara-rdor-rje and Mañjuśri,
Nagarjuna and the *Hūṃ*-Practicer Sabhava;
Bemala Medra and Darna, the Rambu Guha Shan Dhava,
The Secret Buddha Goamadhi,
And King Indra Bodhi and Guru Tilopa,
Guru Naropa, Biwashidhapa, Gu Gu Ripa and Andhaba,
The Holy Being Dhawa Draba,
Madi Tsidar Dhava Zun and Gub Dha —
All these Gurus are not different beings;
They are actually one being.
I, Padmasambhava, am also identical with them.
I am the one who has all perfections,

I am omnipresent and absorbed in all.
One may visualize me either as the Peaceful Buddha or
the Fierce Buddha.
Whatsoever the forms, ornaments, and holdings of the
Yidam[7], it makes no difference [one may visualize me
whatever the form he choose and attain enlighten-
ment like mine];
Do not be confused that sometimes I manifest many
faces and arms,
and sometimes I manifest few.
After all, what difference does the number of faces and
arms make?
You should remember that I manifest all!
I shall transform myself into numerous bodily forms in
the world to benefit the world.
The innumerable transformation bodies of mine
Will fill every corner of the world!
Although I appear myself before every man,
They do not see me,
Because their extremely disturbing thoughts hinder them.
My love and compassion is so great
That I can not delay a single moment to come to the per-
son who calls for help.
Especially for the Tibetans, I always give them my bless-
ing.
Though apparently I am in the Northwestern Land,
My performances and teachings will never cease to exist
in Tibet.
I even appear myself in person before my faithful and
sincere disciples.
My Transformation Body will never cease to exist in
Tibet.

None will get a faster response in praying to other Bud-
dhas than in praying to me.
If a good wish cannot be accomplished by peaceful
means,
I will use the powerful one!
For the welfare of others, I use both the peaceful ways
and the forceful ways —
In the Mandala I am the chief Buddha and am also the
retinues.
I manifest in various forms — [as] many or few deities in
a Mandala —
According to the nature and capacity of the individual.
I will protect my disciples from the affliction of the
Eight Earthly Demons.
I will bestow all the Siddhis like rainfall upon my fol-
lowers.
If one desires to be born in the Pure Land of Non-Re-
gression[8],
He should look to me.
If one wants to help others, he should appeal to me.
If one wants longevity and prosperity, he should pray to
me.
For the afflicted ones, I also destroy demons, hindrances,
sins, and illness.
If one wants power, I grant that to him.
If one wills to conquer the proud enemy,
I will fulfill his wishes.
I give the Siddhis of the Four Performances,
The desirable Lotus of Wish-Granting also comes from
me.
I am the one who fulfills all wishes without delay.
With my body, speech, mind, merits, and performances,

I send forth numerous transformation bodies and sub-
   transformation bodies.
I am the shelter, the refuge, the protector, and Wish-
   granter of all beings.
I am the one who cures all illness, kleśas, and sufferings.
In the dangerous state of Bardo,
When one beholds the frightful scenes
And hears the terrible voices,
I shall be his savior and protect him from fear.
I am the one who creates the Essence of Buddha's Pure
   Land.
I am the Lord of the Lotus, the Yidam of all devas.
I elucidate the Pith-meaning of the radiant Dharmakaya.
I am the Lotus-Born Wish-Granting Guru.
By merely hearing my name,
One's hair stands up and one's tears flow."

(The Guru says:)

"Thus one should have faith in his teaching and lineage.
O the Lotus Lord! Through his miraculous Phurba,
All wishes are granted and accomplishments realized."

Again, you should know that the Father and Mother
Guru are embodied in the P'urbu-dagger. Today's initiation is called the Initiation of the *Ao-rgyng Yabyum*[9] embodied in the Buddha Rdo-rje-gyoun-nu, or the Teaching
of Elimination of Evil through the Fierce Guru with
Phurba.

Says Padmasambhava's prophecy:

*"In the time of sinful, soiled, and corrupt custom — in the
   future —
The demons and spirits of the Planets[10] will infest the world.
At that time, the Demon King Pehar will be very powerful and
   dominant [his teachings will spread afar]."*

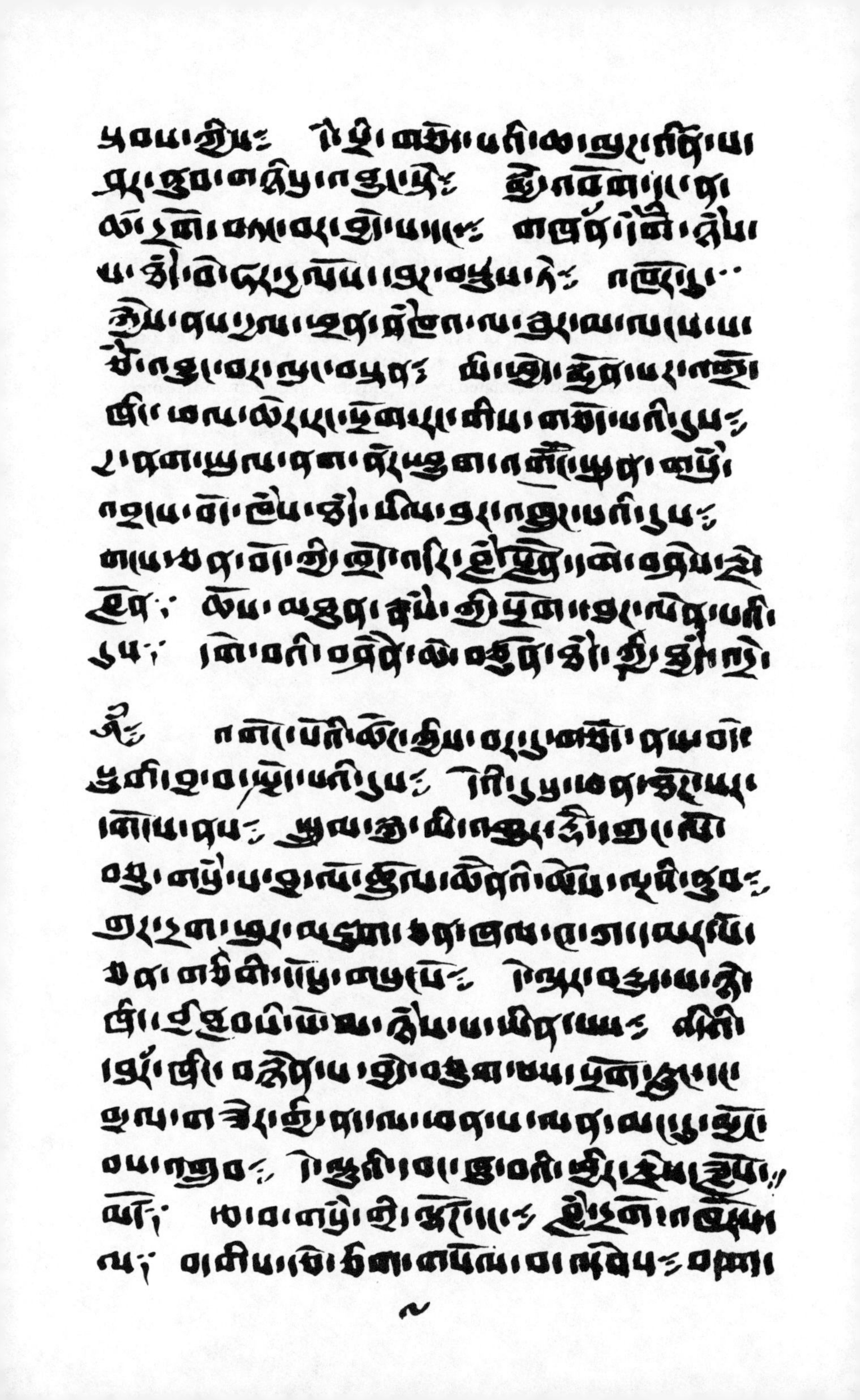

[illegible]

Folios 6 *verso* and 7 *recto* (Muses MS, vol. I) showing the major portion, in the cursive "headless" Tibetan script, of the unique prophecy of Padmasambhava in his role as "The Fierce Guru with Phurba" voiced through the lama prodigy Mi-gyur-rdorje, inspired at the age of 13, as the manuscript relates. The prophecy foretells a time of utter disaster for Tibet, when it will be conquered and decimated by evil and deranged, demon-like men.

Thus he said. Because of the powerful influence of the Demon King Pehar, the cases of insanity [Tib. smyo] and nervous disturbance [abog] will be many, the cases of violent death will also be great in number.

[This remarkable prophecy is now explained further:]

In ancient times, there was an Indian scholar who was very fond of gold. He had devoted his lifetime to practicing the worship of Yamantaka and was about to achieve the Siddhis. But he raised dispute and became very angry; then the Black Yamantaka put him to death. Whereupon he became the Black King Demon called Hala. Later he came to Tibet and enslaved half of the Tibetan population.

Maji Lab Dran[11] (the greatest woman philosopher of Tibet) in her previous life was the Indian scholar Rin-Chin-Drab who subdued and converted many heretic philosophers of India. Among them there was a scholar who became very angry and revengeful after his defeat in debating with Rin-Chin-Drab. He then made a malignant vow and immediately flew away to a cave and died by committing suicide.

By the power of his malignant vow and hate [joined to all other evil], he became a plague-spreading gnome, the one who appeared in the form of life-and-vow-destroyer. He appeared both in the East and in the West. He spread all kinds of disease and made people insane and mentally disturbed. Furthermore, the King Demon Pehar then gathered all the breath of the oath-breakers[12] and made them his retinues, filling many countries like husks scattered by the wind pervading a whole valley.

This was prophesied [also by Padmasambhava]:

At that time half of the populations [of all nations] will become insane; most of the people will cut short their own lives

37

by themselves (suicide); and at that time China will become a dark land. Powerful men and wealth will follow the steps of the evil spirits and their three cousins[13]; all Tibet will be broken into small pieces. At that time, here in the Snow Country, the life and breath of the lamas, the officials, the teachers, the kings, the high officers, and those who follow the Buddhist teachings will be taken away (and persecuted). All the good teachers and virtuous persons will be cut in the middle by the evil demons. People will suffer excessively[14].

Thinking of benefitting the world [later on] at this miserable time, on the evening of the fifth lunar day – a significant date – in the year of Rooster, the Fierce Guru with Phurba himself (red and with one face) appeared before the Living Buddha, Mi-rgyur-rdo-rje, when he was thirteen years old, and imparted to him this initiation and teaching. Therefore this teaching is a very near one (to the original source), and has great power and blessing. If one attains this initiation and practices it many times, he may certainly cure the illness of Life-Prana[15] and the pain of fainting.

To attain this initiation, you disciples should now follow me in reciting the following prayers:
  "I pray the Three Pillars and all Deities,
  I pray the Fierce Guru and his retinues,
  Considering my sincere prayer and earnest request,
  Please grant me the Initiation of the Vase.
  I take refuge in the Three Precious Ones.
  I confess all the sins and evil doings that I have committed.
  I shall view all the good deeds and merits of sentient
    beings with sympathetic joy.
  I pray that all the Buddhas and Bodhisattvas ceaselessly
    remember me in their minds.

From now until the time of attaining the perfect Buddha-
    hood,
I take refuge in the Buddha, the Dharma, and the Sangha.
For the benefit of self and others
I raise the incomparable Heart for Bodhi.
When this prime vow of the Heart for Bodhi is made,
I shall render my services to all sentient beings.
I hope the day I attain Buddhahood will come soon!"
Recite this prayer not less than three times.
(Then the Guru holds the Human Skull, filled with nectar,
and addresses the disciple.)
"You are born in a well-gifted lineage;
I now impart to you the Vajra of Wisdom and grant you
    the Siddhis.
Deyata Jaha Hūṃ Neya!"
(The disciple drinks the nectar from the human skull) and
thinks that he has drunk the nectar that can cure all poi-
sonous disease and bring all prosperity and auspiciousness.
The Guru says:
"This is the Water of Hell for you
If you break your oath or violate the precepts,
It will become a great fire and burn you to ashes.
If you observe the precepts and keep your oath
It will bring you all Siddhis and accomplishments.
Samaya Gahi Hasa Hūṃ!"
Now, follow me in reciting this prayer;
"Oh, Guru. you are the embodiment of all Buddhas;
In you, I take refuge.
In you find shelter.
In the endless and miserable Saṃsara Ocean
I look forward to you – to ferry me to the safe shore!
Ha Ha Ha Ha Ha Ha Ha. Hūṃ Hūṃ Hūṃ Hūṃ!

Now, you disciples should think that nothing any more exists; there is only a vast void. Suddenly from this great voidness you become the Fierce Guru wtth Phurba, four faces all looking in one direction, for this is the manner of conquering and subduing all devils and demons. His first hand holds the thunderbolt with knife; the other hand holds the scorpion. The lower hand holds the symbolic staff, Khadramga, and at the lower part of his body stands the powerful Fhurba with grooves, the weapon that kills the evils, agonizing and tormenting them.

Oṃ Ah Hūṃ!

From the three places, the three words radiate beams of light to the Golden Pure Land in the northwestern direction, and enter the heart of Guru Padmasambhava, who sits on the summit of the hill in the Pure Land. Instantaneously, with great vibration and thundering sound, the Fierce Guru with Phurba descends here. He enters into your body and mind and unites with you.

(Play all musical instruments)

Hūṃ! O Fierce Guru With Phurba, and thy holy retinues,

I pray you to come here and bless me!

I pray you to protect me from the dangers and obstacles
    of my life.

(In addition to the basic incantation add: *Ba-tsa Ah Wei Sha Ya Ah Ah*. Recite it several times.)

The Guru then puts the rdo-rje on the head of the disciple and says:

"*Di Char Ba-tsa!*" (Thus the Initiation of Vases is given.)

"*Hūṃ!* This is the Heaven-Made[16] Phurba,

The powerful and inconceivable one!

This is the illumination of the Fierce Guru,

I now place it on your head. *Ba-tsa Ah Bi Itsa Hūṃ!*"

The Guru then holds the sword in his hand and says:

"*Hūṃ!* This is the blazing sword of the Fierce Guru!

I now place it on your head,

And wish you to obtain the superb initiation of the Fierce Guru."

Then recite the main incantation [not given here *Ed.*] up to [the words] *Dike Ahbi.*

The Guru then holds the scorpion (usually a picture or image) and says:

"This is the nine-headed scorpion of the Fierce Guru.

I now place it on your head,

And wish you to obtain the superb Initiation of the Fierce Guru."

Recite the main incantation and add *Rag Cha Ah Bi.*

[Following the same manner, the Initiation of Staff is given as follows:]

"*Hūṃ!* This is the Staff of the Fierce Guru,

The blazing Staff held in his hand,

I now place it upon your head and grant you the initiation of the Fierce Guru."

Recite the main incantation and add *Dre Shu La Ahi.*

(Thereupon the disciples offer the lamp and recite the following incantation with great sincerity.)

"*Maha Guru Tsida Ma Ma Da Ri Ga Ah Ha Na Haya!*"

Then the Initiation of Fruit:

"*Hūṃ!* This is the fruit of great value.

I now place it on your throat,

I now grant you all the Secret Initiation of the Fierce Guru with Fhurba.

Ah Gei Ha Ge Ge Ge Ge Be Ge Na Savha Ga Ye Ga Ye Hehi Heye Hagadi Gagadi!"

The Guru holds the shell in hand and says:

"*Hūṃ!* this is the right-circled shell [*Ed.:* clockwise] that
symbolizes the perfection and merit of all Buddhas.
I now place it on your heart and bless you,
I wish you to attain the powerful initiation of the Fierce
  Guru with Phurba.
*Ah Ah Ah Ah Ah Dum Dum Dum Dum Ha Ha Ha
  Ha Ha Ha Ha Ga Di Ma Pa Ya Na Ga Go Sen Nga
  Ba Di.*
The Guru holds the wand in his hand and says:
"*Hūm!* my good disciple,
I now place this wand upon your head
And grant you the Initiation of Performance of the
  Fierce Guru with Phurba.
Gehura hasaya de ah mum hūm.
Hūm! This Gtor-ma itself is the Fierce Guru With Phurba;
All the Buddhas and Bodhisattvas dwell in it.
I now place it on your head
And grant you the complete Four Initiations of Tantra.
Bhagavan, the Lord of Infinite Light, Guru Padmasam-
  bhava,
Dakini Ye-shes-mtsho-rgyal, the Superb Deva, Rdo-rje
  Youth —
O all ye holy beings!
You now become embodied in the form of he Fierce
  Guru with Phurba,
I pray, grant your grace and blessing to my disciples.
Please at this very moment cure my disciples' Sickness-
  of-Life-Prana.
Please cure their insanity, psychosis, mania, faintness,
  depression [17] —
In short, please cure all their mental diseases, if any at
  this very moment.

Please protect my disciples from the injuries of the Male
Demon, King-Ghost, Gon-po Demon, Nine Devils
of Bun, white and black devils, the old and new demons, the poisonous devils, evil spirits and all the
malignant ghosts.

From now on until they reach the final enlightenment,
please protect them and remember them!

*Ma Nyan Da Ya Ga Dim Hu, Hasayale Sayaseleye Lei
Lei Sya Deyataya Hūṃ Haya, Oṃ Ah Hūṃ Ahtsi
Netriga Namo Bhagavade Ba-tsa Gi Li Gi La Ya Hūṃ
Pai, Ba-tsa Sa Sa Nan, Ba-tsa Ragcha Nan, Homlan
Nan, Bala Dana Nan, Gu Haya Di La Nan, Ba-tsa Da
Di Nan, Di La Di La Nan, Ba-tsa Ba-tsa Ha Jun Rag
Cha Rag Cha, Sidi U Su Nan, Ratsa Ah Mu Ga, Tsi
Da Be, Mam Sa Be, Ra Dah Be, Gi Ni Ra Di Be, Go
Re Tsa Na Be, Ba Su Da Be, Tsida Jun, Tsida Duob,
Ahdi Labi Dhide Savha!"*

Now you have obtained the initiation of the Fierce Guru
with Phurba. From now on you should always identify yourself with the Fierce Guru, and think that you yourself are the
Fierce Guru inflamed with fire, no evil spirits can harm you.

All the manifestations you should behold as the play of
the Fierce Guru.

All the sounds you should hear as the Fierce Guru's
Mantras.

You should think that no evil spirits can harm you —

In such a manner should you practice.

Now follow me in reciting this incantation:

*Gadiga Samaya Ahr Da Ah Ai Ha La Ha La Sagha
Samaya Ah Di Wa Ah Samaya Na Ra Ga Ga Cha
Savha!*

Then offer the Mandala.

This is a very strict, powerful, and dangerous initiation. It cannot be given to many people. If a proficient Yogi, who has achieved to some extent the Siddhis of Mantra, cannot overcome the illness of life-prana and the mental disturbances caused by the King-Demons, and nothing can cure him: for such an extreme case, this initiation ritual should be practiced, in front of the sick Yogi, one thousand times. It will definitely cure him. The ordinary person, who has not practiced meditation or Mantra, or is merely a beginner, will be much easier to cure. Usually, reciting the Mantra for one or two rotations of the rosary [the Tibetan rosary of 108 beads. *Ed.*] will be quite sufficient to cure him. It is a rare case that a few recitations of Mantra cannot help... Occasionally, when the spittle comes up [18], the Yogi should carefully observe whether the patient has also been affected by the Mantra. In case a great many Mantras have been practiced, but without help, the Yogi should then practice the Visualization with Action and also apply the Frightening Acts together with the recitation of the Mantra. This will definitely help.

If one is not affected by King-Demons' Disease, but merely feels minor mental disturbance because of the time element (at certain times the King-Demons and evil spirits are very active and powerful), he should meditate on this teaching for a little while to protect himself; and reciting the Mantra a few times will certainly help.

The King-Demons (the makers of mental disturbances) are numerous, forming many diabolic families and ranks. Whichever King-Demon harms you, you should visualize that the sharp tip of the Purbu is stabbed into the joiningpart of the white and black part of the demon's heart, torturing him. Absorb yourself in this visualization to recite the Mantra.

The foregoing initiation ritual is one of the instructions from the Heavenly Dharma, which includes not only the initiation ritual itself but also explanations. This ritual was written and arranged by the monk named Brtson-agrus, the Diligent One. If I have ever committed the sin of expressing too obviously and clearly the esoteric teachings which are supposed to be kept secret, I beg forgiveness from the Shelter Berha [19], the Protector and his retinues. If any merits have accrued to me through writing down this ritual, I dedicate them to all the demon-afflicted sentient beings to pacify them and calm their disturbed minds. I also wish them to attain happiness of body and mind.

Good wishes to all.

NOTES

1 Padmasambhava, wishing to combat the demonic evils and mental diseases of this dark time, extended his manifestation as the Fierce Guru into that of Fierce Guru with Phurba (dagger) [actually a ritual dagger of triangular pyramidal blade *Ed.*] for this purpose. This initiation is a sub-initiation of the Fierce Guru.

2 The Golden Mountain is a name for the Pure Land of Padmasambhava.

3 According to Buddhist tradition, there are various ways to subdue evils. The highest teaching, however, urges the disciple to look upon all untoward manifestations and obstacles as themselves representing an aspect of Buddha — in this case, of the Fierce Guru. The yogi, seeing frightful visions or hearing demonic voices, should identify them as a manifestation of the Fierce Guru.

4 *Ao*-rgyng is another name for the Pure Land of Padmasambhava. Padmasambhava is called Ao-rgyng Rimpoche, meaning "the Precious One of *Ao*-rgyng".

5 The Nine Vehicles are (1) the Vehicle of Hearing (Sravaka); (2) the Vehicle of Self-Buddha (Pratyeka-Buddha); (3) the Vehicle of Bodhisattva; (4) the Vehicle of the Tantra of Affairs; (5) the Vehicle of the Yoga Tantra; (7) the Vehicle of the Maha Yoga; (8) the Vehicle of Ah Nu Yoga; and (9) the Vehicle of Adi Yoga. The first two vehicles are Hinayana Buddhism; the third is general Mahayana Buddhism. The remaining six all belong to Tantricism. Among them the fourth, fifth, and sixth are the so-called three lower divisions, or preparatory Tantra. The seventh, eighth, and ninth belong to the highest division of Tantra, the Annutara Tantra, which is practiced in Tibet; while the lower division of Tantra, Tang-Mig (the esotericism of the Tang Dynasty), is practiced in China and Japan.

6 The Fierce and Peaceful Buddhas are both the manifestations of the Dharmakaya.

7 Yidam is the patron Buddha one relies on.

8 Unfavorable circumstances for practicing Dharma will usually cause the disciples to regress. Therefore it is their wish

to be born in a land of favorable circumstances for their practice, so that regression cannot occur.

9 The *Ao-rgyng Yabyum* is the Father-Mother Buddha in the Pure Land of *Ao-rgyng*.

10 Tibetans believe that certain mental illnesses are caused by the demons and spirits of the eight planets.

11 Maji Lab Dran formed her own school, which still prevails in a part of Tibet. She was Tibet's greatest woman philosopher and yogi.

12 Oath-breakers are disciples who violate the Tantric precepts.

13 This is the translation of the prophecy, which is quite clear except for the meaning of the phrase "three evil spirits and their cousins."

14 Tibetan text: *Bde Sdug-ahi Bya Wa Spyod Bai Dus.* Although literally *Bde* means happiness and *Sdug* means suffering, this seems to be an idiomatic expression denoting "the coming into being of the sufferings," or "great changes and sufferings will come to pass."

15 According to Tantrism, most mental disturbances are caused by irregular or abnormal activity of the Life Prana that usually functions in the central nervous system.

16 See previous note on the thunderbolt (Note 30, Chapter I).

17 The Tibetan word for insanity is *smyo-wa;* for neurosis [so changed from the translator's "psychosis". *Ed.*], *abog;* for mania, *srog-rhin-nad;* for faintness, *brgyl-nad;* for depression, *atibs.*

18 The meaning of this statement is not obvious from the text; it may have a hidden meaning. The translator presumes that, when the incantation is effective, the yogi as well as the patient will feel the spittle rise into his mouth.

19 Shelter Berha *(Mgong-b'o Berha)* is the Protector of the Old School.

CHAPTER THREE

THE INITIATION RITUAL
OF THE ALL-MERCIFUL ONE[1]

Obeisance to Guru Devadike.

Pray grant me all Siddhis *Hūṃ!*

This is the Fourth Initiation [of the Tantric Scheme], the Initiation of the All-Merciful One. The Mandala should be arranged as before[2]. The Gtor-ma should be made as the pomegranate in shape and placed in the center of the Mandala. On the right side a glass rosary is placed; on the left side three fossil shells; in the front many precious ornaments; on the west side a white vase boundwith ribbons. On the top of the Gtor-ma, the Tsag'li[3] is installed.

(The aforesaid articles are arranged in preparation for the ceremony. At the time of performing the Initiation, the Vase Ritual and Gtor-ma Ritual may be performed according to the general rules. In the preparation practice for the Initiation, the guru should meditate on the proceeding once: visualize the Self, Front, and Vase as all instantaneously united with the Wisdom Ones[4], and recite the incantation not less than one hundred times. If one wants to practice a more comprehensive and elaborate ceremony, he should perform the Three Purifications[5].)

One should visualize as follows:

In front of me is the Vase-Buddha[6], the All-Merciful One.

He is white in color with four arms and one face.

He folds his two palms together with his central arms.

The two outer arms hold separately the lotus and the
  rosary.
His two feet join together in the Diamond Sitting Pos-
  ture[7].
All the precious ornaments adorn his body.
Robed in magnificent clothes of silk,
He sits solemnly on the cushion of the Lotus-Moon.
Oṃ Ma Ni Be Mi Hūṃ, the All-Merciful One is here!
Sa Ma Ya, Jia Jia Jia!
Recite and visualize as follows:
In the heart-center of the Vase-Buddha before me, there
is a white word, *Shri;* standing straight on the moon disc
and encircling the *Shri* clockwise are the Six Words. From
these Words emanate rays of light shining into the ten
directions. Among all the Bodhisattvas, the rays of light
choose the All-Merciful One and entreat him, with all
Buddhas and Bodhisattvas, to descend here. Because the
All-Merciful One, Avalokiteśvara, is extremely compassionate. He is the special tutelary Buddha of Tibet. Practicing his meditation makes it easier to attain the grace of
bliss. He is nearer to us than other Buddhas. Padmasambhava said, "In the time of defilements, Avalokiteshvara is
the most compassionate one. Especially to us, the Kham
Pa[8], the Six Words of Incantation are most beneficial and
appropriate. The All-Merciful One, His Holiness Avalokiteśvara, is the intimate patron deity of the Snow Country[9]. His Dharma, especially, has a close affinity to the
people of Kham. Therefore, in the region of Kham, one
sees that men and women alike all recite the Six Words
Incantation diligently." This was prophesied by Padmasambhava himself.
About the benefits of remembering and meditating on

the All-Merciful One, *The Thousand-Arms-and-Thousand-Eyes-True-Words Tantra* says, "If one takes the initiation and recites the incantation of Avalakiteśvara, his sins will all be cleansed and his obstacles removed. He will obtain the infinite merits[10]; after his death he will go to the Pure Land (of Buddha Amida)." In *The Sutra of the Ten Countenances*, one reads, "The All-Merciful One himself said, 'If one think of me and call my name, whatever his wishes may be, all will be granted. All injuries to him will be prevented, sins and hindrances will be obliterated; all his fears will be conquered. This man is liberated from the evils and obstacles, and well protected under my shelter. His merits and talents will be promoted. He is hid from all ominous signs and afflictions.'"

In *The Various-Winds-and-Waters Sutra (Chu-rlung-snga-tsogs-mdo)* it is also said, "In the future time, any good man or good woman who has heard the merits of the All-Merciful One will gradually exhaust his or her kleśas; the Great Five Unceasing Sins and their like will be exhausted. If one has nothing in his mind but the All-Merciful One[11] and meditates on the merits of Avalokiteśvara for only one month, he will be able to see the All-Merciful One as well as Buddha Amida face to face. He will thus never regress on the Path of Bodhi[12]. He will recollect his lives in the past, follow the teachings he has heard, and wherever he is born will com across Dharma. He will never depart from Buddhism, and will attain great wealth and enjoy great happiness. Wherever he stays no demons nor illness can seriously harm him."

The Magnificent Casket Sutra states: "Gotama Buddha says, 'Whoever thinks of Avalokiteshvara will attain to happiness; he will be freed from the sufferings of birth, age, illness, and death. He will go to the happy Pure Land to see Buddha Amida. Those devoted to the All-Merciful One will have no Saṃsaric sufferings in their bodies, no leśas in their minds; hunger and thirst cannot threaten them, nor will they undergo ordeal in the womb. With sincere devotion growing in their hearts, they will then be born in the lotus[13]. Those relying on the Victorious Master Avalokiteshvara to be their tutelary Buddha will always be able to go to Buddha's paradise and remain there.'"

The benefits and profit of the Six Sacred Words are thus stated in *The Sutra of the Hundred-and-Eight Symbols:* "Tathagata Buddha says, 'Those good men and good women who contemplate Avalokiteshvara and recite the Six Sacred Words: *Oṃ Mani Padme Hūṃ*, will never fall into the lower Lokas or the Unceasing Hell. Whoever takes this incantation in his mind and recites it with sound, his body becomes immune from leprosy, ulcer, Bra Gyan and Bas Lhag diseases[14], tuberculosis, asthma, and all kinds of disease. Immediately after death, he will be born in the Happy Pure Land. Wherever he is born he will never be separated from the All-Merciful One.'"

Again, *The Magnificent Casket Sutra* states: "The Majestic Red Buddha says, 'That good man or good woman who recites these Six Sacred Words will attain the following benefits: his valor and spirit will never diminish, his wisdom will grow, he will become a man with great compassion and kindness, he will complete the Six Paramitas[15] in his everyday activity. He will become the King of Turning-the-Mystic-Holding-Wheel[16]. He will become a Bodhisattva of Non-Regression. He will eventually attain the perfect, peerless Buddhahood.'"

This initiation practice was revealed by Buddha Amida

to His Holiness Mi-rgyur-rdo-rje in the (year of the) Fire Monkey, Dragon Month, when he was twelve years old. This initiation was bestowed upon me [the original lama-scribe. *Ed.*] by two Living Buddhas; therefore it is a very recent late and close one with great blessing power. Dakinis [17] vowed to give special protection to this instruction. Therefore, together with sincerity and respect you should feel happiness and joy for this opportunity.

The guru says, "You should think that I and the Initiation Symbols are the real embodiment of Avalokiteshvara. With this confidence and devotion follow me in reciting the following prayers:

"I pray to all the Buddhas in the past, present, and future.
Especially I pray to the All-Merciful One!
I pray thee to grant me the invaluable Initiation!
I take refuge in the Three Precious Ones.
I confess to you all the sinful deeds I have done.
I raise my sympathetic joy unto all merits and virtues of
    the sentient beings.
Forever I shall bear the Three Precious Ones in my mind,
From now on till the time of my attaining the Buddha-
    hood,
I devote and submit myself, my whole being, to all Bud-
    dhas!
For the sake of benefiting self and others,
I hereby take the oath for the Devotion for Bodhi [18].
After the growing of the Heart for Bodhi,
I render my service to all beings as a humble servant.
With joy and vigor I practice the Action of Bodhi.
In order to benefit all the sentient beings,
I sincerely pray the day of my attaining Bodhi will come
    soon!"

(Repeat not less than three times, using Ku Sha grass to bless the disciples.)

Now, the disciples should practice the visualization of the Arising Buddha. Follow my instructions and visualize them. (The guru reads loudly and slowly.)

"All of you become Avalokiteśvara, the All-Merciful One.
His body is white in color and he has only one face.
His four arms are poised in the following manner:
The palms of the two center arms are folded together.
One arm holds a rosary, and one holds a lotus branch.
The two feet entwine in the Diamond Sitting Posture.
The rare ornaments adorn his body.
Arrayed in silks, he sits solemnly on the cushion of the Sun-Moon-Lotus.
"In such manner you visualize the Arising Buddha. Now you should meditate on the three places from which to draw the wave of grace and blessing:
"Visualize in your forehead a white *Om* word standing straight;
A red *Ah* word stands in the forepart of the throat;
A blue *Hūm* word stands in your heart.
In the very center of your heart is a moon disc;
Upon the white moon disc stands a white *Śri* word.
The Six Sacred Words circle the *Śri* word.
Because of inviting the Wisdom-Buddha to come here,
From the *Śri* word emanate infinite rays of light.
These rays of light shine forth to the Pure Land of Happiness,
Also shining forth south toward the Holy Potala [19].
There by numerous forms of Avalokiteśvara, big as mountains, small as mustard seeds,

With the Six Sacred Words, and the white *Śri* word in
their bodies,
As snow falling, they all descend here.
They enter your body like the rainfall and penetrate deep
in you."
(Play all musical instruments. All chant in rhythm.)
"*Hūṃ!* I think, I think of the All-Merciful One!
Listen! the All-Merciful One and Buddhas rise up,
From the Great Place of the South the Buddhas arise!
With retinues and assemblies they descend here.
Well dressed is the crown of the head,
The precious ornaments are as glossy as sun rays.
Accompanied with music and dance, you come here.
Your grace and blessing are beyond human apprehen-
sion.
Without any closefistedness, you grant us the Siddhis.
From the great place full of wonder,
With an unlimited compassion you come down here.
I pray thee with my utmost sincerity and yearning
Grant me your grace and blessing!
Pray thee, embrace me in your care under your bound-
less compassion!
Pray look after me and bestow on me the Siddhis.
Come here, thou gracious one!
Safeguard me, you compassionate one!
Oh, father Guru himself is the All-Merciful One!
To whom I pray with one single thought (concentrated
attention).
May all the wishes of ours be granted!
*Oṃ Ah Hūṃ Śri Svaha! Oṃ Mani Padme Hūṃ! Be Tsa
Ah Bi Sha Ya Ah Ah!*"
(Play musical instruments; then place the Vajra on the

head. Visualize the Wisdom Buddha becoming steady.)

Di Tsha Be Tsa!

(Hold the vase in hand and read the following words.)

Hūṃ! the Beyond-Measure Palace

Where the All-Merciful One and his retinue abide,

Whereby the Four Initiations of Vase I wish to attain.

(Place the symbol on disciple's head.)

Oṃ Mani Be Mi Hūṃ Ga La Shu Kura Sar Jia, Tsa Tu Ah Bi Di Tsa Hūṃ!

(Give the water in the Vase to disciples and let them drink it. Then hold the Gtor-ma in hand and read as follows.)

Hūṃ! This Gtor-ma itself is the embodiment of Avalokiteshvara.

His myriad retinues are also contained within it.

To you my disciples, the Four Initiations of Avalokiteshvara

Are now completely being given!

I pray Buddha Amida, the Dharmakaya,

I pray Bodhisattva Avalokiteshvara, the Sambhogakaya,

I pray the teacher Padmasambhava, the Nirmanakaya,

I pray the Dakini and the Victorious Ocean Wisdom, Ye-shes-mtsho-rgyal,

I pray the twenty-eight followers and one-hundred-and-one Treasure Finders,

I pray all accomplished Illumination Holders[20].

Pray the All-Merciful One, Lord of Transciency, One with the Eyes of Compassion,

Mighty being! Also pray all the accompanying holy beings to bless this disciple of Diamond Vehicle, and grant them the Initiation!

Pray to cleanse the Hindrance of Passion, Hindrance of Knowledge[21], and all Habitual Thinking for them forever!

Pray forever close the gate of Sanmara and Lower Path for them!

Pray bestow your gracious blessing to them and deliver them to the West Pure Land at the moment of their departure!

Oṃ Mani Padme Hūṃ! Gaya Waga Tsida Sarva Ahbi Aitsi Hūṃ!

(Recite this incantation three times. Hold the image in hand and read.)

Hūṃ! Pray the All-Merciful One and his accompanied Deities,

Grant you, the disciples, the complete Four Initiations.

(Place the image on the disciple's head.)

Oṃ Mani Padme Hūṃ Gaya Ah Bi Ai Tsa Hūṃ!

(Holding the Vase, Vajra, rosary, and conch in hand read the following prayers.)

Hūṃ! Pray the All-Merciful One grant you, the well-destined disciples, the Initiation of Body, Mouth, and Mind.

Oṃ Mani Padme Hūṃ, Gaya Waka TsiDa Kica Ah Bi Ai Tsa Hūṃ!

(Place all the symbols on disciple's head. Throw the flowers and sing the benediction psalm and dedications.)

Hūṃ! May all the gurus who possess the Trikaya[22] grant us the blessing and prosperity.

May the tutelary Buddha, Deities, and Dakinis grant us the blessing and prosperity!

May all the Guardians of Dharma, the Ocean-like Samaya[23] Holders bless us.

Among the ocean-like teachings in the Mind-Treasury of Heavenly Dharma in the Whisper-Succession there are forty initiation teachings. This one, the Initiation of Avalokiteshvara with Six Sacred Words, is one of them. From now on you should always submit yourself to your tutelary Buddha, the All-Merciful One, and recite the Six Sacred Words regularly; therefore follow me in taking this oath.

From now on, till the time of my attaining Buddhahood, I will regard the All-Merciful One as my tutelary Buddha. *Sa Maya Narayan!*

NOTES

1 *The All-Merciful One:* Avalokiteśvara, patron Bodhisattva of Tibet.

2 The ritual containing these instructions is missing from the manuscript. — *Ed.*

3 *Tsag'-li:* A miniature flag with the device of a mandala or mantram, one of the Tantric ornaments.

4 *Wisdom Ones:* Those Buddhas that give life to the Front Vase, manifestations of the coming Buddhas. See Note 5, Chapter 4.

5 *Three Purifcations:* The ceremony of purifying the body, mouth, and mind.

6 *Vase-Buddha:* See Note 2, Chapter 4.

7 *Diamond Sitting Posture:* Traditional cross-legged posture of the Buddhas.

8 *Kham Pa:* People of Kham, or East Tibet.

9 *Snow Country:* Another name for Tibet.

10 *Infinite merits:* Buddhist term for all virtues.

11 This refers to deep Samadhi in which the thought-flow is stopped.

12 *Path of Bodhi:* The way to Buddhahood.

13 *Born in the lotus:* A term of the Pure Land Sutras referring to those advanced beings having a higher birth than from the womb.

14 *Bra Gyan and Bas Lhag diseases:* Unknown diseases.

15 *Six Paramitas:* Six perfections of Buddhist philosophy.

16 *Mystic Holding-Wheel:* The ruler of a Golden Age holds a golden wheel and rules through love; the king of a Silver Age rules through fear; the king of an Iron Age, whose symbol is the iron wheel, rules through violence. (Asoka is identified with the last type of ruler.)

17 *Dakinis: Tantric goddesses.*

18 *Oath for the Devotion for Bodhi:* The Bodhisattva's vow.

19 *Holy Bodala:* Pure Land of Kwan Yin, traditionally located in this world in a region of the Chinese coast, Chekiang province.

20 *Illumination Holders:* Tantric yogis.

21 One freed of the passions may yet have *Hindrance of Knowl-*

edge, not being omniscient. Such a one is an arhat, but not
yet a fully enlightened being — Buddha.

22 *Trikaya:* The Three Bodies of Buddha.

23 *Samaya* here means the Tantric precepts

CHAPTER FOUR

THE INITIATION RITUAL
OF HAYAGRIVA BUDDHA
THE GREEN RTA-MGRIN'S[1] INITIATION
CEREMONY FROM THE TREASURY
OF PERCIPIENCE

Obeisance to all Gurus!
In obedience to the order of the guardians of Dharma,
I relate these instructions of the initiation ritual of the Green Hayagriva from the Treasury of Percipience[2].

On the top of the Food Vase[3] one should make a Horsehead of butter,
And adorn it with a colored scarf and the proper jewel ornaments.

If one wishes to make a separate symbol[4],
He should prepare a separate figure of the Horsehead mounted upon the complete jewel-like body (of Hayagriva).
This figure should be placed on the Gtor-ma of Initiation.

Besides this, the various offerings should be made and traditional prayers recited as customary in the usual rituals.

As to the process of the Perfecting Device[5], one should practice the Yoga of the Bound and Wisdom Buddhas[6], also meditate on the Arising Buddha[7].

Then practice the inner and outer prayers such as the Three Refuges.

The (Buddha) in the Vase, the Buddha on the offering's Gtor-ma, and I, we three become instantaneously Vajra, the Horsehead, green in color, with two arms and all the adornments of the wrathful deity. One hand holds a human skull. Above the crowned head[8] of Hayagriva a horsehead appears. From the three places shine the three words, and the green *Sri* word standing on the Sun Disc with the rosary of invocation arranged from left to right (clockwise) encircling the (main seed-word) *Sri*. From all these words glorious rays of light shine forth in the ten directions. Immediately an innumerable host of green Hayagrivas descend, like rainfall, from the Pure Land of all the Buddhas to this place (of ritual), entering my body and merging with me fully. They also enter into and merge with the symbolic Hayagriva in the Front Vase. By this the Wisdom Buddha is assimilated with (the symbolic) Buddha; the preparation of the guru for the initiation is completed. From the Perfect Buddha's body flows forth a stream of nectar, filling the whole Vase.

Oṃ Hayagriva Hu Lu Hu Lu Hūṃ Pai!

This invocation would be recited not less than one hundred times.

Ah Rgyam!

The King of the Wrathful Deities, the meritorious Horse Lord,

Yells with dreadful voice, as the horse roaring.

This terrible voice subdues all demons and all evils!

To the King of the Wrathful Ones

I render my obeisance and praise!

After this the disciples should gather together and perform the Cleansing Ritual followed by the Mandala offering ritual.

(The Guru addresses the disciples:)

Now is the time to grant you the initiation of the Green Hayagriva. In the time long past when the Great Bliss-Beyond-Effort, the Lotus Dancing-Master, the Lord Buddha Amida was staying in the Heaven of *Aog-min*[9], a vicious demon named Dregs Byod Tshogs Sprul (prideful actor multitude-conjurer) roamed the worlds (of the Cosmos), committing various evils and doing grievous harm to all sentient beings. Therefore the Lord conjured the Mandala of the Green Hayagriva, and by this subjugated the demon. Whereupon the great Mandala of Hayagriva was elaborated, the Tantra of Hayagriva preached. This caused the king of all demons great distress. In a furious mood, he raised his five burning poisons[10] and deranged the Three Kingdoms[11]. He brought contagious diseases, famine, and war to the world. He destroyed the crops and showered various weapons of destruction upon the earth. At his instigation all the demons displayed dreadful forms; plagues raged, fields were scorched, and great floods covered the corners of the earth. Evil burned continually like furious fire; both the Path of Virtue[12] and the Paths of Liberation[13] were cut; the minds of the people were oppressed; and all the sentient beings throughout the Six Lokas were thrown into immeasurable misery. Thereupon, the Bhagavan (Amida), from his heart center, sent forth the Mandala of the Wrathful Hayagriva, whereby the demon king was subjugated and bound to observe the Precepts.

By the end of the Kasyapa Buddha's[14] time in this Kalpa, the demon king Matram Rutras afflicted all the sentient beings, killing them and eating their corpses. Whereupon the Bhagavan again sent forth the Mandala of Hayagriva, transformed in blue, and plunged it into the chest of the demon, cutting him to pieces. After the extinction of the demon, his demon-body became the abode of Hayagriva. Then he was bound by the Precepts and became known as Mahagala, the Guardian of Dharma. At that time, the *Tantra of the Manifestation of the Superb Horse* was preached. Later on, the Nirmanakaya Buddha, Gotama, preached the *Seven Hundred Stanzas of the Enlightenment of Hayagriva.*

Because of the numerous lineages of Gurus beginning with Hayagriva, preached in these sources, the well-known saying arose: "The lineages of Hayagriva are as many as the Horsehead's conjuration."

For all the sects of the Red-Cap School, a green Hayagriva in a form with four faces and eight arms was introduced also, as stated in the *Tantra of Sambhuda.*

This, now, is the history of Hayagriva quoted from the Treasury of Percipience:

When the Living Buddha[15] Mi-rgyur-rdo-rje (Immutable Vajra), was eleven years old, he captured entirely by intuition thirteen volumes of the Treasury of Dharma from Heavenly Sources[16] within three years. Afterward he also received this one volume of the Treasury of Percipience. Although there was an indication that he might have captured another one hundred volumes from the Treasury of Earth, he did not receive any due to unfavourable influences. His external life was ill-omened. By the age of seventeen, he had completed his work on the Treasury of Percipience. In one of his books of Initiation, this volume was found. As said in the *Sutra of the Emerging of Pure Dharma, Chos-yan-dag-par-sbyun pahi-mdo:*

"There will come a few Bodhisattvas of pure mind and heart who, merely through the observation of their own consciousness, will obtain the inner teachings and the principles of Dharma (the law or nature of reality); from them these inner teachings of Dharma will thence be imparted to the people."

This is evidence that the tradition of the *Dharma from Treasury* finds support in the Sutras.

Furthermore, the *Dharma from Treasury*[17] is deeper and more profound than the *Dharma from Mouth*[18] (preaching). The *Treasury from Heaven*[19] is more profound than the *Treasury from Earth*[20]. Again, the *Treasury of Percipience* is more profound than the *Treasury From Heaven.*

The benefits to the devotee who practices the Yoga of Hayagriva were stated in *The Manifestation of the Superb Victorious Wrathful Great Horse Tantra:*

"To the superb Initiation of the Fierce Hayagriva
And the victorious Tantra of great value!
If one surely beholds the initiation and has a
  fancy for it, he will be emancipated from fear and all
  diseases.
Those who practice the Yoga of Hayagriva, their patron
  Buddha,
Will be immune for seven hundred births from falling
  into the lower path and hell.
Those who have the faith and the pure realization con-
  stantly,
Will in their future life be born in the Pure Land.
If one recites each word of incantation 100,000 times,
Right in this life he shall see the face of Hayagriva.
Even in offering a part of the offerings to the Lord,
He will influence his surroundings and his neighbors.
Those who merely recite the incantation frequently
Will be free from the afflictions caused by evil spirits."

So it is said in this Sutra.

The Tantra of Proud Master Hayagriva states:

"Those who practice the Yoga of Hayagriva will attain the Common and the Eight Superb Accomplishments. They will also obtain the Four Accomplishments of the Illumination-Holding[21] (Yogi). He who does this will likewise attain the Three Bodies, the Four Bodies, the Five Bodies, and so on. He will also attain the Accomplishment of Mahamudra."

The Secret Wrathful Hayagriva Tantra declares as follows:

"When it comes near to the Ending-Time[22]

The Tantric Yogis who desire to perform the inner invocation practice

Will be able to protect themselves from disease and harm

If they invoke this profound ritual.

Whatever intention they have in mind,

Whatever act they wish to perform,

If they visualize the body of Hayagriva clearly,

No one will be able to oppose or afflict them.

For the armor of Śūnyatā[23] is unparalleled,

This is the King of all Protections."

The Precious One, Padma Sambhava, also said:

"Whoever has obtained the complete initiation

At the time of death, when he enters into the state of Bardo,

From the Palace-beyond-Measure[24] of the great burning bliss

Will come his patron Buddha and lead him into paradise."

As stated in the *Sutra for Forming Hayagriva:*

"Whoever, including even the insects, has heard the

name and incantation of Hayagriva only one time will never again fall into the lower paths[25]. Therefore, to those who have taken the Bodhisattva's Vow and obtained the Initiation, to them have accrued merits extremely great. Thus you disciples who have come here for the profound initiation should follow my reading and repeat:

To all the Buddhas in the past, present, and future,
And especially to the Buddha, the Green Hayagriva,
I sincerely pray to grant me the Initiation of Hayagriva."
(Repeat this stanza three times.)

(The Guru says:) Now follow me in repeating the prayers of the Three Refuges, the Confession of All Sins, and the great Vow of Bodhisattva:

I take refuge in the Three Precious Ones,
I also take refuge in Hayagriva.
I confess all the sins and evil doings that I have committed;
I shall view all the good deeds and merits of sentient beings with sympathetic joy.
I pray that all the Buddhas and Bodhisattvas ceaselessly remember me in their minds.
From now on till the time of attaining the perfect Buddhahood,
I take refuge in the Buddha, the Dharma, and the Sangha.
For the benefit of self and others
I raise the incomparable Heart for Bodhi[26].
When this prime vow of the Heart for Bodhi is made,
I shall render my services to all the sentient beings.
I shall treat them as my friends and kinsmen.
I vow to practice the Actions of Bodhi[27] with determination and joy
In order to benefit all the sentient beings.

I hope the day I attain the Buddhahood will come soon!

After this is repeated more than three times, the Guru takes the holy grass of the Vase of Performance and sprinkles water from the Vase over the disciples.

(The Guru then reads the incantation of Śūnyatā:)[28]

Oṃ soubava shuta sarva dharma soubava shutor haṃ!
(The meaning of which is explained as "All the universe becomes a great emptiness.")

From the Emptiness, you, the one who seeks the initiation, and the Front-Arising-Buddha[29] from whom the initiation is given, together with the other Gtor-mas, all immediately become the holy word *Śri*. This *Śri* word is seated on a resplendent Sun Disc supported by a lotus with eight leaves. From the *Śri* word spring beams whose rays touch the Heavens and render homage to all the Buddhas, and again the rays shine forth upon all the worlds to relieve the sufferings of sentient creatures and to benefit all beings. Finally all the beams contract into the *Śri* word.

This *Śri* word now transforms itself into an emerald, in color like the green Hayagriva's body; above, his face, red and wrathful, with three widely opened eyes, stares fiercely as if looking on all obstacles and demons. All the hairs of his head stand up in the midst of a cluster of flames burning vehemently as though blazing in a strong wind. All-radiant, the vigorous horse-face glows green. With the terrible voice of the horse, he yells with such fury that all the universe is shaken.

On his head Hayagriva wears a crown made of five human skulls, the top of each skull adorned with five glowing jewels. His mouth opens wide, exposing his tongue and his four canine teeth that symbolize the subjugation of the four demons[30]. His eyebrows and beard burn with fire.

A new moon stands at his side. In his right hand, he grasps a curved knife with a cross-shaped vajra as its handle. In his left hand, he holds a human skull filled with blood. Large of body, sturdy of limb, he stands posturing on a corpse of the demon enemy which lies above the Sun-Lotus-Disc. Blood-drops, the great ash-bundle, six ornaments of bone, and the snake-tassel adorn his sun-like figure, clothed with elephant skins and wearing the tiger-skin apron. He possesses all the adornments of the wrathful one.

He is posturing in a flame as great in fury as the fire of this Kalpa's ending. On his forehead lies a white *Oṃ*, on his throat a red *Ah*, on his heart a blue *Hūṃ*. In his heart center stands a green *Sri*. From all these words rays of light in many colors reach out unto the Pure Land. By this light the Buddhas in the Pure Land are invited to descend. From the Palace-beyond-Measure of the Great Bliss Master Wrathful One, the green Hayagrivas descend in numbers countless as snowflakes falling — some large as Mount Sumeru[31], others tiny as seeds of mustard. All of them enter into your body and dissolve in you. You should attentively visualize like this.

(The trumpet is blown and musical instruments played.)
(The Guru reads as follows:)
Hūṃ All the Buddhas and the green Hayagrivas,
Pray come here and grant us your blessing!
Please bestow the initiation to these faithful and well-endowed ones;
Pray dispel the obstacles to our longevity.
Oṃ Hayagriva Hulu Hulu Hūṃ Pai! Ba-tsa Ah Wi Sha Ya Ah Ah!
(Recite three or seven times; adjust the Vajra Head.)

The Wisdom Buddha thus becomes stable.

Dee Chr Ba-Tsa[32]!

The myriad initiation Wisdom Buddhas all come!

Ba-tsa Samaya!

I pray you to grant the initiation to my disciples.

After this prayer visualize that the Initiation of the Vase is granted by the Buddhas.

Hūṃ! From the Palace-beyond-Measure comes the Initiation of Vase.

Having obtained the complete Initiation of Vase,

The well-endowed disciples will easily attain the Four Bodies of Buddha;

Also they will achieve the Four Accomplishments[33].

In the future, may they constantly receive the great initiations.

Oṃ Hayagriva Hulu Hulu Hūṃ Pai! Oṃ Sarva Datagada Ahbiuigade Samaya Bri Ya Pai!

The disciples receive the initiation as rays of light. Thereupon the bodies of the disciples are filled with nectar, and all their sins are purified. The nectar received from Hayagriva is so much that the body cannot hold it all. The superfluous nectar swarms up out of the head to form a horsehead. It utters the yell of the horse three times. According to this description, visualize. (The Guru sprinkles water with the holy grass.)

By tasting the water in this Vase, you will attain unlimited Power of Mouth[34]. (Each disciple tastes the water of the Vase.)

Now, in order to attain the Initiation of Body, Mouth, Mind, Merits, and Accomplishment, follow me and repeat three times:

To all the Buddhas and Hayagriva in the Three Times

Especially to the green Hayagriva

I pray you to grant me the Accomplishments and the Initiation of the Five Bodies.

Then think that from the forehead of the Front-Arising-Buddha emanate innumerable small wrathful Hayagrivas white as a white shell. Visualize these entering into your forehead and penetrating fully all parts of your body.

Hūṃ! The one who illustrates the conduct of the great Precept.

I pray to that great fierce one to come here.

I pray you to grant me the accomplishments of Body, Mouth, and Mind;

Also bestow on me the power to exhibit and protect the Doctrine and other Tantric abilities.

Through the attainment of this Initiation of Body

All the sins, hindrances, and illnesses within my body are purified.

Oṃ Hayagriva Hulu Hulu Hūṃ Pai Gayanbidi Tsi Oṃ!

(If available, set up five Hayagriva images in five different colors. Otherwise use the Gtor-ma and discard it afterwards.)

Hūṃ! All the teachings of Buddhas embodied in Padmasambhava [35].

He is the Dharmakaya, the Buddha Amida, the Diamond Doctrine.

From the *Śri* word of the All-merciful One (Avalokiteśvara)

Was formed the Great Speech Body.

May the horse-yelling-laughing-body bring us propitiousness!

Thus the Body Initiation is attained, the defilements of the body are purified, and illnesses and demonic hindrances are dissolved. The seed of the Vajra body is thus planted (or obtained).

Again, disciples, you should visualize that from the throat of the Front-Arising-Buddha emanate numerous Speech-Hayagrivas, red as rubies. These figures are tiny but fully formed. They all enter into your throat and these fierce red Hayagrivas fill your entire body.

Hūṃ! The one who illustrates the conduct of the Great
    Precept,
I pray the great Fierce One to come here.
I pray you to grant me the Accomplishments of Body,
    Mouth and Mind;
Also bestow on me the Power of Showing, the capabil-
    ity of protecting the Doctrine, and other Tantric abil-
    ities.
I pray you to grant me the Superb Initiation of Speech;
Thereby my power of speech will be magnified.
Oṃ Hayagriva Waga Ahbiditsa Ah! (The Guru places the symbol on the disciple's throat).
Hūṃ! Like the King of Initiation who gave the all-es-
    sential initiations,
This initiation is a green one like the fire of Kalpa's end.
This initiation is greatly bright like the hundred thousand
    suns gathering together.
Pray the Initiation Buddha grant us the propitiousness
    of speech!
Thus, through the attainment of the Initiation of the
    Mouth,
All the obstacles of speech are cleared;
The seed of the Speech of Buddha is thus planted.
Again, you should think that from the Front-Arising-Buddha's heart emanate infinitely small Hayagrivas, blue

as sapphires, and fully formed of limb. They all enter into
your heart, and thus the fierce blue Hayagrivas fill your
body.

Hūṃ! The one who illustrates the conduct of the Great
Precept.

I pray the great fierce one to come here.

I pray you to grant me the accomplishments of Body,
Mouth, and Mind;

Also bestow on me the power of appearance, and the
capability of protecting the Doctrine, and other Tantric abilities.

I pray you to grant me the Initiation of Mind;

Thereby the bliss and illumination of mind will be vividly illustrated.

Oṃ Hayagriva... Tsi Da Ahbiditsa Hūṃ! (The symbol is
placed on the disciple's heart.)

Although your mind-essence never moves nor wavers

Nor departs from the immutable quietude,

For the sake of subduing the vicious enemy and obstacles

You arose and uttered the fierce voice in the flame of
Kalpa's end;

Pray that the reverend mighty mind of yours grant us
propitiousness!

Thus the Initiation of Mind is attained, and all the defilements of mind are cleansed. The seed of Mind-Vajra is
thus planted.

Again you should think that from the navel of the Front-
Arising-Buddha emanate infinite fierce Hayagrivas of the
Merits, yellow in color like hemp. These are tiny but com-
pletely formed. They all enter into the navel of your body.
Thus the fierce yellow Hayagrivas fill your body completely.

Hūṃ! The one who...

I pray the...

I pray you to grant me...

Also bestow me the power of Showing...

I pray you to grant me the Initiation of Merits

Thereby I pray that my power and might will be greatly
   augmented.

Oṃ Hayagriva Sarva Ahbi Ditsi Śri!

Having been born from the lineage of non-craving,

And having acted in the manner of a king to subdue the
   demons,

With your flame blazing furiously like the fire of the
   Ending-Time,

O wrathful king, Hayagriva! I pray you to grant us
   prosperity!

Thus the Initiation of Merits is attained. The defilements
of decay dissolve. Hindrances to longevity and prosperity
are subdued. The seed of Merits-without-Effort is thus
planted.

Again think that from the place of generation of the
Front-Arising-Buddha emanate numerous emerald golden
coloured Hayagrivas and enter into the place of generation
in your body; thus the golden Hayagrivas fill your body
[thus impregnated by the Buddha]*.

Hūṃ! The one who...

I pray the...

* We have added this parenthesis to clarify an important
concept, which though stated here in simple form, expresses the
fundamental idea of the new birth of the regenerate man within
the shell or womb of the old self — the renewed man, born of
divine power. The essential *gotra* concept explained in our Introduction in vitally close to the meaning of the text. *Ed.*

73

I pray you to grant me...
Also bestow on me the power...
I pray you to grant me the Initiation of Performance
Pray destroy all sickness, demons and obstacles.
Oṃ Hayagriva Garma Zabiditsa Pai!
Śri! The original nature is beyond appearing and extinction;
The magnificently manifested Horse-Body is never apart from the immutable nature of being.
Through the superb speech of horse-yelling the beings are subjugated.
May the accomplishments without effort and without difference (from Hayagriva) be granted!
May prosperity and propitiousness be bestowed upon us.

Thus the Initiation of Performance is attained, the Obstacle to Omniscience[36] cleared away. All hindrances to things desired are subdued. And planted is the seed of benefitting sentient beings in all actions.

Now that you have attained the Initiations of the Body, Mouth, Mind, Merits, and Performance, let us look into the practice of Gtor-ma by which things desired are accomplished.

Think that the Gtor-ma itself becomes the green Hayagriva with all adornments as described previously. Also visualize the Succession of Gurus[37] sitting on his head. See one after another come quickly to the top of your head like clouds gathering together. Think: Whatever I pray to them, the wish is granted; the wave of grace and the various Siddhis are bestowed on me. Then see all the Gurus vaporized into a great light and see all enter your body as beams of light and merge with you.

Hūṃ! I pray the...
I pray you to grant me...
Also grant me the power of Showing...
I pray you to grant me the Initiation of Gtor-ma,
Thus I shall become identical with Hayagriva.
The Body, Mouth, Mind, Merits, and Performance of
   Hayagriva
Encompass and contain the quintessence of all good-
   ness.
I pray you, Hayagriva, grant me all accomplishments in
   this very moment!
I pray the Dharmakaya, Buddha of Infinite Light,
I pray the Sambogakaya, the All-Merciful One,
I pray the Nirmanakaya, the Guru Padma Sambhava.
Also I pray the Dakini Yishi Tsojar, the great teacher
   Beroo Tsana,
The powerful one Barji Sange, the Immutable Vajra who
   conquers demons.
To those Keepers of the Tantra, the Succession-Gurus,
   I pray.
I pray the Hayagriva of the Performance-Lineage,
The Heruka- (Vajra) of Superb Horse who conjures
   numerous retinues and sub-retinues.
I pray that you all grant me the Wave of Grace,
I pray you to grant me the Initiations.
Pray protect me from the harm of male and female de-
   mons,
Also protect me from the dragon demons and the eight
   divisions of heavenly demons.
Pray protect me from injuries, ulcers, pains, illnesses,
   all four-hundred-and-four kinds of sickness, together
   with all afflictions.

May all these misfortunes be conquered.

May all the virtuous merits, powers, and fortunes increase for me.

Protect me from the fear of suffering Low Birth and Samsara.

Oṃ Hayagriva Hulu Hulu Hūṃ Pai, Hūṃ Hayagriva Hūṃ Hūṃ, Gayavačatseda Ahbiditsa Hūṃ!

Now I am going to grant you the Superb Green Hayagriva's rosary; follow me and repeat:

I pray the perfect Buddha to look after me,

Pray make me your servant.

Throughout these prayers the heart of the green Hayagriva sends forth a green incantation rosary, which enters into your mouth and finally arranges itself in a right-winding circle.

Repeat the incantation three times:

Oṃ Hayagriva Huluhulu Hūṃ Pai:

Thereupon the incantation rosary becomes a flower rosary, which you must see wreathed upon your head.

I pray the perfect Buddha to bless me,

Pray make me your servant.

Oṃ Susra Di-Tsra Ba-Tsa Svaha!

Now you have already obtained the comprehensive Initiation of the Green Hayagriva. Under the blessing and protection of your patron Buddha, Hayagriva, you should repeat with me the following words:

Whatever the admonishments our master has given to us,

We will follow and obey and practice.

From this moment on, please always remember us!

I offer you my whole being and all my possessions,

Pray have pity on me and consider me as your disciple!

Pray be my shelter and refuge at all times!

For beseeching forgiveness, the disciples should offer the Mandala practice and recite the Mandala prayer...

If, in my account of this ritual, there is any mistake or discrepancy, pray all Buddhas to forgive me in my ignorance. I hope that, through the good deeds of this work, all sentient beings will find peace and happiness. Wherever this book is presented, may propitiousness come to that place.

NOTES

1 *Rta-mgrin:* A Tantric Buddha; Sanskrit — Hayagriva. The literal translation of the Tibetan name is *Horsehead* or *Horseneck.*

2 *Treasury of Percipience (Dgons-gter):* One of the four Treasuries of the Red School. Treasury *(Gter)* means the hidden teachings of the esoteric doctrine. These esoteric teachings were hidden in the rocks, caves, and underground. Their discovery is preordained for the right time by the right person, who introduces them to the faithful. This is the regular Treasury, or *Treasury of Earth.* There are other types, such as the *Treasury from Heaven;* that is, the Treasury Finders see the revealed scriptures in dreams or in trances, or hear the reciting of the scriptures, incantations, and prophecy from the deities. The highest Treasury, according to the Red School, is the *Treasury of Percipience;* this type of Treasury does not require even the revelations — from the intuitive sense the Treasury is naturally unfolded.

3 *Vase:* In the Highest Division of Diamond Vehicle (the Anuttara Tantra of the Vajrayana), there are altogether four classes of initiations: the Initiation of Vase, the Secret Initiation, the Wisdom Initiation, and the Initiation of Great Symbol (Mahamudra). This initiation ceremony belongs to the first class; therefore, the symbol of vase plays a very important role. The vase symbolizes the original nature of Buddhahood; it also draws the grace wave and blessing from the real Buddhas (the Wisdom Buddhas), and so the original or Buddha nature can thus be unfolded. The vase is also the center of all symbols used in the initiation performance. The vase or vases are different in number; usually one is enough, but sometimes two, three, four, or even ten are used. The initiation vase has many different names, too.

4 The *separate symbol* is the effigy of a complete body of Hayagriva; the horsehead effigy is molded from tsamba (cooked barley flour) and decorated with colored butter.

5 *The Perfecting Device:* The identification of Buddha nature (the Bound Vase), the praying to Buddha, the coming and blessing from Buddha, the unification of Buddha and vase

(Buddha nature) – these four processes make a Perfecting Device.

6 *Bound Buddha and Wisdom Buddha* (or Bound One and Wisdom One): The original Buddha nature, which is not lost but hidden or "bound" deep within each sentient being. The Bound One (the cause or impulse toward realization) must be merged with the Wisdom or Fruit Buddha to produce the enlightenment.

7 *Arising Buddha:* The Bound Buddha is also called the Arising Buddha.

8 *Crowned head:* One of the thirty-two signs of Buddhahood.

9 *a Og-min:* The highest Buddha paradise (*lit.* "inferior to none").

10 *Five burning poisons:* Lust, hate, blindness, jealousy, and pride.

11 *The Three Kingdoms:* the domains of desire, of form, and of the formless.

12 *Path of Virtue:* The teaching or the path that leads one to a happier life in one's next birth. The precept of Ten Virtues is taught in Buddhism, and by the practice of these Ten Virtues one may go to heaven and live there for a long period. But this practice can never bring one to liberation, because the Ten Virtues are not practiced in the light of non-kleśa or non-discrimination. The kleśas and discrimination are the two main causes of Saṃsāra.

13 *Paths of Liberation:* The Paths of Four Noble Truths and the Path of Bodhisattva.

14 *Kasyapa Buddha:* The Buddha directly antecedent to Gotama Buddha.

15 *Living Buddha:* Tibetan, *Sprul-skur;* literally the Transformation Body of Buddha (Nirmanakaya). But nowadays this name is merely a title or a rank of a Lama; it no longer has any significant meaning in religion.

16 and 17 See Note 2.

18 *Dharma from Mouth:* Traditional Hinayana and ordinary sources of Buddhist doctrine.

19 and 20 See Note 2.

21 *Illumination-Holding:* A title of the Tantric Yogi. *Illumination (Rig)* has a number of meanings.

22 *Ending-Time:* The end of our time. Buddhist tradition says that there will come a time when all beings on earth will be annihilated. Here, however, the author means to emphasize a *Bad Time* — when kleśas and all misfortunes prevail in the world. The Tibetan term *Mtha-ma* means both *the Last* and *the Worst.*

23 *Śunyāta:* The Voidness, emptiness. The teaching of Voidness is the most important in Buddhism.

24 *Palace-beyond-Measure:* The size of the abode of the Buddhas is beyond measurement — infinite. *Ed.*

25 *Lower Paths:* Three lower paths of the six Lokas of Saṃsāra — Hell, Hungry Ghosts, and Animals.

26 *Heart for Bodhi:* The wish to liberate sentient beings, to practice the Six Paramitas and actions of a Bodhisattva.

27 *Actions of Bodhi:* the practice of Six Paramitas and Four Dominations Practices, etc.

28 *Incantation of Śunyāta:* Generally, Tibetan Buddhists never expect to understand incantations or to trans-late them into ordinary language, since the literal cannot contain the whole truth. Tradition does not try to explain the incantations but treats the secret words as sacred syllables and sounds. Being symbolic, each word and sound has many meanings. This sacred statement is called "The Incantation on the Observation of the Emptiness."

29 *Front-Arising Buddha:* The Buddha of the Vase.

30 *Four Demons:* Illness, Obstacles to Dharma, Death, and Kleśas.

31 *Mount Sumeru:* A symbolic huge mountain. According to Buddhist legend, it is located in the center of the cosmos.

32 This short incantation is to stabilize the coming Buddha.

33 *The Four Accomplishments:* To alleviate sorrows and misfortunes; to augment merits; to attract sentient beings; and to subdue demons.

34 *Power of Mouth:* Speech, singing, admonishing.

35 *Padmasambhava:* Founder of the Red [or Nying-mapa] School. This ritual belongs to the Red School, so Padmasambhava's name is always mentioned. The followers of this School believe that the body of Padmasambhava was transmitted from

Buddha Amida; his mouth from Avalokiteśvara; and his mind from Gotama Buddha. Another way of viewing this is to say that Padmasambhava received his Dharmakaya from Amiba, his Sambhoga-kaya. Avalokiteśvara; his Nirmana-kaya from Gotama.

Padmasambhava received his Dharmakaya from Avalokiteśvara; his Nirmanakaya from Gotama.

36 *Obstacle to Omniscience:* Another translation is the *Hindrance of Knowing*. To attain Nirvana, one must annihilate the Hindrance of kleśa, which is the direct cause of Saṃsāra. But to attain the Non-Abiding Nirvana (Mahayana's view of the perfect Nirvana), one must also annihilate the Hindrance of Knowing, or the Obstacle to Omniscience. Since the Bodhisattvas aspire not merely to liberation but also to *Perfection*, the extermination of the Hindrance is necessary in attaining the perfect Buddhahood.

37 *Succession of Gurus:* The Lineage or Rosary of Gurus in direct succession from Hayagriva.

CHAPTER FIVE

*Of the Heart Treasury of Heavenly Dharma, Among the
Oceanlike Teachings in the Whisper Succession, This is*

THE INITIATION RITUAL
OF THE RED GSHIN-RJE[1]

Namo Guru Diwa Dargini Shidi Hūṃ! [Note
Tibetan transliterations of Sanskrit words like
Deva and *Ḍākinī. Ed.*]
If one wants to practice the Three Pillars[2] Red
Gshin-rje, he should arrange the Mandala as
in that of the foregoing rituals. He should prepare a hill-
shaped Gtor-ma. At the back of the Gtor-ma, a vase with
red decorations on its brim should be placed.

Both the preparation for the initiation by the Guru and
the actual initiation ritual (by the deity) require only the
general Gtor-ma and offerings. Before the initiation ceremony takes place, the teacher should perform and meditate at least once on the following prayers, which include
the Self-Front-Arising Yoga, confession, and other prayers.
If one wants to perform a very comprehensive ritual, he may
elaborate by reciting the prayers of the Three Pillars as well
as the Bodhisattva's Vow and the like. After these practices
the Guru should follow the instructions given below:

I, myself, become the Red Gshin-rje;
Three faces, six arms, and four legs, stretched apart.
The right face is blue; the left, black; and the center, red.
The three arms on the right side hold the club, Vajra,
    and knife.

The three arms on the left side hold the bloodskull, bell,
  and stick.
Also adorning him are the complete ornaments of a
  Fierce Buddha.
He (I) sits on the cushion of the Sun-Moon-Lotus Wheel.
Absorbing himself in this meditation, the teacher should
recite the following incantation:
Ah Śri Hūṃ Śri Hūṃ Soha!
(By reciting this incantation the Red Gshin-rje is con-
solidated).
Sa Ma Yu Chia Chia Chia!
"Sa Ma Yu Chia Chia Chia!"
The Guru recites and meditates:
In front of me is the Buddha of the Vase,
In the center of his heart there is a Sun Disc,
Upon which stands a red *Hūṃ* letter.
Around this *Hūṃ* circle the words of this incantation
  in a clock-wise order.
From his body shine forth splendid rays of light.
The Buddhas, Bodhisattavas, Three Pillars, and all de-
  ities in the ten directions and three times, all become
  the red Gshin-rje.
Like rain falling, they descend here and are absorbed
  into the Buddha of the Front Vase.
From the body of the Vase Buddha incessantly flows out
  the Water of Heaven.
Thus should one meditate, also reciting the incantation
as much as he can. Then the disciples should gather near
the Mandala and offer flowers and food. If conditions per-
mit, it is desirable to conduct a complete performance, including the preparation ritual with offerings, confessions,
consecration, and exorcising.

The Guru then addresses the disciples:

Now, you are to be given the Initiation of the Red Gshin-rje. He is identical with Mañjuśri[3] in essence. The Sutra of Mañjuśri says:

"If one repeatedly calls the names of numerous Buddhas as numerous as the total number of sands in the sixty-two Ganges rivers – his merits are great; but if he calls the name of Mañjuśri only once, his merits are even greater." Hence it is obvious that if one attains the Initiation of Mañjuśri, his merits should be greater than the merits of those who attain the initiations of Buddhas as numerous as the sands of the Ganges. Among the Four Divisions of Tantra, this initiation belongs to the most profound Tantra, namely, the Highest Division Tantra (Anuttara Tantra). Of the two forms of Mañjuśri, this is the fierce one. Among all the Fierce Buddhas, this one is most powerful and effective. As said in a Tantra:

"When some fierce deities behold the Fierce Gshin-rje,
they are frightened, they tremble, and the weapons
they brandish slip from their hands."

Furthermore, we, all the scientist beings, are going to see the Gshin-rje, for he is the King of Death for everyone. No one in this world is immortal; therefore everyone is destined to see the Gshin-rje one day.
As said in the Sutra:

"From the Buddhas of the three times
Down to the lowest animals, the insects and worms,
All should be wise to keep good relations with the
King of Death, the Life-eater, the powerful one!

This Deva Yama is conjured by Bodhisattva Mañjuśri. If one attains the initiation of this Deva, all the retinues of Yama will not harm him. He is freed from the Untimely

Death. He will also be immune from illness and sufferings at the moment of his death. The hostile demons, such as Dur-mi, Dun-zur, She-yi, and She-ga never harm him. This Deva Yama is an extremely formidable one; therefore, keep on good terms with him."

Thus the Sutra says.

This initiation of Deva Yama, extremely powerful and dynamic, yet easy to practice and to accomplish, was given by the All-Perfect Buddha to my first Guru*, Mi-jyur-rdo-rje (The Immutable Vajra), early one morning in the Dragon Month of the Monkey Year when he was twelve years old. I obtained this initiation from him, the Adi-Buddha like Illumination-Possessor, directly. Hence, this teaching has a very close and warm succession – the conduit through which the grace-waves are transmitted. Therefore, you should all join the initiation ceremony with great reverence and high spirits. You should now think that I and all the initiation symbols are identical with the Red Yama himself.

In the preparation of the initiation, the disciples are to follow the Guru in reciting the following prayers.

I pray to all the Buddhas in the three times,

I especially pray to the Red Yama,

I pray Thee to grant me the Initiation.

(Repeat three times. Then the disciples should recite the prayer of taking the Three Refuges and the confession, and so on).

I take refuge in the Three Precious Ones,

I take refuge in the Red Yama.

I confess all the sins that I have committed.

*The Guru-Scribe is speaking. – *Ed.*

I raise the sympathetic joy toward all good deeds.
To the Buddhas and Bodhi, I aspire.
From now on till the time of my attaining the Bodhi,
I shall take refuge in the Three Precious Ones,
For the sake of benefitting others and self,
I now raise the all-virtuous Bodhi Heart.
I will serve all sentient beings as their servant.
I will practice the all-virtuous Action-of Bodhi[4].
For the benefit of sentient beings,
I offer my heart in the pursuit of Bodhi-Fruit.
(Recite three times; bless the disciples with the holy grass.)
Now, disciples, you should visualize the Red Yama as follows:

You all, each of you instantaneously, become the Red Yama,
Three faces, six arms, and four feet extending apart.
The right face, blue; the left, black; and the center, red.
The three right arms hold club, Vajra, and knife.
The three left arms hold blood-skull, bell, and long club.
You become completely adorned with all the Fierce ornaments
And sit on the Lotus-cushion of the Sun-Moon disc.

In this manner you should visualize yourself as the Red Yama. See a white *Oṃ* placed at your forehead, a red *Ah* at your throat, a blue *Hūṃ* at your heart. From them emanate infinite rays of light reaching to the Buddha's Pure Land and also the Land of Self-Nature[5] inviting all the Buddhas and the Red Yama together with infinite incantation, tantric symbols and seeds[6] to come here, and they all enter and are absorbed in you as the rain falls into the ocean and merges with it.

(Play all musical instruments.)

Hūm! the Red Yama and all deities!

I pray you to come down here and to bless these
faithful and gifted disciples!

I pray you to grant them the highest initiation;

Thus they may eschew temptations and not go astray,

Thus they may be freed from all the causes of
accidental and untimely death[7].

Om Śri Hūm Śri Hūm Savha Betsa Ah Bi Sha Ya Ah Ah

(Recite this incantation as much as possible and play the
musical instruments. Next, the Guru places the Diamond
Flower on the heads of the disciples.)*

Now the disciples should think that the Wisdom Buddha
is consolidated.

Di Cha Ben Tsa!

Thereupon the Guru holds the vase in his hand and
     says:

This is the vase in which the Red Yama resides;

I now place it on your head,

I now grant you the Four Initiations of the Red Yama.

*Om Śri Hūm Śri Hūm Savha Ga Na Sha Gu Haya Tsa
Dur Ah Bi Ai Tsa Hūm!*

(He places the Vase on the heads of the disciples and
baptizes them.)

Then the Guru holds the Gtor-ma in hand and says:

Hūm! This is the body of the Red Yama,

This is the complete body of the Red Yama.

By him, the Four Initiations are given to you.

---

* In the "Diamond Flower" the symbolism of the combined
natures of active love (upāya) with the lotus of wisdom (prajñā)
or padma. The same symbolism exists in the sacred phrase "The
Jewel or Vajra-Diamond is in the lotus." — *Ed.*

Pray! that you will attain all the accomplishments of the
Four Initiations.

I pray the Dharmakaya, the All-Perfect Buddha; I pray
the Sambhogakaya, the Buddha Amida; I pray the Nirmanakaya, the Guru Padmasambhava; I pray Dakini Yeshes-
mtsho-rgyal; the twenty-five disciples; the hundred-and-
eight Treasury Finders; and all the Ocean-like Illumina-
tion-Holders. I pray the peaceful and wrathful tutelary
deities. I pray the Red Yama and the Ocean-like Dakinis,
Guardians. Pray all of you to bless my disciples. I pray you
to grant your grace-wave to them, and to bestow the initiations upon them. I pray you to protect them from the
afflictions of the self-demon, others-demon; the demon of
Dun-zur, Drug-drum, Gshed-bzhe; the demon of illness,
death; the demon-afflictor of Mdung-bsu, Rjes-rgyal – in
short, all the three-hundred-and-sixty different demons.
I pray you to protect them from the eighteen different kinds
of untimely death. I pray you to grant them the one hundred Siddhis, the Four Performances[8], the mundane and
transcendental accomplishments. I pray you to give them
these accomplishments without delay!

> *Oṃ Śri Huṃ Śri Hūṃ Savha Gayawaga Tsida Sarva Ah*
> *Bi Ditsa Hūṃ!*

(Recite this incantation three times.)

Thereupon, the Guru holds in his hand the consecrated
white shell whose curve is clockwise and says:

> *Hūṃ!* The Body, mouth, and mind of all Buddhas in the
> Three Times,
> Are embodied in this right-direction-circled shell.
> I now place it on the four centers of your body.
> Pray that you will attain the Four Initiations of the Red
> Yama.

Oṃ Śri Hūṃ Śri Hūṃ Savha Gayawaga Tsida Guna Garma Ah Bi Ditsa Hūṃ!

(At the same time, the Guru places the shell on the four centers [chakras] of the disciples.)

Thereupon, all should throw flowers and recite the auspicious wishes and prayers. Among the Ocean-like Teachings in the Whisper Succession, this is the Initiation of the Red Yama of "The Heavenly Dharma Treasury of Heart," in which one may find forty different Initiations at the concluding section. This Initiation of Yama which has just been given to you is one of them. From now on, you will be protected and be taken care of by the Red Yama. Therefore, let us all recite this prayer:

Whatever you have admonished us, we shall all obey
  and practice.
From now on you are my master,
Pray consider and remember me as your disciple,
Pray bless me and grant me the superlative Siddhis.

Thereupon the disciples should render their gifts and perform the Mandala Offering.

This initiation belongs to the teachings of the Heaven Dharma. It is based on the sayings of Buddha in its ritual and arrangement. No alterations or modifications were made. If, however, I have made any mistake in recording it, I pray that the Buddhas and all the Guardians of Dharma will forgive me and allow me to make apology.

Good wishes to all sentient beings.

NOTES

1 *The Red Gshin-rje (Yama):* How does Buddhism come to have a "judge of the dead" if, according to Buddhist doctrine, the Law of Karma responding to the individual's action brings of itself full punishment or reward? To understand why the position of Yama as Judge of the Dead is not contradictory, we must examine Buddhist thought on this doctrine. First, it should, however, be pointed out that while deities like Yama, Mahakala, and others may found in Hinduism, their meaning and interpretation is quite different in Buddhism.

There are three Buddhist views on the subject of Yama. One, briefly stated, is that Yama is not an objective god but the subject manifestation of an individual's conscience, which punishes him. Certain Sutras offer another explanation; that often a Bodhisattva declares he will transform his body into that of the Fierce Yama, in order to benefit many sinful people. For instance, in order to reduce a murderer's retribution, the Bodhisattva takes the place of the slaughterer. A third theory is that a number of sentient beings are connected to Yama by Karma. Because of their Karma, they must stand judgment in the after-death state. This is not necessary, however, for humans who have taken certain initiations or reached a certain enlightenment. The doctrine concerning Yama will be understood best, perhaps, if the reader remembers that Buddhism is very fluid in its teachings which best fit the different levels of human development.

2 *Three Pillars:* Guru, Patron Buddha, and Garuda.

3 *Mañjuśri::* A great Bodhisattva who represents the wisdom of all Buddhas.

4 *Action-of-Bodhi:* The Wish-for-Heart-of-Bodhi must be followed by *Action-for-Bodhi*, practical application of the Bodhisattva's precepts.

5 *Land of Self-nature:* Reality, the eternal world.

6 *Seeds:* The 'seed-words' such as *Śri* and *Hūṃ*, which the disciple visualizes placed in the various centers of the body according to the initiator's instructions.

7 *Untimely death:* According to Buddhism, there are two kinds of death. The first is that arising from the inevitable decay and running down of the bodily machine and its functions. The second, or untimely death is that which results from Karma of this or a previous life. This kind of death might have been prevented. Examples are death from accident, war, poison, capital punishment, or other man-made causes. This kind of death can be prevented by certain Yoga. Untimely death cannot be prevented by hygiene; Yoga is the antidote.

8 *Four Performances:* (1) to subdue ominous evils; (2) to increase whatever is auspicious, such as Wisdom and Merits; (3) to gain the power to attract human beings and animals; (4) to uproot and finally conquer various stubborn evils.

CHAPTER SIX

From the Treasury of Heaven This is

THE SUPERB INITIATION RITUAL
OF AHM GTSUG[1] VAJRAPĀNI

*Obeisance to Vajrapani!*
For the performance of the Initiation Ritual
of Vajrapani general preparations are required,
and the Vase and Gtor-ma should be arranged.
The yogi should think that both he and the
front Gtor-ma instantaneously become Vajrapani, whose
hair is as white as a shell, appearing in a form of Drang
Strong[2]. His right hand lifts up in a threatening manner of
conquering all the hindrances, and his left hand holds the
bell in front of his breast as a sign of attracting and increasing longevity, merits, and prosperities.

His body is greenish-grey adorned with silk scarves;
He wears a tiger-skin apron at the lower part of his body.
He stretches the left leg and bends the right.
Vajrapani stands vividly on the lotus-moon.
A *Hum* word stands on the moon disc in his heart center;
Circling the *Hum* word clockwise is the garland of
   Mantra,
From it emanate beams of light to the ten directions,
Inviting all Vajrapanis, the Masters of Tantra,
To come down here, entering into both the front Gtor-
   ma and the yogi's body.
The nectar in the vase now is overflowing.
Om Ba-tsa Pani Nama Hum!

(Recite this Mantra several hundred or thousand times, or recite it as much as one can. After the recitation of Mantra, the Eight-Offerings ritual should be performed.)

(Then, the guru addresses the disciples:)

Now, I am going to impart to you the initiation of Vajrapani, the Son of Buddha Samantabhadra. In fact, Vajrapani is identical in essence with Buddha Samantabhadra, who is considered to be the First Buddha or The Buddha, who came into being before all other Buddhas. Vajrapani has different forms, as clearly stated in the *Tantra of One-Hundred-and-Eight Praisings*. These different forms can be classified as the Wrathful Ones, the Peaceful Ones, and the Wrathful-Peaceful Ones. This initiation belongs to the Wrathful-Peaceful form. According to the *Heart Treasury of the Heavenly Dharma*, Vajrapani has thirteen different of the Heavenly Dharma, Vajrapani has thirteen different forms; this Vajrapani is the one appearing in the form of Ahm Gtsug. He is not known heretofore on earth.

At one time, Vajrapani transformed himself as a sage deity (Tib. Drang Srong) named Gon-b'a-skyes, and engaged himself in deep Samadhi at the west side of Mount Sumeru. At that time Buddha Rnam-gzigs came to this world. When he was about to manifest the manner of realizing the Perfect Enlightenment, numerous demons, together with their great armies, came to afflict him. They threw myriads of weapons like rain to hurt the Buddha. The Buddha then waved his Dharma-rope as the eagle flaps its wings, and said:

"O wrathful Drang Srong, please come here to subdue these demons!"

As soon as Buddha had spoken, from the west side of Mount Sumeru the deity Gon-b'a-skyes, holding a nine-spoked thunderbolt in his hand, with his whole body enveloped in great flames, descended from the sky and conquered all demons. The numerous Buddhas and Bodhisattvas were much pleased. Thereupon they blessed Vajrapani and named him the Thunderbolt-Holder, the Master of the Cosmos, and handed him the thunderbolt as the symbol of initiation. Then Vajrapani said to the Buddha, "O my Lord Bhaghavan! I am the protector of all Buddhas in the three times; I was the protector of the seven Buddhas in the past; I am the protector of the present Buddha and will be the protector of the nine-hundred-and-ninety-two[3] Buddhas in the future. I shall be their protectors until all of the one thousand Buddhas in this Kalpa have completed their missions. I shall protect them from all hindrances. I have besought the Buddhas in the past to preach the Dharma, and shall beseech the Buddhas in the future to preach the Dharma; also I shall beseech all the present Buddhas to preach the Dharma. I pray you, the Perfect One, grant me your blessings."

Then said the Buddha, "You have been blessed as both Bodhisattva and Wrathful Deity by all the Buddhas in the past. The Buddhas-to-come will also bless you in both of these two forms. Now, I shall also bless you. You will become the master of all the great devas. You should emancipate all sentient beings from Saṃsāra and from miseries."

So this is the story of the origination of Vajrapani of Drang Srong form. His Mantra is unique and superb. *Oṃ* symbolizes the Five Buddhas and Five Wisdoms. *Ba-tsa pani nama* means "pay homage to Vajrapani". *Hūṃ* is the word that destroys all the sufferings. Says the *Tantra of the Supreme Origination of Vajrapani:*

"If the disciple renders one obeisance to Vajrapani, he attains more merits than he would have secured through rendering numerous obeisances to myriads of Buddhas as many as the total grains of sands in ninety-two million Ganges Rivers. Thus, we know if he recites the mantra of Vajrapani with faith once only, he attains more merit than he will attain through paying homage to Buddhas as many as the total grains of sand in millions of Ganges Rivers. If he relies on Vajrapani as his Yidam Buddha and recites the Mantra, he will surely be protected by Vajrapani from all hindrances. No demons can hurt him, all illness will be cured, his merits will be increased and prosperity augmented. All his wishes will be fulfilled. Thus, the benefits of practicing this ritual are beyond description, nothing can afflict those who practise it.

The practitioner of this ritual will also accomplish all the four performances, namely, the Performance of Subduing, of Increasing, of Attraction, and of Conquering. He will encounter no obstacles. Therefore, one should always rely on Vajrapani, take him as one's shelter and refuge. Also, those who have chronic diseases will be cured through reciting the Mantra of Vajrapani.

Now, you should all think that these initiation symbols prepared for you are all Vajrapanis themselves, and follow me in reciting the prayers:

"I pray to gurus and to the Three Precious ones and to
   the Yidam Buddhas,
Especially, I pray Vajrapani.
Please grant me the superb initiation."
[Recite this prayer three times.]
The guru then addresses the disciples:
Follow me and recite the prayer of Raising the Bodhi
   Heart:

"I take refuge in the Three Precious Ones.
I confess all my sinful doings and transgressions
To all virtuous deeds of sentient beings,
I raise the sympathetic joys.
I devote my heart to Buddhas and to the Enlightenment.
Till the day of my final enlightenment,
I take refuge in Buddha, Dharma, and Sangha.
For the sake of benefiting self and others I aspire to
    Bodhi.
From now on I will serve all sentient beings;
And practice all Actions of Bodhi with earnestness and
    joy.
For the sake of benefiting all beings,
May I come to the realization of Perfect Enlightenment."
All you disciples should think that you have now be-
    come the Ahm Gtsug Vajrapani,
Appearing in a form of Drang Srong,
Holding in his hand the skull;
His braided hair is as white as the seashell.
His right hand holds the thunderbolt upflung toward
    the sky;
That is the symbol of subduing all hindrances.
The left one holds the bell in front of his breast;
That is the symbol of increasing longevity, merits, and
    prosperity.
His body is greenish-grey, adorned with silk scarves.
On the lower part of his body
He wears an apron made of tiger-skin.
He stretches his left leg and bends his right leg.
Vividly and distinctly he stands on the lotus-moon disc.
On the moon-disc at his heart-center there is a *Hūṃ*
    word.

Clockwise encircling the *Hūṃ* word is the garland of
   Mantra.
From this garland of Mantra emanate infinite beams of
   light,
Inviting the numerous Vajrapanis from the Pure Lands
   in ten directions.
Thus, the beyond-number-Vajrapanis all come down
   here,
They all enter into you and unite with you.
[The guru says:]
Hūṃ! All the Vajrapanis in Ahm Gtsug form,
Pray come down here and bless us!
Pray vouchsafe my disciples your supreme initiation!
Pray protect them from all evils and hindrances of
   life!
Recite the main incantation:
Oṃ Ba-tsa Ah Wei Sha Ya Ah Ah!
Recite this incantation many times, and play the musical
   instrument.
The guru then puts the thunderbolt on the head of dis-
   ciples and says the following Mantra:
Déé Tsha Ba-tsa!
Now in order to attain the main initiation the disciples
should follow the guru in reciting this prayer:
I pray to gurus, the Three Precious Ones,
The Yidam Buddha and all deities.
Especially I pray to the Ahm Gtsug Vajrapani.
I pray you grant me the Initiation of Body, of Speech,
Of Mind, of Merit, and of Performance.
The guru then holds the Vase in his hand and says:
"This is the Vase of Initiation; adorning its surface are
the precious stones; its body is light, its neck long; it is

full of the sacred water. It is decorated with the heavenly clothes; a blue silk scarf is also fastened on its neck. In the inner part of the Vase stands the Buddha Vajrapani in his Beyond-Measure Palace. From the body of Buddha Vajrapani gush out streams of nectar flowing into your body through the Gate of Heaven in your head. Thus the defilements of your body are purified, and all the four hindrances of mouth are cleansed. Therefore, you should understand that you have now received the four initiations and also attained the capability of realizing the Buddha's body [in future time].

Hūṃ, this Vase itself is the Beyond-Measure-Palace!
In it the great Ahm Gtsug Vajrapani resides.
Now, I put it upon your head
And impart you the Initiation of Vajrapani.
Oṃ Betsapani Nama Hūṃ Grum Bha Ahbi Ahi Tsa Hūṃ!
Also recite "O, the Braided-Hair Vajrapani... till...
    [text obscure and broken here]
Through the power of the body of Lord Vajrapani,
May I attain the blessing and prosperity".

You have now attained the Body Initiation of Vajrapani; all the hindrances of sickness and demonic afflictions of your body are thus purified. From now on you will be able to meditate on the Body of Vajrapani, and you will have the capability of attaining the supreme body of Vajrapani with its perfection of the Thirty-two Signs and Eighty Beatifications.

Then the guru holds the white shell in his hand and says:
From the throat of the Front-Buddha in the shell emanate infinite beams of light,
Shining upon the Pure Lands of all Buddhas in all directions,

And attracting the merits of speech of all Buddhas, including the sixty voices of Perfection,
Through which the eighty-four thousand Dharmas were introduced.
This shell symbolizes the expression of all Buddhas,
The clockwise curves on its surface are a symbol of prosperity.
It also has the eight signs of auspiciousness.
Spontaneously this shell broadcasts the voice of Dharma.
Now, you should think that the waves of the voice of Dharma delivered from this shell all enter into your throat.
Hūṃ! This is the shell which perfectly represents the expression of Buddha Vajrapani,
I now put it upon your throat
And impart to you the Initiation of Speech of Vajrapani.
Recite the main Mantra and add: *Shan Kha Lam Ah Be Ahi Tsa Mong!* Then repeat the basic prayer:
"O Lord Vajrapani
Manifesting in a form with braided hair...
Through the power of speech of Lord Vajrapani,
May I attain the blessing and prosperity."
The hindrances of your speech are now cleared; thus, you have attained the power of expression and the capability of achieving the unique sixty merits of the voice of Buddha.
Then the guru holds the thunderbolt in his hand and says:
"From the Heart-Center of Vajrapani emanate infinite beams of light shining upon Buddha's Pure Land in the ten directions and attracting numerous thunderbolts with five spokes, which symbolize the wisdom of Buddha, to

come down here. All these thunderbolts then enter into your heart and unite with you.

Hūṃ! This thunderbolt itself is Vajrapani,
Possessing all qualities of Buddha's wisdom.
I now put it upon your heart
And impart to you the complete Initiation of Wisdom.
Recite the main incantation and add: *Ba-tsa Ah Bi Ahi Tsa Mong!*

Also recite the basic prayer: "O, Lord Vajrapani...
Through the power of wisdom of Lord Vajrapani
May I attain the blessing and prosperity."

Now you have attained the Initiation of Wisdom; thus, the hindrances that block your mind are cleared; from now on hundreds and thousands of Samadhis will grow within you.

Then the guru holds the picture of Vajrapani in his hand and says:

"This picture clearly represents Buddha Vajrapani himself. From it emanate infinite beams of light shining upon the Pure Lands in the ten directions, and attracting numerous Vajrapanis from the eternal Heaven Aog-min and also from the Pure Land of the North to come down here. These Vajrapanis are in different sizes and numerous forms: the large ones are as big as Mount Sumeru, and the small ones are as tiny as mustard seeds. Now you should think that all these Vajrapanis enter into you and merge with you.

Hūṃ! This picture is Vajrapani himself
I now put it upon your head
And impart to you the Initiation of Merits of Vajrapani.
Recite the main incantation and add: *Gaya Ahbi Ahi Tsa Mam!*

Plate II

Folio 10 (ii) *recto* (Muses MS, vol. II), the second of two folios bearing the same number. The Holy Thunderbolt, Vajra or rDorje, symbolic of the power of wisdom, especially in its most potent or esoteric form; and hence symbolic of the entire Tibetan Tantra (rGyud) or Vajrayāna.

Also recite the main prayer:
"O, Lord Vajrapani...
Through the power of the merits of Vajrapani
May I attain the blessing and prosperity!"
Now you have received the Initiation of Merits; thus the hindrances that cause the degeneration of merits are cleared. From now on you will be able to increase all your merits and wisdoms.

Then the guru holds the Gtor-ma in his hand and says:

This Gtor-ma itself is Vajrapani; from it emanate infinite beams of light in white, yellow, red, and green, shining upon you and merged with you. Thus, from now on you will be able to perform the Four Acts without any difficulties or hindrances.

Hūṃ! This Gtor-ma itself is Vajrapani;
I now put it in your hands,
And impart to you the Initiation of Performances.

Recite the main Mantra and add: *Shandan Sudam Sashang Maraya Bendha Ahbi Ahi Tsa Mang;* also recite the main prayer:

"O, Lord Vajrapani...
Through the power of the performance of Vajrapani
May I attain the blessing and prosperity!"
This Gtor-ma itself is identical with Buddha Vajrapani, the Master of the Esoteric Teachings. From it emanate infinite beams of light shining upon Buddha's Pure Lands in the ten directions, attracting hundreds of thousands of Buddha Vajrapanis, large and small, from the Aog-min Heaven and also from the north side of Mount Sumeru, together with infinite Garlands of Mantra and five-spoked thunderbolts to come down here. They all enter into your

heart, and eventually they are transformed into lights and merge with you.

"O, the Dharmakaya Samantabhadra,
The Sixth Buddha, the Great Rdo-rje-chang,
The Guru Padma Sambhava and the Dakini Ye-shes-
  mtsho-rgyal,
The Gurus Bal-ji-sen-ge and Mi-rgyur-rdo-rje,
All the demon conquerors and all gurus in the lineage,
And then the beyond-number Buddhas in the universe,
Buddha Vajrapani, the host-Buddha of this initiation, in
  numerous numbers and forms,
I beseech all of you!
I pray you bless my disciples!
I pray you protect them from all kinds of demons and
  sickness from the planets⁴... [and] epilepsy,
I pray you increase their merits and advance their med-
  itation experiences.
I pray you safeguard them from the miseries of Saṃsara
  and all fears.
*Oṃ Ba-tsa Pani Nama Huṃ Balinda Gaya Waga Tsida
Ahdirdana Samaya Tsa Huṃ Bam Ho!*
Now you have well received the initiation; hence you should rely on Vajrapani as your Patron Buddha.

At the end of this initiation the disciples all say to the guru:

"We shall obey all your instructions and follow all your admonishments."

NOTES

1 *Ahm Gtsug:* This word is obviously a mistake made by the copyist. The translator presumes that this word should be spelled Ahm Gtsigs, which means using the upper teeth to press the lower lip when one is in despair or anger.*

2 *Drang Srong:* The sages, hermits, or anchorites. Also means the *Rishi*, the deific sages who can perform miracles.

3 According to Buddhist tradition, one thousand Buddhas will appear in this world in this Kalpa. Eight Buddhas have already appeared, therefore the Buddhas-to-come total nine hundred and ninety-two.

4 That is, astrologically indicated illnesses. — *Ed.*

---

* The editor disagrees here. The same (Gtsug) spelling is repeated in the ritual consistently. The editor believes this to be a technical tantric term designating one of the thirteen forms of Vajrapāni, and specifically the one with the braided hair. — *Ed.*

[A COMPENDIUM OF THE INITIATION RITUALS OF PERFORMANCE OR ALL-ACCOMPLISHING WISDOM PRESIDED OVER BY AMOGHASIDDHI]

FOLIO I

Picture: Buddha Amoghasiddhi (Tibetan *Don-yod-grub-pa*, meaning Buddha of Performance). This Buddha abides in the north of the Mandala. He is the fifth Buddha of the Five Buddhas of Tantricism and usually belongs to the last of the initiation series[5].

Text

Hūṃ! This is the Bhagavan, Buddha of Performance.
I now give to you, the well-destined disciples, his initiation.
Have faith and devotion toward him!
Through the power of his speech and wisdom,
Your envious nature naturally dissolves and becomes his
  holy body.
May you attain the complete initiation of Amoghasiddhi.
Dagarma Abhi Ditsa Ah!
If you understand, O disciples, that everything is the man-
  ifestation of consciousness,
Or that consciousness makes everything,
Then you will truly attain the Initiation of the Dissolution
  of the Envious Nature.
(And you should know that) the green wisdom-light sym-
  bolizes the Buddha of Performance, himself.

FOLIO 2

Picture: Very unclear; presumably it is the robe which
Buddha wears.

Text

Buddha's body feels no cold,
But following the fashion of sentient beings —
Needing this and needing that —
Buddha, likewise, robes himself.
Putting on this Buddha's robe, you will become
resplendent:
Ahdi Sabuya Svaha.

FOLIO 3

Picture: The Tiger-skin apron and ornaments for the
Fierce Buddha.

Text

You should think that you offer the Tiger-skin apron
and ornaments to the Fierce One.
Hūṃ! Although Buddha's mind is fearless,
He wears these terrifying ornaments
On his wrathful body
To cleanse the sins of sentient beings
And bring them to the Path of Liberation.
By your wearing this Tiger-skin apron and fierce orna-
     ments,
The demons will be conquered and all your fears routed.
Oṃ! Sher Bi Yo Di Sar Su Yy Svaha!

FOLIO 4

Picture: The Fiery Water [which conquers both cold
and heat]

Text

(The Guru hands over the picture of the Fiery Water to they
   disciple.)

Hūm! This is the protection from heat and cold – the Fiery
   Water with qualities of both warmth and coolness.

I now impart to you well-destined disciples, this initiation.

You will be immune to the cold and heat-torments of Hell;

Thus you will be forever freed from the sufferings of Hell.

Du Da Ha Da Ha Sarwa Nara Gade Heru Hūm Pai!

FOLIO 10

Picture: The Five Wheels.

Text

Hum! These are the Precious Wheels

The Cross Symbols[4] on the human heart.

I now impart this initiation to you, good disciples.

May you attain the Initiation of the Five Wheels.

Batsa Matna Bema Garma Ah Be Ditsi Ah!

SECOND FOLIO 10

(as marked in Tibetan on the folio. *Ed.*)

Picture: The Thunderbolt.

Text

Hūm! This is the Precious Wheel – the Cross Symbols of
the lotus on the human heart.

I now impart this initiation to you, good disciples,

May you attain the Initiation of the Five Wheels.

Batsa Darna Bema Garma Ah Be Ditsi Ah!

FOLIO 11

Picture: A water vase, a hat, a thunderbolt, a bell, and a
Buddha.

Text

The Vase Initiation is the annihilation of Hate.

The Initiation of Head-Adornment is the subduing of the Pride-poison.

The initiation of Thunderbolt is the destroying of the Lust-poison.

The Initiation of Bell is the conquering of Enviousness and Arrogance.

The Initiation of Name is the dispelling of the Ignorance-Darkness.

I now bestow upon you the Initiation of Eternity.

Hūṃ Batsa Ah Dar Shu Jana Samaya Ahbi Yi Tsa Mum!

(Use the water vase.)

Sar Rana Jarna Sobhawa Ahbi Yitsa Mum!

(Use the thunderbolt.)

Da Di Cha Ah Bu Di Jana Sadna Batsa Ahbi Yi Tsa Mum!

(Use the bell.)

Om Dar Tsi Da Ma Di Ahme Jaha Batsa Ahbi Yi Tsa Mum!

(Use the thunderbolt and bell.)

FOLIOS 12–13

Picture: The Yab-Yum (literally Father-Mother) of All-Perfection or Adi Buddha Yab-Yum.

Text

Hūṃ! to you well-gifted disciples
I now grant the Initiation of Adi Buddha Yab-Yum. With the annulment and purification of the "mind complex",
May you attain the Initiation of the Immense Dharmakaya.

Darmakaya Ahbe Yitsa Oṃ Ah Hūṃ Hri!

(Then the Guru makes the wish for the disciples.)

O, well-gifted disciples: Through attaining the Initiation
Of Adi Biddha Yab-Yum, your mind will be purified in the

Dharmadathu (the universal whole). May you thus attain the Initiation of the Immense Dharmakaya.

(Then the Guru bestows the Pointing-Out Practice[5] upon the disciples.)

O, well-destined disciples: You should not think that the so-called Yab-Yum Adi Buddha is other than the Alaya Bodhi Heart[6] of your own mind. Oh! the aware thinker at this very moment, bright, radiantly aware, transparent, itself is the absolute body of Adi Buddha, the original, the primordial Immutable Shelter.

The awareness of your own mind, devoid of any characteristics and substantialities, the lightning awareness itself is the Mother Adi Buddha: its over-flowing manifestation and play. The versatile actor itself is the Father Adi Buddha: Now, recognize it and become acquainted with it!

FOLIOS 14–15

Picture: The Five Buddhas.

Text

(Thereupon the Initiation of the Five Father Buddhas of the Five Groups is given as follows:)

Hūṃ! To you well-gifted disciples,

I now impart the Initiation of the Five Buddhas in the Five
  Groups.

Your Five Aggregations [the skandhas or five modes of
  consciousness] will thus be purified.

May you obtain the Initiation of the Universal

Reward Body (Sambhogakaya)!

Oṃ Hūṃ So Ahm Ha Sambhogaya Ahbi Aitsa Ah!

(The Guru blesses as follows:)

Having received the Initiation of the Five Buddhas, I wish that all your Five Aggregations will be purified and that

the Initiation of the Universal Reward Body be attained
by you.
(The Guru now executes the Pointing-Out Practice.)
O well-gifted disciples: The so called Five Buddhas are
nothing else but your own Five Skandhas. The non-extinct
but purified [natures] of your own Five Skandhas are the
Five Buddhas themselves: — The non-extinct but all-manifest Form, clear and vivid, is the Buddha of All Manifestations. (Tib. Rnam-b'ar-snang-mdzad; Skt. Vairochana).
The non-extinct but all-manifest Feeling (Tib. Rin-chen-
byun-gnas; Skt. Ratnasambhava) clear and vivid, is the
Buddha of Treasury. The non-extinct but all-manifest
Conception (Tib. _Adushes), clear and vivid, is the Buddha
of Infinite Light. The non-extinct but all-manifest Volition,
clear and vivid, is the Buddha of All-Performance. The
non-extinct but all-manifest Consciousness, clear and vivid,
is the Buddha of the Diamond-Mind. This, you should
understand.

FOLIO 16

Picture: The Five Mother-Buddhas or the Five God-
desses.
Text
Hūṃ! To you well-destined disciples.
I now impart the Initiation of the Five Mother-Buddhas.
Having purified but not abolished the five elements,
May you this attain this Initiation of the Five
Mother-Buddhas.
Mum Lam Mam Syam Tayam Ahbi Aitsa Ah!
   (The Guru now bestows a wish as follows:)
Having received the Initiation of the Five Mother-Bud-
dhas, I wish that all your five elements may be purified and

that the Initiation of Generating All Buddhas be attained
by you.
(The Pointing-Out Practice follows.)

FOLIO 17

Text

O well-gifted disciples, the so-called Five Mother-Buddhas
are nothing else but your own five inner and outer elements. The non-extinct but purified five elements are the
Five Mother-Buddhas themselves. The manifested earth-
element is the Mother-Buddha Spyng-ma. The manifested
water-element is the Mother-Buddha Ma-ma-ge. The manifested fire-element is the Mother-Buddha Gos-dg'ar-mo.
The manifested air-element is the Mother-Buddha Dam-
tsig-sgrol-ma. The manifested space-element is the nature
of the Mother-Buddha Dbyings-pyug-ma.

FOLIO 18

Picture: The Eight Boddhisattvas.

Text

The Initiation of the Eight Bodhisattvas:
Hūṃ! To you well-destined disciples,
I now impart the Initiation of the Eight Bodhisattvas.
Having purified but not destroyed the eight conscious-
    nesses,
May you obtain the Initiation of the Great Bodhisattvas.
Bu Dhi Sa Ta Ah Bi Yi Tsa Ah!
(The Guru makes a wish as follows.)
O well-gifted disciples, through the attainment of this
Initiation your eight consciousnesses are purified. Thus
having attained the Initiation of the Eight Bodhisattvas,
you will act as the Eight Bodhisattvas to carry out the

great career — to further the welfare of all sentient beings.

FOLIO 19

Text

The Pointing-Out Practice:

O, well-gifted disciples, the so-called Eight Bodhisattvas are nothing else but your own eight consciousnesses. The non-extinct but brightened eight consciousnesses of one's self are the Eight Bodhisattvas themselves. The eye-consciousness, aware and non-extinct, is the Bodhisattva *Earth-Essence*. The ear-consciousness, the one that hears, is the Bodhisattva *Space-Essence*. The nose-consciousness, the one that smells, is the Bodhisattva *Self-Seeing*. The tongue-consciousness, the one that tastes, is the Bodhisattva *Thunderbolt-Holder*. The body-consciousness, the one that penetrates all[7], the illumined wisdom, is the Bodhisattva *Purger-of-Obstacles*. The kleśa-bound Mind-Consciousness, the one that perpetuates the ego, is the Bodhisattva [called] *All-Merits*. The base-of-all consciousness, the all-pervading and illumined, is the Bodhisattva [called] *Meritorious Youth*.

FOLIOS 20–21

Picture: The Eight Consort-Bodhisattvas.

Text

The Initiation of the Eight Consort-Bodhisattvas:

Hūṃ! To you well-gifted disciples

I now impart the Initiation of the Eight Consort-Bodhisattvas.

Having purified but not destroyed the eight (outer) objects,

May you obtain the Initiation of the Eight Consort-Bodhisattvas.

Ahbi Yitsa Ah!

(The Guru makes a wish as follows:)

O, well-gifted disciples, through the attainment of this
Initiation of the Eight Consort-Bodhisattvas, the eight
objects are purified but not abandoned. Thus, you will act
as the Eight Consort-Bodhisattvas to further the welfare
of sentient beings.

(The Pointing-Out Practice.)

O, well-gifted disciples, the so-called Eight Consort-
Bodhisattvas are nothing else but the purification of the
thought of the eight objects. The eye-object, the appearance of form, in its purity, is the Consort-Bodhisattva La-
ser-Dkar-mo. Likewise, the Ear-object, the sound in its
purity, is the Consort-Bodhisattva Ma-le-ser-mo. The nose-
object, the odor in its purity, is the Consort-Bodhisattva
Ge-di-mar-mo. The tongue-object, the taste in its purity,
is the Consort-Bodhisattva Ni-ti-ljang-gu. The purification
of thought in the past is the Consort-Bodhisattva Su-si-
dkar-mo. The purification of thought in the present is the
Consort-Bodhisattva Dub-se-ser-mo. The purification of
thought in the future is Bodhisattva Ah-loga-mar-mo.
The insubstantial, the not-definite nature of the elements,
the purification of phenomena, are the Consort-Bodhisattva Green Gha-ne. This you should understand.

FOLIO 22

Picture: The Six Transformation Bodies of the Six Buddhas.

Text

The Initiation of the Transformation Bodies of the Six
Buddhas.

Hūṃ! To you well-destined disciples
I now impart the Initiation of the Six Buddhas.
Having purified the six Kleśas,
May you obtain the Initiation of the Nirmanakaya Buddhas.
Nir Ma Kaya Ahbe Yitsa Ah!
(The Guru makes a wish as follows:)

O, well-gifted disciples, through the attainment of this Initiation of the Six Nirmanakaya Buddhas, the Six Poisons – five kleśas and stinginess – are purified. Thus may you be able to transform numerous bodies to further the welfare of sentient beings in the Six Lokas.
(The Pointing-Out Practice:)

O, well-gifted disciples, the so-called Six Buddhas are not something else – the purification of Pride is the Buddha of Heaven, Dwan-b'o-brgya-bying;

FOLIO 23

(Continues the text of Folio 22.)
the purification of envy is the Buddha of Asura Tag Zang-ris; the purification of lust is the Buddha of Human beings, Shakyamuni; the purification of Blindness is the Buddha of Animals, Sen-ge-rab-brteng; the purification of stinginess is the Buddha of Hungry Ghost, G'a-*a*bar-ma; the purification of Hate is the Buddha of Hell, Chos-gyri-rgyal-b'o.

FOLIO 24

Picture: The Initiation Buddha of the Four Meanings.
Text
Hūṃ! To you well-destined disciples
I now impart the Initiation of the Four Meanings.

Having purified the realistic and nihilistic Four Extremes[8]
May you obtain the Initiation of Infinite Performances.
Shen Da Su Da Ahn Wa Shm Ma Ra Ya Ahbi Aitsa Ah!
(The Guru makes a wish as follows:)

O well-gifted disciples, through the attainment of this Initiation of Four Meanings, the Realistic and Nihilistic Four Extremes are purified. May you be able to benefit sentient beings through the power of the Four Great Performances without the slightest hindrance.
(The Pointing-Out Practice:)

O, well-gifted disciples, the Buddhas of Four Meanings are not something else – the purification of the Realistic View is the Buddha Victor (Rnam-b'ar-rgyal-wa); the purification of the Nihilistic View is the Buddha of Death. Gshin-rje-gshed-b'o; the purification of the Ego-View is the Buddha of Horse [-Head] (Rta-mgrin); the purification of the Form-View is the Buddha of Nectar-Flowing.

FOLIO 25

Picture: The Female Buddha of the Four Meanings.
Text
Hūm! To you, the well-destined disciples,
I now impart the Female Buddhas of Four Meanings.
Having purified the four ways of birth,
May you attain the Initiation of the Four Performances.
Batsa Om Gu Sha Ja Sa Sha Mo Da Gen De Ahbi Aitsa Ah!
(The Guru makes the wish for the disciples:)

Now you, the disciples have attained the Initiation of the Four Female Deities. Thus, the gates of the Four Births will be shut off, the four Infinities will arise from your heart – the four great performances through which you

will be able to benefit sentient beings without the slightest
hindrances. Thus you will accomplish the career of benefiting others. May you attain all these merits and powers!
(The Pointing-Out Practice:)

O well-destined disciples, the Four Female Buddhas are
but the natural purification of the Thought of the Four
Births[9]. The birth from metamorphosis is the Iron-Chain
Goddess; the natural purification of the thought of birth
from the womb is the Rope Female Buddha. The natural
purification of the thought of birth from eggs is the Iron-
Fetter Female Buddha. The natural purification of the
thought of the warmth-wetness is the Bell Goddess.
From the very beginning they are identical! O well-gifted
ones! You should definitely know these thruths — as they
are unmistakably true — and bear this conviction with you.

FOLIOS 26–41

Are not of first importance to initiation *per se* or are idea-
tionally repetitious and hence have not been translated. *Ed.*

FOLIO 42

The Pointing-Out demonstration for the complete [com-
pany of] Fierce Buddhas
The Guru says to the disciples:

O well-gifted disciples, these sixty Blood-Drinking
Deities are not something else, they are one's own kleśas-
group, purified but not abandoned. The insubstantial or
the perceiver that is devoid of any self-nature awareness
manifests itself as the sixty Blood-Drinking Deities. As
illustrated, in the Palace-Beyond-Measure in one's skull-
brain, a group of Blood-Drinking Deities now actually
and vividly dwell[10]. The forty-two Peaceful Deities with

their illuminate bodies, all now dwell in the Dharma Chakra in the heart center. Furthermore, all the hairs over your body are identical with the nature of Db'a-wo (Brave Deities). All the Pranas are the nature of Dakinis, all the White-Drops [11] manifest in the form of the infinite Peaceful and Wrathful Sambhogakaya of the Father Buddhas. All the Red Drops [12] (Ragda) manifest in the form of the infinite Peaceful and Wrathful Sambhogakaya of the Mother Buddhas. The numerous nadis [13] of the body are the Dakinis. Therefore, your very body itself is the nature of the Mandala of the Peaceful and Wrathful Buddhas. Hence, you should never despise, abuse, or injure your body, nor should you overstrain your body, practice asceticism, or commit suicide. When you eat or drink you should think that this is the Tantric Sacrament and duly make the offering. If you remain without attachment, you may always wear fine and lovely clothes and adorn yourself as a manner of

FOLIO 43

[Continuing the text of Folio 42.]
practicing Tantric offerings. At the time of death, the Peaceful and Wrathful Buddhas will come out of your body, extending over all space; thereupon the Bardo visions will begin. Remember! At that time do not be frightened or terrified by the thundering voices and the Three Lights! You should remember that all these Buddhas are your tutelary Buddhas whose initiations I am right now giving to you! You should remember and recognize them. As soon as you recognize them, you will be instantaneously emancipated!

Thus the Pointing-Out demonstration is extensively given to the disciples.

Plate III

The number 5, entering Mahayāna Buddhism via Hindu Tantric forms of the Sāṇkhya doctrine, pervades Tibetan Buddhism. This detail, depicting the five Dhyāni Buddhas, is from a tanka of the sambhogakāya aspect of the Buddha Amitābha. *(Reproduced here by courtesy of the Newark Museum, Newark, New Jersey.)*

The foregoing initiation-ritual is given to the disciples
to make them understand the teachings of initiation; as
said in the Prime King-Initiation Tantra of Vajrasattva:

The Mandala-Offering practice is to be done [now.]
For the unwise disciples,
The Vajrasattava gives the Skull-Initiation,
To elucidate the symbolic teachings.
The disciple should try to understand the Wisdom Ini-
    tiation,
The Secret Initiation will elucidate the self-experience.
While the Word-Initiation elucidates the non-existence
    of self.

FOLIO 43 b

(The text written on the reverse side of Folio 43.)
Thus says the *Tantra of Vajrasattva*.

Of this Skull-Initiation (a simpler type or Rite-Free Initiation), that Tantra gives the following explanation:

"The Initiation tells the disciples whether the Outer
Objects in the material world and Inner Essence [14] within
oneself are existent or non-existent, and in what sense they
do or do not exist, by giving many symbols and explanations, such as the Sumeru Mountain, the Four Continents
and the Vase Buddhas. In the Wisdom Initiation, the
Thunderbolt, the Precious Wheel, the Cross-Thunderbolt,
the Three-Pointed Knife, the Purba Dagger, the bow and
arrows, the mirror, the forms and colors – these things
are shown to the disciples, to give them a sagacious
view, by the Guru in the Initiation ritual." Thus states
the Tantra.

The Tantra explains the Extreme Rite-Free Initiation in
the terms of the Secret Initiations; its objective is to elu-

cidate self-Illumination – if one knows himself, he has attained the Secret Initiation.

The Tantra also says:

"If one knows one thing he knows all.
O, marvelous is the Nature of Equality![15]
If existent – Equality from the beginning!
If non-existent – Equality from the beginning!
If abstract – Equality from the beginning!
If concrete – still Equality from the beginning!
If one realizes the Nature of Equality,
He has attained the Secret Initiation!
Oh, marvelous is the Nature of Equality!"

Now, the ultimate-Rite-Free Initiation:

As said in the Tantra: "Through the Words-Initiation the Non-ego truth is elucidated to the disciples: Wherever there is ego, there are always confusions (Saṃsāra). The word of no words is the highest initiation. Without I, without ego, none sinks into Saṃsāra!"

Now, the Great Vase Initiation with Rite, the Rite-Free Initiation, the Extreme Rite-Free Initiation, and the Ultimate Rite-Free Initiation are all given to you; thus the sins, hindrances, and habitual thoughts of your body, mouth, and mind are all cleansed and actually become the Four Bodies of Buddha. Hereafter, you will benefit sentient beings in a natural way, without any strenous effort.

To obtain pardon and give thanks, the Mandala should be offered; the assemblage should be intertained and exalted with dancing and singing. What remains after the festival should be given away as charity.

Those who want to have a comprehensive sacramental

festival and celebration should consult the Annotations of the Four Initiation Rituals.

Samaya Chia Chia Chia!

May the message of the Argument-Free Adi Doctrine[16] reach all the corners of the world at all times. May this teaching be spread and magnified on the earth and last for ages.

This is the teaching from the Treasury of Garma Linpa, the accomplished Yogi.

Blessings to all!

NOTES

1 The manuscript of these initiations presents a series of colored images of god-forms, with explanatory text on the verso sides and on supplementary folios containing the most profound ideas, most explicitly expressed, of any of the seven initiation texts here given. – *Ed.*

2 The translator believes the folios of the other four Buddhas are missing. The first few lines of the text are indiscernible.

3 *Fiery Water:* For human beings, fire is fire and water is water. This is not so for sentient beings in Hell. For them, cool water they try to drink turns to fire, and fire by which they try to warm themselves turns to cold water. Hence the term "Fiery Water" is used to convey the absence of self-nature in this nether-world phenomenon.

4 *Cross Symbols (Rgya-gram):* In Tibetan, this term may refer either to the symbol of the crossed thunderbolts or that symbol we call the swastika. Here it means crossed thunderbolts.

5 *Pointing-Out Practice:* This is the practice by which the Guru points out (illustrates) to the disciple, during the initiation, his original Buddha-nature. This is a special practice of the Red and White Schools of Tibetan Buddhism.

6 *Alaya Bodhi Heart:* "Alaya" is the term meaning "foundation of all." Here the term is used in connection with Bodhi-heart, implying that the Vow of Bodhisattva is the foundation and source of all Buddhist teachings.

7 This refers to the most active and versatile consciousness, generally called mental, which Buddhists classify as the Sixth Consciousness.

8 *Four Extremes:* (1) The Extreme of Existence; (2) The Extreme of Non-Existence; (3) The Extreme of both Existence and Non-Existence; (4) The Extremes of neither Existence nor Non-Existence.

9 *Thought of the Four Births:* From the transcendental viewpoint, there is no birth nor death. The Four Births of Samsara are dreamlike and unreal; they are merely thoughts, not the real beings.

10 This is the esoteric teaching of this initiation: that all the

Wrathful Buddhas are reflected or manifested through the psychic center in the head.

11 *White Drops:* The life-force (physically, semen) of the male.

12 *Red Drops:* The life-force of the female.

13 *Nadis* (Skt.): Follicles; all the tubes and nerves in the body; Tibetan, *Rtsa.* [Actually the nadis (rTsa) are not part of the physical body, but are subtle channels for the conveyance of prana. — *Ed.*]

14 *Inner Essence,* here, refers to the disciple's consciousness.

15 The Nature of Equality is one of the most important aspects of the Prajna-Paramita. From the viewpoint of absolute enlightenment, all things appear equal. [Instead of "equal," to say "partaking of the same ultimate nature" would probably be more accurate. — *Ed.*] Therefore, Tantrism declares that declares that Nirvana is Saṃsāra and Saṃsāra is Nirvāna.

16 *Argument-Free Adi Doctrine:* Traditionally, this term carries two meanings: (1) It refers to the nature of the Adi Doctrine beyond arguments, opinions, and "play words"; (2) It refers to the tradition of the Red School which, in contradistinction to the Yellow School, disregards scholastic opinions and arguments.

PART II

THE SIX YOGAS OF NĀROPĀ
[IN TSONG-KHA-PA'S COMMENTARY]*

Entering the Profound Path Through the Successive Teaching of *The Six Yogas of Naropa*, Which is Named *The Book of the Three Faiths* [1].

---

* We have, in the text, allowed the translator's *Naropa*, frequent *Milarepa* and *Dumo* to stand, instead of correcting to Nāropā, Milaraspa and Gtum-mo, since the loose orthography in such instances does no severe violence to the actual pronunciation. Similar instances were treated likewise. *Ed.*

With great respect I bow down to the Lotus-Feet of the
revered gurus who are identical with the great Vajra Dhara [2].

I prostrate myself in front of His supreme Body, Mouth
and Mind!

I bow down to my guru and his omnipresent miraculous
powers!

He who grants all wishes (of ours),

He who possesses all the merits and virtues,

He who is the mighty master, the embodiment of Vajra
Dhara!

To him, the mighty lord of eight merits, I render my
obeisance,

Gathering all the quintessence of the profound Tantras.

The accomplished masters Deropa and Naropa, through
their lineage, handed down this teaching!

It is known as the Six Yogas of Naropa,

It is the teaching heard in all directions!

Following its path, the hard-working and well-gifted
disciples

Are led to the plane of the saviours!

Through a careful and continuous study

Of the teachings by the successive gurus in the lineage,

I now elucidate for you the way to liberation!

CHAPTER ONE

INTRODUCTION

It is the intention of the author to relate the secret, yet famous teachings of the profound Six Yogas of Naropa in two steps. First, the preparatory practice. Second, the main practice of the teaching itself.

The first step includes two groups of teachings, the ordinary preparatory works of Mahayana Buddhism, and the extraordinary preparations for the Supreme Vehicle. About the first group two questions must be answered: (1) Why is it necessary to make an effort in the ordinary practice of Mahayana Buddhism? (2) How should one actually practice them? Let us discuss the first point. It is absolutely necessary to work step by step on the preparations both for the Paramita Vehicle and the True Word Vehicle. As admonished by Lama Rngog-pa[6], the one who held the traditional way of preaching of Marpa (he quoted from the Tantra of Two Forms):

The disciple must first give and offer ... till...

....

After that, he is to be given
The teaching of the Middle Way[8].

Both schools (exoteric and esoteric) of Mahayana Buddhism exhort the disciples to observe the basic practices and teachings of Buddha, there is no exception, even in Tantra. The Jetsun Milarepa also said that if one wants to know how to liberate oneself in Bardo, one should first practice the prayer of Taking the Three Refuges, then bring forth the Bodhi Heart of Vow and the Bodhi Heart of Performance (see note 15). Even then it should be known the misfortune-bringer always turns out to be one's close friend. The fallers in the abyss are the men who follow the cattle.

Thus, if anyone does not observe the precepts strictly after having taken the oath of Tantra, both he and his guru will fall into danger. It is also said that by merely hearing the advantages of the esoteric teachings one may apply (the initiations) in an easy-going manner which is very dangerous and often leads to disasters. The Jetsun Mila was blessed by the Goddess[9] for having preached the Bardo preparation in such a manner. Thus we know that the fundamental teachings of Buddha are essential and necessary to all schools. His holiness Gampopa also urged in his Commentary on the Four Dharmas that all Buddhists should follow the Three Gradual Paths of Lam-rim[10] in the beginning stage of his way to Buddhahood.

Some disciples may raise the question: Why did not Jetsun Pag-mo-grubpa and other great masters mention any of these preparations in their books on the Six Yogas? This is simply because the preparatory teachings had already been given, and the teachings of the Six Yogas were to be given to those who had already completed the preparatory practice. In their admonishments to the monastic orders, the masters clearly emphasized the importance of the preparatory practices. If one follows these instructions one will be freed from partiality. This is the vital point of both esoteric and exoteric Buddhism; the reader should especially note it.

Now the second question. How should one actually practice the preparatory teaching? According to the Great Jetsun (Adisha), the disciple should first find a qualified guru of Mahayana Buddhism, think of his teachings and practice them under his instructions wholeheartedly.

After this, he should then follow the guru's instruction to contemplate the difficulties of attaining this present precious and meaningful human birth. Thus he fervently determines to make right use of this human body; he also learns that to make the most of it is to enter the path of Mahayana in which the first step is to awaken the Heart-for-Bodhi. If the Heart-for-Bodhi is actually awakened in one's heart, he is then able to practice Mahayana Buddhism truly and naturally, otherwise his Malayana will merely be a word. Therefore, the wise Buddhist must strive step by step to put an end to the wrong thoughts adverse to the Heart-for-Bodhi.

If he does not completely give up thoughts concerned with the wordly affairs of this life, he will encounter many difficulties in the practice of both Hinayana and Mahayana. Always he should remind himself that this life is short. Always he should think of his inevitable death and warn himself of the possibility of falling into a lower birth after his departure from this world. Furthermore, he should realize that to strive for a happier birth in his next life is still of no avail, for everything in Saṃsara is transient and untenable. Rather he should exert himself to attain Liberation, he should continously make an effort to widen his compassion and kindness as these qualities are the roots of the Heart-for-Bodhi. He should try to reach a state in which the compassionate Bodhi-Heart arises spontaneously without effort.

With a desire for learning the way of the Bodhisattva's actions, he should gladly undertake the Bodhisattvas' responsibilities and compassionate deeds. With this in mind, he is to observe the precepts of the Bodhisattva and study and practice the Six Paramitas in general. He should particularly pay attention to the preparatory works for Dhayana [13], namely, the fitness and readiness of his mind for meditation. He should also study and practice the teachings of the Prajana Paramita, contemplating on the magic-like and space-like [14] nature of all beings. Thereafter, if he is capable of taking the Tantric precepts on himself, he should study the *Guru's Fifty Stanza* and follow its instructions to serve his guru. In this manner, he should set about the practices of Tantra.

If he has not undergone these preparatory works step by step, he can never conquer the craving of this life. Thus he has no chance to become a steady and unwavering devotee. By no means then shall he possess unfeigned faith, or an absolute devotion in his heart. He is uncertain about the law of Karma, and he will become an unscrupulous Buddhist who observes no precepts whatsoever. He will have no abomination for Saṃsara. There will be no tranquility in his mind; therefore, his striving for liberation is merely a talking with no meaning at all. Since kindness and compassion cannot grow within him, he has no chance of developing the spontaneous Wish-for-Heart-of-Bodhi [15]. At most he is a nominal Mahayana Buddhist. He lacks a strong desire to learn the actions of a Bodhisattva so that the peacefulness of abiding-in-goodness will never come to him. A steadfast understanding of Meditation and Wisdom will never come to him; he will always be confused at the delicate discriminations on Samadhis. Nor is there a chance for him to attain an unwavering understanding of the non-Ego truth. If one wants to avoid the aforementioned dangers, he should work hard on the preparatory practices for Mahayana. This is clearly advocated and elucidated by His Holiness Adisha, who received the teaching from the Maitreya-Asanga lineage and also the teachings from the Manjusri Nagra-juna-Ziwala lineage, and put them together as if to combine the three rivers into one to show that preparatory works are necessary both to the Paramita Path and to the Diamond Path.

SPECIAL PREPARATIONS

The Jetsün Milarepa also said in his song:
"Good and evil do never fail
To bring about corresponding fruits;
Hence, one should be extremely careful to avoid evil
    deeds.
Even petty misbehaviours, one must forbid;
For the law of retribution never fails,
And the misery in the Lower Paths is hard to bear!
If anyone realizes not the faults of desire
And the consequences of pleasure,
He can never resign ardent longings!
Then, from the Saṃsaric Prison he has no way to escape.
One should therefore remind oneself:
All these desires are delusions!
Bearing this understanding in mind
One may work on the cure of the kleśas!»
If one remembers not the gratitude one owes
To the father- and mother-like sentient beings in the Six
    Paths,
One is liable to fall down to the Small Vehicle,
    (Hinayana).
Therefore one should foster great compassion,
And learn to nourish the Bodhi-Heart."
Milarepa said in another song:
"I am so much afraid of the Eight Non-Freedoms [16]
That I continously think of the faults of Samsara
And the transiency of beings!

I submit myself completely to the care of the Three
    Precious Ones!
I strictly discipline myself in all karmic doings.
By repeatedly practising the Heart-for-Bodhi,
I dispel the enduring shadow of Habitual-Thinking[17],
Realizing that all the manifestations are delusory magic
Of the Three Miserable Paths, I have no fear nor alarm!"

In view of these admonishments (by the celebrated
masters), one ought to work hard in the preparatory practices until one's mind is consolidated. One should bear in
mind that to complete a perfect journey, a clear knowledge
is needed of the route and what is required for the journey.
This is not a light matter. In fact, the most important and
crucial of all the teachings is the preparation work, or the
"Common Foundation of All Practice."

In the second group of teachings, the extraordinary prep-
parations for the Supreme Vehicle, there are also two types
of preparations, the general and the special. The general
preparation for the Supreme Vehicle means to attain a
complete initiation, and to observe the precepts of Tantra.
I want to expound the attainment of initiation first.

According to the tradition of the Marpa lineage, as demonstrated by Me-sdon and Ngo-sdon[18], whoever aspires to
the practice of the Arising Yoga and of the Secret Doctrine
Perfect Yoga[19] must first obtain the complete Four Initiations. When Milarepa first saw Gambopa, he asked
Gambopa whether he had obtained the complete initiations before importing to him the teachings of the Six
Yogas. Gambopa said, "Like a fine copper utensil ready for filling with butter, I am quite ready." Thereupon,
Milarepa bestowed upon him the teachings and Pith Instructions[20]. Milarepa also urged Gambopa to encourage

the Bari Translator to come for initiations. Many instances like this have been told.

The great master Pag-mo-grub-pa also considered the attainment of the Four Initiations was necessary for the disciples. In accordance with the teachings of these great masters of the Marpa Lineage in the past, a disciple must have the complete Four Initiations before the bestowal of Tantric teachings. This point is emphasized in many Tantras; for instance, the *Second Ti-Li of the Mahāmudra Tantra* says:

"When the disciple starts to learn the teaching,
He should first try to obtain an initiation.
After the attainment of initiation,
He will then become a candidate
Capable of receiving the grand esoteric teachings!
"Without Initiations there will be no accomplishment!
If he grinds sand, no butter will ever come out of it.
If he has obtained no initiation
And unscrupulously relates the teaching of Tantra,
Both he and his disciples will go to hell immediately
    after their deaths,
Even if they are accomplished beings!
Therefore, all diligent persons should look for a Guru
    for Initiation."

The *Second Tantra of Rdor-bred* says:
"The most important matter is initiation;
All the accomplishments depend on it.
I now tell you this essential truth;
To it, you should pay first attention.
When one intends to be a follower of Tantra,
One should first attain a perfect initiation.
Having attained this initiation, one is thus

Capable of practicing the Perfecting Yoga!
If a disciple has all knowledge about Tantra
But never attained the initiation,
Both he and his followers will fall into the great hell!"
Both the acquisition of the Pith-Instructions, and (the transformation from common capacity to) the competency-in-Tantra depend on initiation. Therefore, initiation is the root of all accomplishments. Without initiation, no matter how diligently one may strive, he will achieve no accomplishments whatsoever. Also, there is a definite danger that both the guru and disciples are liable to fall into hell.

The Tantra of Bde-mchog says:
"If a Tantric Yogi who desires to practice a certain
Yoga, has never seen the Mandala,
All his efforts will be in vain,
As a man trying to beat the sky with his fist,
Or a fool taking the mirage for water."
According to these sayings, the disciples should first be sent into the Mandala and given the complete Water and Crown Initiations. This is necessary, for if one depends on the Partial Initiation, such as the consecration from one particular Buddha and the fragmentary performance of initiation, it can only be considered a preparatory work preceding the "real, complete Initiation." Although there is no fault in depending on the Partial or Concise Initiation, it is by no means sufficient. A great and complete Initiation is necessary, as admonished in many Tantras and by many learned and accomplished teachers.

Having attained the Initiation of Hevajra[21], if one can also obtain the initiation of Bde-mchog, it will be very useful to him, because these two teachings are very closely connected with each other.

The explanation for the necessity of observing the Tantra precepts follows.

During the ceremony when the Guru and all the Buddhas' Sons imparted the initiation to the disciple, the disciple had sworn to observe the precepts and to follow all the admonishments. Having been shown how the precepts should be observed in the initiation ceremony, he was made fully aware of his responsibilities. He should observe the precepts accordingly. As said in the basic *Tantra of Bde-mchog:*

"The experts in Dhyana, the advanced Yogis,
Should always observe their precepts carefully.
Whoever violates the Tantric precepts
Will never accomplish anything in Mandala,
He will attain no Siddhis whatsoever."
The Tantra of Mnyam-sbyor (Balanced Actions) says:
"If one has never entered the Mandala,
If one violates one's oaths,
If one knows not the esoteric Pith-Instruction,
No matter how hard one practices,
There will be no accomplishment!"

It is clearly stated that if the disciple has not entered the Mandala and obtained the initiation, or if he does not observe the precepts and know the teaching of the Two Steps of the Arising Yoga thoroughly, he will never attain any accomplishments – even if he practises a long time.

If he has attained the teachings of the Highest Division of Tantra and claims to be a Tantric Yogi, he must know the Fundamental and Secondary Precepts of Tantricism[23]. Therefore, he should discipline himself well and observe the precepts carefully.

After these general preparations we now consider

special preparations, which are the supreme preparation practice. After the disciple has learned the necessary prac-preme preparation practices such as the general virtuous deeds, the attainment of Initiation, and the observation of Tantric Precepts, he should then begin the essential Tantric practice: the *Guru Yoga, Vajrasattva Yoga,* and the *Mandala Offering* Performance. Based upon the traditional sayings of the Gurus in the past, the explanation of the Vajrasattva Yoga and the Guru Yoga follows:

Vajrasattva Yoga is designed for cleansing the sins and removing the obstacles of the disciples, while the Guru Yoga is designed for the bestowal of blessing and grace on the disciples. First, the Vajrasattva Yoga:

He should earnestly devote himself to taking refuge in the Three Precious Ones like a hunted prey. He should also think of his fellow men, the infinite sentient beings, who are drowned in the ocean of suffering with him. As a matter of fact, they were all once his own mothers[24]. Hence he should remind himself of the immense debt of gratitude that he owes them — think how much work has to be done by a mother to bring up a child; think how a mother protects her child from dangers, illness, hunger. By constantly bearing such thoughts in mind, a resolute will to benefit the mother-like sentient beings will arise in one's heart. Then he should think further that all the seeming pleasures they may enjoy in Saṃsara will end in vanity and pain, and he should make a fervent oath: "I will bring all happiness by all possible means to sentient beings. I will set them free from all sufferings and unhappiness." He realizes that to materialize this wish there is no other way but to look for attainment of Buddhahood; thus a genuine Heart-for-Bodhi may arise within him. He fully understands that it is for

the sake of sentient beings that he hopes for the Supreme
Enlightenment and practices the Yoga of this Tutelary
Buddha – Vajrasattva. The Tantra of the Essence of Adorn-
ment says:

"He (Vajrasattva), who is the body of all Buddhas,
Sits on the Moon Wheel upon the white lotus
Holding the Thunderbolt and Bell with all ornaments.
A devotee should visualize the Vajrasattva in this man-
ner.
He should also practice the Incantation of the Hundred
Words[25]
For twenty times in one performance.
By doing this, even the sinful ones will be blessed."
Those accomplished masters also said:
"In between the meditation periods
One should recite the incantation.
If one recites it one hundred thousand times,
one's sins will be completely purified."

This means if he practices the Hundred Words Incantation of Vajrasattva twenty-one times in the interval of
meditation periods, his transgressional sins in the Yoga
practice will not grow; if he recites the incantation one
hundred thousand times, his sins will all be cleansed. Thus
one should practice this Yoga according to the following
procedure.

Visualize a white lotus on the top of your head. In the
center of the lotus is an *Ah* word which is transformed
into a Moon Wheel. Upon the Moon Wheel stands a *Hūṃ*
word, which transforms into a Thunderbolt, and from this
Thunderbolt's lower part a *Hūṃ* word radiates infinite
beams of light (by which the Two Acts[26] are performed).
It shines forth reaching to the Buddha's Pure Land and

renders offerings and services. Then it returns and shines downwards into the lower Lokas to relieve the sufferings of the sentient beings. Then the light retracts to the *Hūṃ* word and instantaneously becomes the Budhha Vajrasatt-va – his body is white, his right hand holds a Thunderbolt, and his left hand holds a bell. He also holds the Mother Buddha, the White Mother of Elegance. She has all the ornaments adorning her body and holds the Curved Knife and Human Skull. Her beauty and elegance are beyond description. She sits in a Lotus Posture and her body bears the thirty-two glorified marks and eight subsidiary signs of Buddha's body. In the Mother's heart lies a moon, upon which the white *Hūṃ* word radiates infinite light to the Buddha's land inviting the Wisdom Buddha to come down. When the Wisdom Buddha descends, remember to perform the Five Offerings and say *Tsa Hūṃ Boṃ Hoo* – to consolidate the Buddha. And, from the Mother's heart, the light again emanates to invite all the Buddhas in the universe to come down. You should earnestly pray them to grant you the Initiation. Then think that from all the nectar-filled vases held in the hands of all the Mother Bud-dhas, there begins to flow out the nectar to fill your body. Thus the Initiation is given to you. Meanwhile you should recite: *Aum Sarwa Da Ta Ga Da Ah Bi Ke Gada Samaya Shir Ye Hūṃ!* After the initiation, the over-flowing nectar gathers over your head and crystallizes into an image of the immutable Buddha (Me Gy Ba) to adorn your head. Thereupon, with the greatest sincerity of your body, mouth, and mind, you should pray as follows:

"O! Bhagavat Vajrasattva! Pray cleanse all the sins and transgressional evils of mine and of other sentient beings!"

Moved by your sincere prayer, Buddha Vajrasattva

radiates beams of light from his heart, which shine upon the bodies of all sentient beings in the cosmos; thereby, their sins and hindrances are cleared. The light again shines forth to the Buddha's Pure Land, rendering service and offerings, and finally collecting the merits of Buddha's body, mouth, mind, virtue, and performance before retracting to the *Hūṃ* word. Having been enforced by the merits of all the Buddhas, the Vajrasattva becomes more grandiose, powerful, and compassionate. Circling the *Hūṃ* word in his heart-center is the following sacred incantation:

Oṃ Ba-tsa Heruga Samaya Manubabaya Heruga Delobaditsa Dri Dor Mabawa Sudokayo Mabawa Subodayo Mabawa Ah Hu Rado Mabawa Sarwa Sidhi Mebaryatsa Sarwagarma Su Tsame Tse Dar Shirya Guru Hūṃ Ha Ha Ha Ha Ho Bhagavan Bentsa Heruga Mamemutssa Heruga Bava Mahasamaya Satta Ah Um Pai!

When reciting the incantation, you should visualize the incantation-circle rotating on and on. As the speed of the rotation steadily increases, beams of light emanate from this incantation-spin and shine upon the bodies of all sentient beings, cleansing their sins and removing obstacles. The light again travels to the myriads of Buddha's Pure Land, rendering offerings to the Buddhas and gathering the wave of grace* from Buddha's body, mouth, and mind before returning to the incantation letters. (Through this inspiration) a stream of pure nectar begins to flow out from the body of Vajrasattva. It flows into your body through the Pure Gate on the top of the head, until the whole body is full of nectar. At the same time, this incoming stream of nectar washes away all filthy and putrid mat-

* This term is common also in the initiation rituals. It is a term from the Hindu Tantra. *Ed.*

ters — which symbolizes the sins. One should think that through the pores over all the body the filthy matters, representing the sins and kleśas, are squeezed out and washed away. The body is filled with nothing but the pure and clean nectar. Thereupon, with a confidence of benefiting others and self, you should recite the incantation. When the recitation is finished, the devotee should apply the principle of the Four Mighty Ways [27] to confess all his sins and wrong doings to Buddha. Then he should think that all his sins of the Three Wheels [28] — the sin, sinner, and the act of sin — are cleansed thereby.

(At the end of this meditation) the Yogi reads the following prayer:

"O my protector! Because of my ignorance and desires
I have committed certain transgressions and evil deeds.
My Guru, my refuge! Save me and protect me!
O my lord, the one who holds the immutable Vajra!
Thou art the essence of great kindness and compassion!
The supreme lord of all, in whom I take refuge!"

After reciting this prayer, Buddha Vajrasattva smiles at him and says, "Good man, your sins, transgressions, and hindrances are all cleared." Then the Buddha Vajrasattva transforms himself into great light and enters into the body of the disciple. Then the disciple should think that his body, mouth, and mind are united and identified with the Buddha Vajrasattva. At the end of this meditation, the disciple should dedicate the merits and make an expression of good wishes toward all sentient beings.

In order to obtain blessing and grace from the Guru, the instructions for the practice of Guru Yoga are given as follows:

1. To view the Guru as the Field of Merits [29].

2. To serve and revere the Guru.

1. The disciple should think that in the firmanent in front of him there is a lion-shaped seat of gems with lotus-moon cushions upon it. On this sits his own Guru, who is the embodiment of the Thunderbolt-Holder, the Great Rdo-rje-chang, the Primordial Buddha of the Six Buddhas[30]. His blue body has one face and two arms. His right hand holds the Thunderbolt and his left hand holds the bell. With heavenly clothes and jewels adorning his body, he embraces the Mother Buddha in a Lotus-Sitting posture. From his body radiates resplendently the five-colored aura. On his forehead is a moon and a white *Om* word, at his throat there is a lotus and a red *Ah* word, in his heart there is a sun and a blue *Hūṃ* word. From these three words emanate beams of light shining forth to the Buddha's Pure Land and inviting the great Rdo-rje-chang and all the Gurus in the lineage to descend here. They all enter the disciple's body and become unified with the disciple.

As said in the *Tantra of Sdom-abyung:* "Guru is the Buddha, Guru is the Dharma, Guru is also the Sangha..." One should thus regard his own Guru as the embodiment of the Three Refuges. The *Five Steps Tantra* also says:

"The self-born Bhagavan

He who is the supreme heaven of all.

He gives the teaching and Pith-Instructions.

But there is one who is superior even to the Bhagavan,

He is the actual teacher, one's own Guru of Vajrayana."

According to these sayings one must regard one's own Guru as much more important even than the Great Buddha, for only through him can one be benefited. As Buddha says:

"When the appropriate time comes, I shall embody myself in a proper person. Whoever serves him will be blessed, his sins and transgressions cleansed."

This convinces us that whenever we serve the Pith-Instruction-Giver, our Guru, all the Buddhas will embody themselves in him to accept the offerings and to purify the disciples' sins. In the ordinary practice when one renders the offerings to Buddha, no doubt he attains the due merits of serving the Buddhas; however, he cannot be assured that the Buddha will actually come and accept his offerings[31]. Therefore, we know that the very best Merit-Field is one's own Guru. Thus, we should regard the Guru as the embodiment of all Tathagatas, possessing all the merits. In this manner, a pure faith toward one's Guru will grow. If a disciple thinks ill of his Guru or is fault-finding towards his Guru, he is sure to encounter the hindrances in his quest for enlightenment. If a disciple esteems and pays homage to his Guru, he will soon attain the enlightenment. With this and other right manners and considerations, one should think much of the gratitude that he owes to his Guru and faithfully respect and venerate him.

2. To serve and revere the Guru, as said in the Tantra of Five Steps:

"He should give up all other services and offerings
And concentrate on serving and offering to the Guru
    alone.
If his Guru is pleased,
The disciple will soon attain the All-Knowing Wisdom.
If the disciple serves and offers to his Guru
As he offers and serves the real Buddha,
What accomplishments and merits cannot he attain then?
What easier way to enlightenment can he find?"

One should know that among all the offerings and services, these made to one's Guru are the best. Hence, with great faith, one ought to make the best effort to serve one's Guru.

The practice of Mandala [32] (a ritual of offering) is briefly expounded as follows: The Mandal, of clay or gems, should be smeared with incense and the Five Nectars. The Yogi then recite the invocation: *Oṃ Ba-tsa Bume Ah Hūṃ!* By reciting this invocation the great iron wall is laid up. Within the enclosure of the great iron wall are spread clusters of gorgeous flowers, from which emanate the fragrance of perfume and the agreable odor of the Five Nectars. In the center of the earth looms the great Sumeru Mountain; encircling the Sumeru Mountain are the Four Continents – the East, South, West, and North; and between the continents are scattered small islands. East of the Four Continents is a sacred elephant (The Precious One); in the South, a sacred Family Overseer; in the West, a sacred Supreme Horse; in the North, a sacred Girl Rinbochi; in the Northeast, a sacred Warrior; in the Southwest, the precious Wheel; in the Northwest, the precious Jewel; in the Southeast, a great treasury. In the farther inner circle the sun, moon, planets, and stars are situated in their respective locations.

"This great Mandal, which includes the entire wealth of the cosmos, is now visualized clearly by my mind. Now I offer it in its entirety together with all the pleasures, merits, and happiness of mine and others in past, present, and future to the Gurus and Deities. I pray you to pity me, to accept my offer, and to grant me your blessing." Thus the yogi should pray. He should also render the Outer Offerings, the flowers and so on; the Inner Offerings, the offerings of nectars; and the Secret Offerings [33]. Thus he should praise Buddha and take Tantric precepts, both general and special, before his Guru. He should pray with earnestness and respect to his Guru to grant him a speedy arising of the understanding and realization of the Mundane and Transcendental Siddhis, to keep him apart from obstacles and bring him to agreeable conditions for his practice. Moved by this sincere prayer, the Guru is pleased. Therefore, he radiates successively from the Three Words *(Oṃ Ah Hūṃ)* the white, red, and blue lights which enter into the Three Places (forehead, throat, and heart) of the Yogi in order and eventually fill his body wholly. The defilements and sins of body, speech, and mind are thus cleansed, and the Vase Secret and Wisdom Initiations are attained.

The Yogi should also think that he has attained the accomplishments of the Three Vajras[34]. Thereupon, from the Three Places of the Guru simultaneously emanate the Three Lights. They enter into the body through all the gates[35]. By means of these lights, the subtle defilements[36] of the body, speech and mind are cleansed; the fourth initiation is thus attained by the Yogi. The Yogi should think that he has attained the Accomplishment of the Identity of the Three Vajras.

The Three Words *(Oṃ Ah Hūṃ)* are the symbol of the Three Vajras, having the ability to cleanse the defilements of the three gates. Therefore, it is permissible to consider that the three initiations are attained by this practice. And inasmuch as the thought of attaining the Absolute Fourth Initiation (Identity of the Three Vajras) is able to cleanse the Subtle Defilements, thereby the Fourth Initiation is attained. However, these so-called initiations are merely accepted for convenience and are by no means the actual initiations.

"Thereupon, the Guru above and before me descends upon my head, enters my body, and becomes one with me. Thus the Guru's body, speech and mind are identical with mine." Thus the Yogi should think; and then he should recite the Mantra of One Hundred Words to consolidate this unification. This practice should be performed at the beginning and end of the meditation, especially at the beginning.

CHAPTER THREE

THE ARISING AND PERFECTING YOGA

In the second part, the actual practice of the Path, there are two divisions – *the Arising Yoga and the Perfecting Yoga.*

We have heard some ignorant sayings from schools in Tibet that the Arising Yoga is necessary only for the Mundane Accomplishments. Nevertheless, according to the Mes-mds'ur and Rngog [37] schools of the Marpa lineage, the teaching of the Arising Yoga is given first. Milarepa said:

"In the course of the arising and extinction of manifestation,

For the sake of developing the illuminated mind,

One should diligently practice both the Arising and the Perfecting Yoga."

Many great teachers of the past said that to practice both the Arising Yoga and Perfecting Yoga is necessary. Therefore, to dispense with the Arising Yoga is against the teaching of Tantra and its authoritative commentaries. It is also against the teaching of their own [i. e. the ignorant objectors'] schools; hence, before the practice of Perfecting Yoga, we must study and practice the Arising Yoga. As said in the *Tantra of G'ye-rdo-rje*:

"If one says the two Yogas are equal [38],

It is a Tantra-infant's preaching."

The same Tantra also says:

"Through practising the Arising Yoga,

The Tantric Yogi [39] first practices the Yoga of Forms [40]

Knowing the Yoga of Forms is dreamlike –

The Yoga of Form itself eventually becomes the Yoga
   of Non-Form."
The Holy Nagarjuna says:
"First one should master the Arising Yoga,
Then one should aspire to the Perfecting Yoga,
This is the teaching given by the Perfect Buddha,
It is like a ladder with rungs."
Thus in many sutras we find stated the necessity for
practising the Arising Yoga first. The main reason for this
necessity is that the Arising Yoga will lay a good foundation for the Perfecting Yoga, and will ripen and produce
in the Yogi's heart the complete enlightenment experience
of the Perfecting Yoga.

If the disciple has attained a stable Samadhi of Arising Yoga, he can then begin practicing the Perfecting Yoga. In the
course of this practice, he first meditates solely on either the
Father or the Mother tutelary deity for the sake of convenience and ease. In such case he may not be wrong. However, to think that this process can also be adopted by the
beginner is certainly against the principle of Tantra. Then,
how should one practice? According to those who retain
the traditions and principles of this teaching, the foundation of the teaching of the Six Yogas is the Heat Yoga.
This view is based mainly on the doctrine of Hevajra, in
which it is stated that any one of the four castes[41] can be
led to practice this teaching.
Those revered masters in the past who devoted themselves mainly to practicing this teaching acquired their
Pith instructions from the Tantra of Bde-mchog. From

Gambopa, through the transmission of Ladak and Mar, the Bde-mchog teaching of Ladak was transmitted. In his youth, the Glorious Pag-mo-grub-pa practiced the Bde-mchog teaching from Mar-do. Transmissions were derived from the Bde-mchog Mandala of Sixty-two Tutelaries of the Lu-I-Pa School. Although there are two such different transmissions, they both (provide the methods of) producing bliss and joy; therefore the practice of either one will do. One should thus practice the Yoga of Four Periods [42] which will lead to the unfoldment of the Mandalas from the feet – the Five Buddhas and Bells – to the head.

Now, these experiences will be encounterd during the practice of Arising Yoga as the appropriate instructions are followed:

At first, (the yogi) should visualize the tutelary deity through the gradual steps till the whole body of the tutelary is completed. If the tutelary deity visualized has many faces and arms, the yogi may disregard the others and concentrate on visualizing the two main arms and the main face. There are two ways of visualizing the tutelary one's body: the upward process from the feet to the head, and the downward process from the head to the feet.

The tutelary-body should be envisioned as a whole, clearly and vividly. At first, however, the yogi should visualize the body not in specific detail but the body at once complete; then softly and loosely hold onto the visualization without any distraction. If any disturbing or diversified thought arises liable to cause the meditator to follow it, the meditator should beware, and bring his mind back to the object of meditation. If the visualization (mind-picture) becomes unclear, the yogi should freshen it by seeing it vividly until it becomes clear again. In the process of his meditation, the yogi will have the following experiences; that part of the tutelary-body he intensifies will appear clearly and vividly, the part to which he pays no attention will never appear in his mind-picture. Finally, the mind-picture will become so clear that he will think that not even the actual eye could see it better.

If the yogi wants to rest his mind stably on the clear picture, he must overcome drowsiness and distraction. Throughout the whole period of meditation he must possess the power of concentration.

Having mastered the above-mentioned "sketchy visualization"[43], the yogi should then visualize the other faces, arms, adornments etc., until all the details are complete and perfect. Thereafter the Mother tutelary deity should be visualized, then the other deities. Eventually the yogi is able to picture clearly and vividly all the deities (in the Mandala) and the objects in the complete Beyond-Measure Palace, general and specific, all at once in perfect concentration. The yogi is required to reach this stage.

Now the teaching of the Tutelary Pride[44]:

The yogi should raise the Tutelary Pride and think to himself, "I am the Buddha so-and-so," and concentrate on this. If the vision becomes unclear, the yogi should freshen it again. In the beginning, this meditation-with-effort-and-stress is needed. Later on, the yogi will be able to maintain a stable feeling of the Tutelary Pride after the meditation period in his daily activities. When he reaches this stage, his mental power of retaining the visualization will be strong enough to withstand the fluctuating circumstances, and he will maintain the Tutelary Pride in between meditation periods. The Visualization Practice and Tutelary Pride Practice should be exercised alternately. Working on this superb meditation, consisting of both deities and their dwellings, will eventually prevent the arising of the Samsaric visions; only the Superb Visions[45] will appear in the yogi's mind. The spontaneous Tutelary Pride – capable of maintaing itself in all fluctuating circumstances – is the cure which purifies the vulgar (or Saṃsaric) attachments in the yogi's mind.

When the yogi arises from his meditation, whatever he sees – living beings or the material world – he should think of as Buddhas and Buddhas' dwelling-places. If he can stabilize this feeling, he can attain the steadfast Samadhi. When he reaches this stage, he is admitted to have purified the Common Visions through the practice of the Arising Yoga.

It is said in the *Tantra of Sdom-aḥyung:*

"The nature of the Three Kingdoms is the Beyond-Measure Palace. All the living beings are the deities of the Mandala."

The saintly *A*pags-b'a-Iha said, "If you understand that the myriad manifestations are the Mandala itself, how would it be possiblle for your mind to become confused?" This understanding is applicable to both the Arising and the Perfecting Yoga. According to the principle of Vajrayana, all manisfestations are the Mandala of Heaven; all feelings and experiences are the Great Bliss; all thoughts are the Uncreated. To follow and to identify this principle is the main function of the Arising Yogi. In the Arising Yoga, the Great Bliss of Perfecting Yoga – produced by the entering of Life Prana into the Central Channel – is not found. Nevertheless, since the practicer has attained a very stable and clear visualization of Yab-Yum Buddha, he is able to unify wisdom and skill, to stop wavering and fluctuating Bodhi-heart, as symbolized in the *Pad* word [46]; and he will exprience a variety of blisses in Arising Yoga.

In short, the main objective and function of the Arising Yoga — the practice of visualizing the Mandala — is to ripen the yogi, to bring his consciousness forth to the realization of the identity of Buddha and sentient beings.

The instruction of the Practice of Perfecting Yoga is given in three parts: the basic principles, the step-by-step path, and the realization of the fruit or accomplishment.

In the first part there are two divisions:

1. The basic principle or real-nature of the mind.

2. The basic principle or real-nature of the body.

For the sake of exposing the principles behind the complete practices, the first exposition is introduced. For the sake of explaining the points in the body with respect to which the visualization should be carried out, the second exposition is introduced.

1. The basic principle of the mind.

The Tantra of Two Forms says:

"The mind, the perceiver, is formless in its essence.

There is no sound and no hearer, no smell and no smeller,

no taste and no taster, no touch and no feeler.

Likewise there are no mind and mind-functions [47]."

"One should understand that the organs, the outer-objects,

and the consciousnesses of the organs

Are all the Goddesses.

Thus, the eighteen dhatus [48] are preached.

From the very beginning, their essence is uncreated — never did they come into being.

They are neither false nor real;
Therefore, they are like the moon's reflection in the water.
Thus should you understand the Dakinis."

The [visual] form, sound, smell, taste, and [touch] stimuli are the five outer objects, from the seer to the feeler are the five senses, from the eye to the body are the five organs. In the terms of Skhandas, they all belong to the Aggregation of Form. In the terms of Ayatana [47b] they belong to the ten Ayatanas of form; the Nonself-nature of them is thus pointed out by the stanza. The so-called mind (Sems) is the Aggregation of Consciousness, or the Ayatana of Consciousness. The so-called mind-function is the Aggregation of Feelings, Perceptions, and Emotions. The above stanza explains the Non-self-nature of sense-data or the Ayatana of Dharma. The form-seer and the sound-hearer mentioned in the stanza denote the egotistic conception of beings. In short, this stanza illustrates both the Clinging of Ego and the Clinging of Dharma.

The stanza says that the non-existence of essence means the absence or the non-existence of self-nature in all Dharmas and living beings. These sayings are the philosophy of the great master Mds'o-sg'yes as mentioned in his commentary. They imply the Voidness or non-existence of the self-nature or the non-existence of the definable nature of being – the self-being as expressed in many other sources.

This truth of the non-existence of self-nature, or the non-existence of essence, or the never-come-into-being-self-nature, is by no means previously untrue but intentionally and subsequently verified through human reason and the holy edifications. This truth exists from the very beginning, as said in the stanza "to understand the truth as it is";

this clearly demonstrates the aspect of the "Originally true".

Guru Marpa said:

"On the bank of the Ganges river in the East,
Through the grace of the great Medrepa[50],
I fully realized the original reality of the never-come-
into-being.
This enlightenment kindles the void-nature of mind.
Clearly I beheld the original essence – the truth devoid
of play-words,
And clearly saw the Three Bodies,
Whereby all the conceptualistic ideas in my mind were
forever cleared up."

Thus Marpa's understanding of Mahamudra was procured mainly from the great master Medrepa, who, in this connection, particularly referred to the *Thatness* among the *Ten Solenesses*. As he said in a stanza: "It is neither with form nor without form." By this he meant the *Soleness of the Originally True*, not the *Soleness With Form* nor the *Soleness Without Form*. His disciple Lhan-j'ig-sg'yes-pai-rdor-rjes gave the exposition to this stanza in his commentary:

"Without-Form means the doctrine of the Sutra School. These terms also imply the True Form or Illusory Form of Yogachara, as favored by the School of Yogachara of True Form and the School of Yogachara of Illusory Form. This is also applicable to the Madhyamika Yogachara School – its doctrine allows the mind-only philosophy, either With Form or Without Form, of Yogachara in the field of mundane truth[51].

The doctrine of Two Truths should be established in a manner such as the Great Yogi Milarepa explains:

(The printing is not clear in the two first lines.)

153

"Buddha says that all do exist.
But, in the category of Transcendental Truth,
There are no hindrances and even no Buddha.
There is no meditator nor meditation.
There is no practice nor experiences.
Neither is there any Buddha-body nor Buddha-wisdom –
Therefore there is no Nirvana.
All such terms are merely names and conceptions."

According to the Middle-Way doctrine of Nagrajuna, Aryadeva, Zla-wa-grags-b'a, the very nature of causation itself is Soleness. So this stanza implies that only these sages' doctrine is acceptable [52]. Nagrajuna and Aryadeva, the Savior and the Holy One, were both middle-wayists after the Sutra period. Subsequent to the period of these two sages, there were many people who talked about Middle-Way philosophy, but these people can only nominally be regarded as middle-wayists. The superb being, Master Medrepa, and the meritorious Dhawadrapa were two outstanding sages who really held Nagrajuna's and Arydeva's view in a correct manner. Furthermore the *Treatise of the Ten Solenesses* says: "Without the adornment of pith-instructions from one's Guru, one can be considered only a mediocre follower of the middle way.

Zla-wa-zhaba said that, if a teacher has no pith-instruction as if an adornment for himself, he can be only a mediocre follower of the middle way. This right explanation of the ultimate truth by Zla-wa-zhaba should be rightly followed.

Now, the explanations of "neither true nor false."
Says the *Sutra of the Sixty Rational Stanzas:*
"The beings that depend on and are caused by other be-
     ings,

Their nature is insubstantial like the moon's reflection
  in water.
All the stable and unstable living beings in Saṃsara
Are originally unborn and non-existent.
There is no fundamental truth nor Innate Wisdom[53],
There is neither Karma nor the effects of Karma.
Therefore, the Saṃsara never existed — even its name is
  meaningless!
O, the absolute truth is like this!"
Thus it is said that in the Transcendental Truth nothing
whatsoever exists, Saṃsaric or Nirvanic — not an iota ever
existed. But immediately the Sutra continues:
"Alas, if there is no sentient being,
From where have the Buddhas in the Three Times come?
If there are no causes there will be no effects.
In the sense of Mundane Truth
Both Saṃsara and Nirvana exist.
This is said by Buddha Shakyamuni himself.
The existence and the non-existence,
The entities and the emptiness,
The manifestations and the reality,
Are identical and of one taste.
In essence there is no difference between them at all.
There is no self-awareness nor other-awareness,
All and all are absorbed in the great two-in-one.
The sages who have realized this truth
See no consciousness but wisdom.
The sages who have realized this truth
See no sentient beings but Buddhas,
See no Dharma Form but Dharma Essence.
They are neither true nor false
One should not fall into these views."

Sentient beings and materials are all produced through respective causes and conditions; they are consolidated through conceptualization; therefore, they are not real, nor have they any substantiality. In other words, all beings are void in their self-nature in the sense of the actual existence of self-essence. If there were an independently-solid self-nature in beings there would be no need for depending on any cause or conditions (to form the beings themselves). Thus there never existed even an atom of sense-data (outer-object) upon which the Clinging of Existence arises[54].

This very truth does not impair the order and functions of the causation-bound events in Saṃsara and Nirvana; as dream, magic, and shadow, all the transpiring events manifest. Based on this view, one should know that those who claim the Voidness as the non-existence of the horn-of-a-rabbit [i. e. the non-existence of false notions *Ed.*] are mistaken. One should also know that those who claim non-existence of the delusory snake-perception arising from the rope, are also wrong. Thus, one should know that this absolute non-existence of the sensedata upon which the Clinging of Existence arises is the correct understanding of Sunyata. Without such a horse-of-right-understanding, even if one rides on a horse-of-Buddha, one will not be able to cross the stream of Saṃsara.

Says the *Tantra of Rdo-rje-bgur:*

"In order to destroy the clinging of ego,

The Buddhas have preached the teaching of the Voidness."

This means that in order to destroy the Clinging of Ego and the Clinging of Dharma, Buddhas have preached the philosophy of the Voidness. Though the principle of the Transcendental Truth is as mentioned above, even in the category of Mundane Truth, if one decisively or unalterably identifies existent things with dreams, magic, and illusory visions, one will eventually come to the point of the Nothingness[55] which is not allowed in my school. If one follows the wrong views of other schools one is liable to fall into endless dangers.

Some hold that all manifestations are magic-like, and accept the existence of all happenings in Saṃsara and Nirvana — such as the attainment of Buddhahood. They also claim that all manifestations are merely names and words denominated and conceptualized by human beings, that the manifested beings in the causations are identical in essence with the Voidness of non self-nature, that the existence and the non-existence have never separated from each other. They further claim that this is the special teaching given by the great masters in the past, and that it is not necessary to follow the Two-Truths System of the Middle Way doctrine. This kind of saying is not right; it is against the teachings of the Buddhas and the exposition of them by sages. Not only that, these sayings contradict their own doctrine, for on the one hand they deny the Two-Fold Truth and on the other hand they accept the principle of the identity of bliss and voidness. In short, one should definitely search for the understanding of Voidness which is briefly explained above.

2. The basic principles or nature of the Body.

In the center of the Transformation-Wheel (Chakra) at the navel and the other main Wheels in the body is pivoted the Central Channel; the upper end and the lower end of it, together with other points of the Wheels, are the most important centers. These centers are viewed as vital points and are emphasized in the Skill-in-Yoga-Teachings of Tantra.

According to the pith-instructions of Marpa, one should put emphasis on the Heart and Throat Centers during sleeping, and should know the critical teachings on the Navel and Forehead Centers during the practice of Heat Yoga and Karma Yoga in the awakening stage. This is because during these different times the Thig-le* upon which the consciousness relies concentrates at these four different centers. According to the teaching of Dus-*a*kor (Kalachakra) the Head Center and Navel Center produce the Thig-le in the awakening stage; the Throat and the Secret Center produce the Thig-le in dreaming stage; the Heart and the Precious Center produce the Thig-le in the deep-dreaming stage. This agrees approximately with the saying that at the end of the navel and genital center, the Thig-le is produced in the four different times.

At the time of falling into sleep, the pranas will gather at the Heart Center and the Precious Center. When they are heavily concentrated, one will fall into sleep; thereafter, the pranas in these two parts gradually become thinner and thinner. When (most of) the pranas come to the Secret Center and Throat Center the fleeting dreams will appear; when the pranas have gathered in these two parts for some time the actual dreams (or steady dreams) will arise. When the pranas rise up to the Center Head and Navel Centers, one will awake. From the Head Center the Thig-le drops to the end of the precious organ; as it reaches the different

* *Thig-le* is equivalent to the Sanskrit *bindu* and signifies a seed and source of life-power. — *Ed.*

centers as mentioned above it will produce the various blisses (or so-called Four Blisses).

This is the meaning of the four times:

Through the power of the prana the Yogi manipulates in exercise, the Downward-Bliss produces the Dim Innate when it reaches the center of the navel; when it reaches the end of the precious organ the Bright Innate is produced.

That these four centers are very important in the meritorious exercises of dream and sleep by no means implies that they are not essential points upon which the exercises of mental concentration should be carried out during the daytime. Among all the centers in the body, the Navel Center is the one upon which the Yogi should begin. One should also know that to concentrate upon the different centers will produce different effects and specific advantages.

CHAPTER FOUR

THE STEPS OF PRACTICE IN THE PATH

First, the preparatory exercises of *A*krul-*a*kor and Stong-ra are given; second, the process of the actual practice.

Some in the Marpa School say that with the protection-practice of the *Hūṃ* word during the inhaling, exhaling, and holding periods of breathing, or with the moderate wrathful deities as protection, or with the practice of the Guru Yoga to accumulate the merits, the Yogi may do without the practice of *A*krul-*a*kor and Stong-ra. This kind of saying is given by the later followers; but His Holiness Milarepa and Gampopa never so declared in the old days.

The practice of *A*krul-*a*kor has two aspects: First, the practice of Taking the Refuges and Arousing the Bodhi Heart; and second, meditation on the Guru who sits upon one's own head and sincerely praying to him. These practices are definitely in accordance with the teachings of Tantra. The Yogi should first vividly visualize himself as the Father-Mother Patron Buddha.

Master Pag-mo-grub-b'a exposed, in his *Stanzas on the Skillful Path*, the methods and physical exercises as follows:

1. Making the body full like a vase.
2. Turning like a wheel.
3. Bending like a hook.
4. With the Vajra Mudra shooting the sky and tightening the lower part.
5. Like a dog vomiting, shaking the body.
6. Shaking the head and body, and stretching the limbs.

These are the famous Six Exercises of Naropa.

1. *Making the body full like a vase:* The Yogi should sit on a comfortable seat in a lotus posture, his body and spine erect; put his two palms on his two knees; inhale the air with the right nostril, and then look to the left and exhale all the air very slowly and gently. Take in the air with the right nostril and look toward the right, and slowly, gently, let all the breath out. Then take in the air with the left nostril and look toward the left; gently let the breath out as before. Next take in the air with both nostrils and let the breath out while the body remains sitting in a normal position. Repeat this manner of breathing three times. Altogether nine repetitions are required to expel all the defiled air within the body. During the inhaling and exhaling, the mouth should not be opened. The yogi should keep his body straight and turn his two fists inward. Then he should inhale very gently and slowly and send the air down below the navel. Meantime he should gulp down the air without any sound, using the diaphragm to press the Upper Prana down and to gently pull up the Lower Prana. Thus, the Upper and Lower Prana meet and unite. The mind should concentrate on the center of the navel Chakra, and one should hold the breath as long as he can as if holding the air in a vase to its fullness. During this breath-holding period, all the body movements should be carried out. Although not a real *Akrul-akor* exercise, this exercise is called a form of *Akrul-akor.* At the moment when the yogi cannot hold the breath longer, he should very gently let the air out through the nostrils, but never through the mouth. While doing this, the mind should not think of anything.

2. *Turning like a Wheel:* Sitting in the Lotus posture,

use the fingers of the right hand to hold the large toe of the right foot and those of the left hand to hold the large toe of the left foot. Hold the body erect, and turn the waist and stomach clockwise three times; turn them counter-clockwise three times. Next bend the body from left to right and from right to left three times; then bend the body forward and reverse it to the looking-up position. Repeat the body-bending three times.

3. *Bending like a Hook:* Put the two fists, in the vajra-fist manner, upon the Heart Center and stretch them forward with great force, then stretch both arms forward. Use the right fist to make a circle around the head from left to right. As the arm and fist come down, use the elbow to strike the side of the chest. Do the same movement with the left arm from the opposite direction. Then holding the Vajra-fists and putting them on the Heart Center, again stretch them forward with force. Next, stretch both arms to the right, as before, and strike the side of the chest.

4. *With the Vajra Mudra shooting the sky and tightening the lower part:* Cross the two knees and hold the body erect. Join the fingers of both hands and massage the body from the lower part up to the head; then use the fingers to support the whole body and lift it up. Then suddenly loosen the fingers, and let the body drop down vehemently.

5. *Like a dog vomiting, shaking the body:* Cross the knees and keep the body straight. Put the two hands on the ground, and then successively lift up the body and the head. As the hands release the support and the body drops down, the whole body should be waved and shaken as though trembling. At the same time exhale the air and utter a prolonged *Ha* sound, turning round at the waist. Repeat three times.

6. *Shaking the head and body and stretching the limbs:* Put the right hand on the left knee and the left hand on the right knee. Use the fingers of both hands to pull up the knees, then shake the head and body.

The yogi who practices these exercises must be acquainted with the art of holding the breath. He must be at ease and gentle. The best time to practice these exercises is before eating, or some time after the meal when the stomach is not too full. These exercises should be practised until the body becomes very flexible and energetic.

The Practice of the Visualization of the Stong-ra (the Empty Body)

The Yogi should visualize the image of the patron Buddha as before, but now he should especially visualize the interior of the body as clear and transparent, like crystal, from the top of the head to the soles of the feet. In this manner, the yogi should try to stabilize the visualization. The practice of mental visualization and the physical exercises should be carried out alternatively.

The Stong-ra practice is to visualize the body without the slightest shadow or obstruction as if one were seeing a clear rainbow. Altbough one's body cannot at this stage actually become (a body of rainbow), the stabilization of this visualization will enable the yogi to overcome the hazards — the nerve pains and prana pains — which he may encounter during his practice. Because of this Stong-ra practice, the greater pains or hazards will not arise; even if these pains do arise they can be subdued by the practice of Stong-ra visualization. This is the special advantage of practicing Stong-ra as well as the physical exercises.

Although there are a number of different statements and arrangements of the Stong-ra practice, the teaching of Pag-mo-grub-b'a says no more than the instruction given above; therefore, one should know that to follow this instruction is quite sufficient.

Though one may not find many accounts of the Stong-ra and physical exercises in the main Tantras, these are the pith-instructions taught by the masters. Furthermore, in the practice on Rtsa[56] and prana it is sometimes difficult to attain Samadhi through the gentle or soft practice; therefore, the radical or strong practice is needed. In that case it is believed that these preparatory practices will minimize hazards and obstacles.

The Actual Successive Practice of the Path

This is expounded in two sections: The classifications of the Path; and the instruction of entering into the Path.

There are different ways to classify this teaching – some divide it into two groups; some, into three, four, six, or ten. However, from the viewpoint of befitting the different dispositions or capacities of human beings, the teachings can be classified in three groups. First, the teaching that enables one to become the perfect Buddha in this very life; second, the teaching that enables one to become Buddha in the Bardo state; third, the teaching that enables one to become Buddha in future lives[57]. From the viewpoint of the nature of the practice, the teaching can be divided into the ordinary Perfecting Yoga, and the outstanding betterment practice of the Perfecting Yoga The latter is not usually found in the teachings of the masters of this school (Kargyupa), who mainly depend on the pith-instructions alone.

However, those masters in the Marpa school who held the tradition of preaching the Tantra do accept this type of teaching.

Marpa said:

"From the great master Naropa, the guard [58],
I have heard the profound *Tantra of Hevajra*
I also received the pith-instruction of
  joining, transformation and unification [59]
  (*Bsre, rpo, mtsams-sbyor*).
Especially have I learned the teaching of Heat Yoga and
  Karmayoga.
Thus, for me, was the essence of the teachings of the
  Whisper Succession illustrated."

Thus, Marpa said, was illustrated for him the joining and transformation practice of the Whisper Succession. In particular, he relied on the practice of the Heat Yoga of the Vajra, which produces the four blisses. Later on, through the practices of Karmayoga, the four blisses were also raised within him. From this we know that, in the teaching of Hevajra, he relied mainly on the Heat Yoga and Karmayoga.

Again Marpa said:

"In the city of Lagkedar, in the west,
I bowed down at the feet of the holy
Ye-shes-snying-po.
From him I heard the teaching of
Gsun-wa-*a*dus-b'a of the Father Tantra [60].
And also received the pith-instructions
Of the Illusory Body and Great Light.
Thus have I learned the teaching of the
Path of the Five Steps."

According to Naropa there are four outstanding Tantras from which the superb pith-instructions are derived; one of them is the teaching of the Path of the Five Steps of Gsun-wa-*a*dus-b'a. Thus Marpa learned the teaching of the Illusory Body and Great Light of Gsun-wa-*a*dus-b'a from both Ye-shes-snying-po and Naropa. As for the teaching of Transformation Yoga and Yoga of Entrance, he mainly derived them from the masterly *Gdan-bizh Tantra*.

According to the classification of the Six Yogas of Naropa, the yogas are: Heat Yoga, Yoga of Illusory Body, Light Yoga, Transformation Yoga, Yoga of Entrance and Bardo Yoga. Both the Dream Yoga and Bardo Yoga are ramifications of the Yoga of Illusory Body. It is better to appropriate the Light-of-Sleep[61] to the Yoga of Illusory Body; also it is more convenient to classify the Transformation Yoga and the Yoga of Entrance as one. The pith-instruction of Milarepa stated:

"... This teaching contains the Arising Yoga, Head Yoga, Karmayoga, the Knowledge of Reality, the Symbolic Light in the Path, and the Symbolic Illusory Body and Dream in the Path. These six teachings are the heart-like pith-instruction of Marpa, the final teachings of the Whisper Succession. No other teachings of any Path-with-Form can be found superior in essence to these. There is no other temporary or final instruction that does not belong to this teaching. The teaching of the Six Yogas is itself the Perfecting Yoga."

Those who follow and hold the traditional instructions of the Marpa School all hold this opinion. Those who declare that there are other teachings more profound than tha Six Yogas of Naropa, speak nonsense.

Here it is proper to point out that, in general, the highest Perfecting Yoga must first provide the method of inducing the [prana] of the Roma and R-kyang [62], to enter the Central Channel. This teaching is indispensable, though there are a great many different methods given by accomplished yogis who relied on different Tantras. In this teaching (of Six Yogas), the method of meditating on the [g Tummo] [62] or the short. *Ah* at the Transformation Center of the navel is used to gather the Live-Dynamic Prana into the Central Channel. Through the entrance of the air into the Central Channel, the four blisses are produced, and finally, the Mahamudra Innate Wisdom. Ii this profound Teaching of Skillfulness [63] is not relied on, but, instead, the practice of the Samadhi of Absolute-No-Thought, the Yogi will reach the state of Mind-Consolidation in which bliss, illumination, and non-thought are experienced. This state of Mind-Consolidation, however, is a common stage: Hinayana, Mahayana, Paramitayana, and Vajrayana all have the knowledge and experiences of it. It is by no means special; therefore, it is of great importance that one should not confuse the teaching of this Mind-Consolidation state with the special Tantric Skillful Path. This view can be verified by the instance of Gampopa's [Sgam-po-pa] meeting with Milarepa. Whon Gampopa first met Milarepa, he told Milarepa that he was able to remain in Samadhi with perfect concentration for many days in a single period. But Milarepa told him that no butter can be produced by squeezing the sand; moreover, the Samadhi he had engaged in was by no means enough. Milarepa then told him that he should practice the Small *Ah* of Life-Energy of the Heat Yoga. One should well understand this important point [64].

We have always heard it said that the teaching of Heat Yoga of the Kargyutpa is the very best; however, this should only be understood to the effect that the primordial and fundamental principle of the Perfecting Yoga is to make the life-prana enter into the Central Channel to produce the Innate Great Bliss. Consequently, as the prime goal is reached, there is no need to pursue any other teachings of the Perfecting Yoga. By the practice of the meditation on the Dumo fire, the air enters into the Central Channel and goes through the progressive process of entering, remaining, and dissolving. By means of this power the Bodhi-Heart is brought under control. No more leakage of the Bodhi-Heart will occur; therefore the Yogi is able to practice the Karmayoga which provides favorable conditions for producing the Four Innate Blisses. The teaching of Heat Yoga and Karmaycga is mainly needed for the purpose of producing the Innate Bliss. Relying on this Innate Blissful-Emptiness while awake, the Yoga of Illusory Body should he practiced in the daytime. At time of sleep in the night, exercise on the Illusory Body of the dream state should be stressed. To practice this, one should first exercise the Light Yoga; then one is able to enter into (and master) the dream. In order to be capable of holding the prana during the time of (the unfoldment of) the Light-of-Sleeping State, one must first have the ability to gather the pranas during the waking state. For both of these practices, the best preparation is Heat Yoga.

The Yogi must first completely master the Dream State. After that he is able to recognize the Bardo State; for this the Heat Yoga is also the best preparation. Also because of the Heat Yoga these three practices converge into the Yoga of Illusory Body.

In the art of mastering the special Transformation Yoga and the Entrance Yoga, one must first be able to gather all the pranas into the Central Channel. Practicing Heat Yoga is the best method to accomplish this.

If he knows the different ways of allocating these teachings, he will have no difficulty in understanding the various ways of classifying them. If he possesses sound understanding of them, he may arrange them in any manner.

The Successive Steps of the Teachings in the Path

This will be expounded in two categories: first, the basic teachings in the path; second, the teaching of improvement. In the first category lie (1) the principle of the Path and (2) the ramification teachings of the path-Transformation Yoga and the Entrance Yoga. In the former there also lie two divisions: (1) The exposition of the gathering of prana in the Central Channel and the manner of the arising of the four blisses. (2) Relying on the foregoing experience, instruction on practicing the Illusory Yoga and Light Yoga. Of the first there are also two divisions: (1) The inner practice of Heat Yoga. (2) The outer practice of Karmayoga. The first again has two divisions; (1) Through the practice of Dumo the prana is led to the Central Channel. (2) By means of the entrance of the prana the manner of the arising of the four blisses. The first, again has two divisions: (1) How to practice Dumo. (2) The manner of the entrance, remaining, and dissolving of the prana in the Central Channel resulting from the Dumo practice. The first is divided into three groups: (1) Meditation on the Three Pillars. (2) Meditation on the Clear Words. (3) The practice of Vase-Breathing.

Meditation on the Three Pillars: Visualize clearly that sitting in the front sky are the Chief Gurus and the Succession Gurus, together with the Goddess and the Brave ones[65]. To them render the comprehensive offerings without the slightest regard for one's own possessions. Then pray to them in general terms many times; especially on this occasion one should pray fervently for the arising of the two-in-one bliss-voidness experience and realization. Also one should think that it is for the purpose of enabling all the mother-like sentient beings to become the perfect Buddha Rdo-rje-chang that he now practices the Heat Yoga. One should put all one's heart into thinking of the Bodhi-Heart. Then visualize, clearly and vividly, the image of the self-Buddha[66]. Thus the foundation of Samadhi is laid.

The Yogi should put on the meditation-belt[67], cross his legs (in the sitting posture), hold his spine erect, slightly bend his chin, and rest naturally the eyes. The tongue slightly touches the upper palate, the teeth and lips rest naturally as they are. Alert the body and mind; thrust the chest forward; put one hand on top of the other and poise them below the navel. Clearly visualize the three channels. Then think of the Dumo situated about four fingers' distance from the navel, close to the spine. More explicitly, the Dumo is situated in the Central Channel at the joining point of the three channels — namely the Central, Right, and Left Channels. They are situated in a parallel position, and the Central Channel extends from the place below the navel up to the top of the head, as the supporting pillar of the four Chakras.

The reason for meditting in such a manner is to lead the pranas to enter into the Central Channel. Three different ways of practice were suggested. Some say that the three Channels all end at the place four fingers' distance below the navel. Some say that the Right and Left Channels do not end there, but extend down to the end of the precious organ. In the upper part, some claim, the Central Channel extends up to Smin-mds'ams, the center of the two eyebrows, and the Right and Left Channels extend down to the nostrils. Through correct practice, the Right and Left Channels which encircle the Central Channels in the center of the four chakras will eventually be straightened. As for the diameter of the Channels, there are no definite rules. Meditate on various diameters. When the Dumo is meditated upon, the color of the Central Channel should be visualized as the color of the oil lamps' flame. This whisper-given pith-instruction is found in the *Tantras of Mka-spyol;*; however, before reaching this stage, the color of the Right Channel should be visualized as red, and the Left Channel as white, and the Central as blue.

Then the four Chakras should be meditated upon. First the Transformation Chakra of the Navel Center: its outer shape is triangular and has forty-two red nerve-leaves (Rts'adabs) extending upwards. This is a general way of meditating on these nerve-leaves. Though it is not specific, it is quite sufficient to serve the purpose. Second, the Dharma Chakra in the Heart Center; its outer shape is round, like the shape of the *Boṃ* word. It has eight white nerve-leaves extending downward. Third in the Throat Center lies the Chakra of Reward. Its outer shape is rounded like the *Boṃ* word. It has sixteen red nerve-leaves extending downward. The Yogi should understand that the last two Chakras symbolize Wisdom and Skill, and duly meditate upon them.

At the beginning of visualizing the three Channels, one should know that the process of visualization consists of two practices:

1. Seeing the Channels vividly, or forming a clear picture in the mind.
2. Holding on to this picture.

The mind should concentrate in the Central Channel at the point where the three channels join. This is very important. Then, one should proceed to visualize all the nerve-leaves, complete in number, of the different Chakras. Keep on with this practice; the nerve-leaves will become clearer and clearer in the mental picture.

If one has made every effort to visualize the nerve-leaves, but cannot get a clear picture of them in mind, one should concentrate on visualizing the three Channels, putting emphasis on picturing the portion above the Heart Center. If the mind concentrates without a slight rest for a long period, it will incur great hazards and hindrances. In that case, one should only meditate on the point where the three Channels join. According to this teaching, it is said, the yogi will experience two different stages: the emergence of a very clear and durable picture of the nerves, and the emergence of an obscure picture of the nerves. Whichever the case, it is advisable to follow the above instructions. This is verified by the teachings on visualization of nerves given by the accomplished yogi, the great Lawabi.

During this visualizing practice, if the yogi wants also to practice the breath-holding exercise, he may do so as instructed before. The way of alternately practicing the visualization, body movement, and Stong-ra will be expounded later.

The Practice of Visualizing Words

In Heat-Yoga, a teaching of meditating on different words in the three Channels and four Chakras is provided. This teaching is found in both the fundamental *Tantra of Hevajra* and the *Expounding Tantra of Sambhuda*. Many great accomplished yogis, such as the Black Practitioner (Nagbo-Spyod-pa), taught this teaching.

The practice of visualizing words includes two ways — the comprehensive way and the simple. The comprehensive way is to meditate on the words both at the center of the Chakra and at each different nerve-leaf. But in this teaching (of the Six Yogas), we find no clear instructions on this. The simple way is to meditate only on the words in the center of the four Chakras. This is clearly stated in the *Expounding Tantra* and the teachings of the great accomplished beings. Reflecting on this principle, one finds that merely meditating on the small *Ah* word in the Navel Center and the *Hūṃ* word in the Head Center is not sufficient nor desirable. To meditate on the words in the Heart Center and Throat Center is also necessary. It is of great importance.

To meditate on the words, one should follow the aforementioned instructions on keeping posture. Visualize the small *Ah* word at the center of the Transformation Chakra of the navel, or in the center in the Central Channel, which is close to the core of the spine. The Yogi should concentrate only at this point.

The visualization procedure is as follows:

Visualize a small red, Sanskrit *Ah* word. Its shape is similar to the Tibetan word *Shad* of the printed alphabet, standing upon a moon-wheel.

To locate the visualization in the Heart Center, the yogi should see the word at the center of the eight nerve-leaves of the Dharma Chakra of the Heart Center near the central point between the two breasts.. He should meditate only on the point in the Central Channel that is near the spine. Visualize a blue *Hūṃ* word standing on a moon-wheel, head face down, the Bodhi-Heart like snow about to melt.

To locate the visualized word at the Throat Center, the yogi should visualize only the center-point of the sixteen nerve-leaves of the Throat Center in the Central Channel 'near the spinal column. Visualize at this point a red *Oṃ* word, its head facing up, standing on the moon-wheel.

To locate the word at the Head Center, the yogi should visualize the word at the center of the nerve-leaves of the Head Center in the Central Channel near the spinal column. Visualize at the point a white *Haṃ* word, facing down, standing on the moon-wheel.

It is of great importance that the yogi should visualize the points in the center of the Central Channel, entwined by the knot of the Right and Left channels, at the cross sections of the four Chakras.

Says the *Expounding Tantra Sambhoda:*
"The lotus that reaches the inner part of the heart
Is the principal one, which has eight nerve-leaves.
The nerve that reaches the inside of it is like a lamp.
In shape, it resembles the plantain flower,
Leaves opened and facing downward.
The god who dwells within it
Is as small as the mustard seed.
The indestructible seed – the *Hūṃ*,
Trembles like the snow about to melt..." [cf. the Upaniṣadic and the *gotra* teaching.]

The nerve that reaches the inner part of the heart is the principal nerve, which implies the Central Channel; the *Hūṃ* world should be visualized in it. The other words in the other three Chakras should be visualized as well.

Although there are many different teachings on the word-visualization in the four Chakras, the essential point is to visualize these words in the center of the Central Channel. Nevertheless, this point is not clearly stated in some teachings. If it is not clearly understood, one will not be able to gather the pranas at the Central Channel; consequently one will miss the essence of the pith-instruction.

The size of the words on which the yogi meditates should be as small as the mustard seed – as the Tantra describes the *Hūṃ* word. This size applies to the other four words as well.

The smaller and clearer the word as visualized and held by the mind, the easier it is to control the pranas. This is a very important factor in mastering the pranas.

Although the Sambhodra Tantra does not mention it, the small word *Ah* should be visualized with a head. According to the pith-instruction given in the *Tantra of Bde-mchog*, all the four words should be visualized with the half-moon head, the Thig-le and Na-da melting like the female Bodhisattva about to weep. This teaching is important because it produces and will enhance the Great Bliss.

If the Yogi visualizes the word as very bright and glowing, he will be able easily to overcome drowsiness and promote his illuminative experience of Samadhi.

When any visualized object is meditated upon, the yogi should put all his mind into the subtle object as if his mind (or rather his whole being) enters into the object. He should never visualize the object as if he merely sees it before him[68]. For the correct practice, mind and object become as one; thus the experience of the unification of mind and Thig-le will come to pass, and, the gathering of the prana will become easy. In the practice of this meditation one should neither overstrain nor be too lax in his effort. Overstrain or laziness will bring drowsiness and distractions; therefore, the yogi should avoid both extremes.

The beginner should not meditate on the three words above the heart center for too long; he should meditate on them for only a short while, and devote most of this time to concentrating on the small *Ah*. If he finds it difficult to concentrate on the minute object, he should visualize it a little larger. When a larger picture can be stabilized in the mind, the yogi will then be able to visualize smaller or more subtle objects.

The purpose of practicing the Heat Yoga is to produce the Four Blisses. When the Bodhi-Heart in the nerves begins melting and the two pranas[69] start gathering at the head Chakra, the (first) Bliss [ananda] begins to arise. Thereafter, the Bodhi-Heart begins to disperse into the nerves. When the Bodhi-Heart gathers at the Throat Center the (second) Extreme-Bliss [paramananda] arises; then the Bodhi-Heart disperses again through the different nerves, and when it is gathered at the Heart Center, the (third) Superb Bliss [viramananda] arises. Again, the Bodhi-Hearth disperses through the nerves, and when it is gathered at the Navel Center, the (fourth) Innate Bliss [sahajananda] arises*. Following this

*We have inserted the four technical Sanskrit terms.

The *Hevajra Tantra* states also the alternative tradition of this highest bliss as third in order, thus implying its correspondence with the Heart Center of the Sacred Light of Vairo-

principle, if one meditates upon the words in the center of the Central Channel in the four Chakras, the mind-prana will be easily gathered at the four centers; thus, the Four Blisses will arise from the four centers. It is necessary for the Yogi to recognize these Four Blisses in experience.

When the Bodhi-Hearth begins to melt and drop down from the upper center to the lower centers, if the Bodhi-Heart cannot remain at each center for a longer period, it will be extremely dificult for the yogi to recognize the differences between the Four Blisses. Especially will it be difficult to recognize the Innate Bliss. Thus one should know that if the mind can concentrate a long period on the four Chakras, the melted Bodhi-Heart will also remain at the different centers for a longer period. This is a very important point. If the *Haṃ* word at the Head Center that is the center of the white Bodhi-Heart can be stabilized, the white element will be greatly enhanced and multiplied. If the word at the Throat Center, the place through which

čana and his co-power, the Lord of the Center of the five Dhyani Buddhas. This tacit identification with the heart, and not the usually given hair-splitting reasons, is the true esoteric basis for the alternative order, which is thus seen not to be "artificial" as D. L. Snellgrove *(Hevajra Tantra*, Oxford, Vol. I, p. 137) surmises, saying hence not correctly that "it is associated with no improved interpretation of them (the Four Blisses) as a coherent set." This conclusion is understandable, however, for anyone not familiar with the relation of the Four Blisses to the Chakras, for that relation provides the only solid and practical basis for the non-arbitrariness Snellgrove rightly sought. The moment the Chakras are taken into account, the only proper position for the Highest or Innate Bliss is seen at once to be third, placing it in direct correspondence with the Heart Center, where it uniquely belongs. – *Ed.*

the Right Channel multiplies the blood-element, can be stabilized, the secretion of the Dumo which comes from the
Navel Center will produce great power.* Consequently, it
will promote and improve the practice of Dream Yoga.
The Heart Center is the center of light. If the *Hūṃ* word
at the heart center is stabilized the great light will unfold.
Meditation on the Heart Center will help the emergence
of the light in both the waking and the sleeping states.

The small *Ah* word should also be stabilized at the Navel Center, since through it the Left Channel multiplies the
fluid. From the Navel Center the White-Bodhi-Heart re-
vitalizes the whole body. Furthermore, this center is the
special place where the Dumo resides. It is well known
that the Navel Center is the place where the fire, that melts
the Bodhi-Heart, is kindled.*

It is of great importance that the yogi should acquaint
himself with the teaching of the meditation on the Chakras and their words. Until all the words in the different
Chakras appear vividly in the mind, the yogi should continue his effort.

* We would rather say, as better agreeing with practice: Which
comes from the Heart Center, and in mediated through the
Navel Center. *Ed.*

* Both from conversations with other practitioners of yoga
and from personal experience, the editor can unequivocally
state that the greatest heat (gTum-mo) can be generated and more
easily controlled through the use of the Heart Center rather
than through the navel plexus, allowing the latter to function
unconsciously under orders of the Heart Center, as it were, and
as a distribution point — but not bestowing any direct attention
on the navel *per se*. Even on a cold night the bodily heat thus
generated with comparative simplicity is pervasive and in-
tense. — *Ed.*

The Practice of Vase-Breathing

Following the preceding instructions, the yogi should first clearly visualize the nerve [nadi = Tib. rtsa. *Ed.*] system in general, then concentrate on the center of the Central Channel at the cross section of the three channels. Next, the yogi should meditate on the four words in the different nerves; especially should he concentrate on the small *Ah* word in the Central Channel at the Navel Center. If this mind-holding object can be stabilized, the mind and prana will converge to it. Thus the mind reaches the state of concentration and the pranas are collected. This is stated in the *Tantra of Bde-Mchog* and *the Expounding Tantra Sambhodra* of Hevajra.

During the practice of Vase-Breathing, the yogi should also meditate on the four words in the four Chakras. This is taught by the great accomplished yogis the Black-Practitioner, Lawaba, and Ocean-Born, as well as in many holy, scriptures, especially in those important pith-instructions of the Perfecting Yoga given in the Tantras. But that the four words should all be visualized, is not given, even in the instruction of Vase-Breathing Practice in the Whisper Teaching.

The Yogi should well acquaint himself with the meditation procedure as given in the preceding instructions. Through this practice the pranas will enter into the Central Channel and by the power of the fire of Dumo the Bodhi-Heart will be melted – thus the Four Blisses will definitely arise. But there are many Tibetan teachers who give the teaching of Dumo in a manner which combines all the practices of nerve (Rtsa), word, and Vase-Breathing at one time and declares that it is for the sake of promptly producing the Dumo experience that the combined practice is given.

"The taking-in, the filling-up, the dissolving,

And the shooting like the arrow are the four steps."

This stanza shows the four special steps of the Vase-Breathing practice that was found in the pith-instructions of the gurus in the past and favored by them. There is a certain commentary which says that "the four" means the four bases; this is a mistake, however, that was made through overlooking the text of the Tantras.

The physical preparations for the breathing exercise are the same as given before. The best time to practice this breathing exercise, according to the instructions of the accomplished Yogi Pag-mo-grub-pa is the time when the breathing runs equally (in both nostrils).

Pag-mo-grub-pa adds: "Although many gurus say that the best time to practice this breathing exercise is the time when the air runs equally (through both nostrils), (in the light of serious meditation) the breathing practice should be carried on day and night." In order to make the proper time explicit, this instruction is given first.

In general, the prana[70] is the essence of the expression of the Buddhas. In this practice the exercise should be carried out when most of the Lotus-Shelter-Air ascends. This is stated in the Lotus Commentary of the *Dom Tyun Tantra*.

Now, the explanation of the taking-in-air: The yogi should not inhale through the mouth but through the nostrils. He should not breath in roughly, but inhale gently and slowly.

Filling-up the air: After taking in the air, press it down and hold it. As the yogi inhales, he should think that the air comes in through the two nostrils and enters into the

Right and Left Channels, filling them up (like breath inflating balloons made of entrails.)

Dissolving-the-air: When both channels, Right and Left, are full, all the air enters into the Central Channel with a "Whoosh."

At this time the yogi should swallow the spittle in the mouth and press the upper air down and pull the lower air up from both the lower gates[71] to the small *Ah* word. Then the yogi should concentrate on his visualizations and hold his breath as long as he can. The holy Pag-mo-grub-pa said in his instructions-stanza: "From the Right and Left Channels the air enters into the Central Channel and fills it. When the breath can be held no longer, the yogi should release it for a very short time — the duration of snapping one's finger. The air left in the body should be used for the dissolving practice."

Though this instruction is somewhat contradictory on two points with the instruction given before, except the fourth step (the dissolving step), the other three (taking-in, holding, and exhaling the air) are expounded. The filling-up practice means inhaling the air that fills the Right and Left Channels, and the dissolving practice means the departure of the air from the two channels and its entrance into the Central Channel; thereby the Central Channel is filled with air, but the air in the Right and Left Channel is dissolved or emptied.

As to the manner of practicing the Vase-Breathing at the Navel Center, some claim that the lower air should not be pulled up, merely pressing the upper air down will do; others say that the yogi should press the air down at first, then, after a while, pull up the lower air three times. These sayings are wrongfully given through ignorance of the sesence of Vase-Breathing practice. The right practice is to combine the Live-Prana above the navel with the *Tur Sel Prana*[71a] below the navel. As the *Dom Gyun Tantra* says:

"The up-going air and the down-going air
Should be joined together by the mind."

This stanza explains the way of practicing the Vase-Breathing by combining or uniting the up-going and down-going prana. Thus we know that the up-going and down-going air should be combined and that they should not be pulled up simultaneously, but one after another. If there is no special reason for a particular meditation, the up-going air should be drawn and pressed first; afterwards, pull up the down-going air. It is not necessary to pull the down-going air three times.

"Shooting the air like the arrow." This illustrates the manner of expelling the air from the body. When the yogi exhales the air, he should visualize it arising through the Central Channel freely, like gas through a pipe. One should not visualize the air going out of the body through the crown of the head.

About the practice of drawing the up-going and the down-going air together at the Navel Center, one important point should be mentioned: some say the yogi should visualize the whole body full of Prana; some say the Prana should be visualized only full above the Heart Center or above the Throat Center. These instructions are unsound – because the true and sound teaching is to visualize the small *Ah* word whereupon the two pranas unite*. There

---

* There is a third and synthesizing view and doctrine here not mentioned in the text; namely, to maintain the conscious concentration of the prana at the heart center, letting that center be the means for the (unconscious) command to the Navel Center for its (the prana's) distribution. – *Ed.*

are two reasons for this. First, through leading the Prana into the Central Channel, the Life-Prana and the down-going prana are unified. Second, through visualizing words, the essential mental concentration process is automatically completed. Furthermore, whenever the mouth of Ro-ma and Rkyang-ma are open, the mouth of the Central Channel is closed and vice versa.

Through the practice of Vase-Breathing, the out-going breathing from the Ro-ma and Rkyang-ma is stopped; and through visualizing the air entering into the Central Channel, the yogi eventually will be able actually to lead the incoming air into the Central Channel.

The manner and the duration of holding the breath are explained by Pag-mo-grub-pa as follows: In the beginning stage, practice on taming the nerves is emphasized. The yogi should not hold his breath to the point of strain. The yogi should hold the breath easily and not for too long. Gradually, he should increase the duration of the holding period. Until the breath becomes very smooth and submissive, he should not engage in the stronger breathing practices, such as shaking the upper part of the body and forcibly pulling up the prana. He should release his breath before he feels uncomfortable, and not try to hold it too long. Even if he tries to do so, it will not help the gathering of pranas in the Central Channel, for the prana will remain in the Transformation Wheel only a moment and then go outside. Although to hold the prana outside the Wheel Center for a long period will produce a little warmness and bliss, it does not help the prana to enter into the Central Channel.

In the practice of visualization, the yogi tries to visualize the subject clearly, but a clear image appears in his mind for only a short moment. To visualize a steady picture is difficult. In the after-meditation period, however, he will sometimes experience the appearance of a steady picture in his mind clearly, without any effort. In the same way he will learn that natural and easy breath-holding cannot come without practice and effort. Therefore, until the natural breath-holding or breath-remaining comes to pass, he should try to prolong the breath-holding exercise gently. Even if he exerts himself in holding the breath for a long period the prana will not remain at the place desired. Furthermore, too much exertion will cause many troubles and do little good, so, until the prana can be easily and naturally placed in the Navel Center, the yogi should gently prolong the breath-holding exercise. If one knows how to practice this exercise proficiently, one will be able to know whether the prana naturally remains and whether the prana can be led to the desired place.

The best time to practice Vase Breathing is neither just before nor just after eating, but when the stomach is neither too full nor too empty. The practice should be carried out without interruption, yet not for too long a period. At times the yogi should rest for a while.

During the Vase Breathing, word-visualization should also be practiced. The yogi should clearly visualize the four words – *Ah*, *Hūṃ*, *Oṃ*, *Haṃ* – at the four respective centers of navel, heart, throat and head that are knotted (by the nerves) as mentioned before.

Thereupon, the yogi should visualize an *Ah* word, the essence of fire and Dumo, blazing with brightness. This word-of-fire is then fanned and stimulated by the wind from the Privy Wheel, and its heat rises up and ascends to the *Hūṃ*, *Oṃ* and *Haṃ* words. The three words begin to melt, and the melted drops all fall to the *Ah* word and unite with it, becoming one. This one drop is the self-nature of the Innate Bliss, whereupon the yogi should concentrate. In this process of holding mind to the subject, the yogi should visualize the Dumo-Ti-Le burning with the tiny fire-tongue.

The yogi should visualize the melting Bodhi-Heart begin to drop from the respective Wheels and fill up the *Ah* word, and then concentrate on visualizing the *Ah* word until the signs of a stable visualization appear.

If the visualization becomes stable, the light of Dumo will shine. The body, both inside and out, and the things in the house can all be seen clearly as one sees the olive fruit in one's own palm. Thus it is important to visualize the *Ah* word shining with its burning tongue, clearly and vividly. Through this practice the brightness-aspect of Samadhi will increase, and a perfect Samadhi will be obtained.

CHAPTER FIVE

*The entering, the remaining, and the dissolving process
in the Central Channel:*

THE ART OF GTUM-MO OR HEAT YOGA

Through the above-mentioned three practices, prana will enter into the Central Channel, but in this connection one may ask what are the unmistakable signs of the prana entering into the Central Channel? (In other words, what are the right signs one should expect to experience if the pranas are on the point of entering into the Central Channel?) This is an extremely important question; there is a great number of different answers. Among them the definite and unmistakable sign is the following experience. After the meditation period, the yogi identifies the particular nostril from which the breathing (or most of the exhaled air) runs. Then he applies the mental and bodily practices as before. In a very short time, the breath running through both nostrils becomes even, and it should not alter within one or two breaths. If there is no other hindrance, the breath should remain even in both nostrils; the strength of both nostrils should be equal. If the yogi is able to do this, he may be considered as having a little strength in leading the prana into the Central Channel. However, this does not mean that, by doing this practice once (attaining even runs of the breath in the two nostrils), the ordinary breathing-process, which unequally stresses the two nostrils, will be forever stopped.

Having learned how to make the prana enter into the

Central Channel, the yogi is taught the practice involving the prana remaining there.

In accordance with the teachings, the yogi carries on his practice and carefully observes the manner of the breath running in the nostrils. Gradually the breath will become more and more subtle, and finally it will stop. The Jetsun Milarepa said:

"Happy is the entering into the Central Channel by the air of Ro-ma and Rleyang-ma!

Happy is the cessation of the outgoing and ingoing breathing!

"Happy is the vast experience of the cessation of breath!"

As to the subtle breathing, for some it is difficult and for some it is easy. If the yogi finds it difficult to absorb the air, he will in a few minutes feel it filling up his entire belly, but then it begins to dissolve. Immediately after the dissolving, he will feel an extraordinary warmness taking place in the fire-place of the Navel Center and Secret Center; thereafter, the Melting Bliss will take place.

A cessation of the subtle running breath will tend to accumulate the subtle distractions, whence great distractions often occur. In this connection those who do not know how to concentrate on the central point of the Wheels, and who engage themselves in various kinds of Vase-Breathing exercises, will neither help the prana to enter nor remain inside [the Central Channel], because these practices can not tame the pranas and make them gather in the Central Channel. Consequently, neither the entering into nor the remaining in the Central Channel will come to pass; therefore, one must discriminate carefully.

As to the length or the duration of holding the Vase-Breathing, the *Dom Jun Tantra* says:

"Knowing the way of practicing Vase Breathing
   as instructed before,
The yogi then sits in a lotus posture.
One hand rubs the other three times,
And then he snaps his fingers six times.
The duration of thirty-six snappings
Is the length of time of Vase Breathing.
The best are (able to hold on) three times as long;
The length of more than one hundred snappings."

The left hand is supinely placed on the knee and is rubb-
ed by the right hand three times; then six snaps are made
with the fingers. This is one complete process. If one is
able to hold the breath for 108 times of such duration, it is
the best; to hold seventy-two times is the medium, and
thirty-six times is the minimum. It is also said that whoever holds the breath for any of these three durations will
be able to conquer death.

Now, the second:
The manner of the Arising of the Four Blisses
through the Prana Entering into the Central Channel.
Of this, three expositions are given:
1. The appearance of the signs.
2. The manner of the firing of Dumo
3. The melting of the Bodhi-Heart.

The manner of the arising of the Four Blisses that are
produced by the melting of the Bodhi-Heart will be discussed, and also the practice on the meditation of the
Innate-Born-Wisdom. Now, the first: Through concentration on the central point of the Navel Center, the live
prana enters into the Central Channel, whereupon signs
will appear. These signs are explained by the accomplished
Yogi Lawaba:

"The first sign is like the bewildered animals.
The second sign is the smoke.
The third sign is like the light of the firefly.
The fourth sign is like the lamplight.
The fifth sign is without any form,
It appears like the clear firmament without any clouds."

The first sign — the bewildered animals — means the phantasm. That is, in comparison with the other four signs, which are successively brighter one by one, the first sign is hazy and unclear like the phantasm (seen by bewildered animals in the distance). Some say this stanza cannot be interpreted literally, that the signs do not appear as the stanza relates. Some say it merely symbolizes the stability of the sign-appearing-consciousness, whether the experiences are stable or wavering. Some say the signs are like smoke. Of these three opinions, the last one is best. The intensiveness and stability (of the smoke and light) will depend on the alternation of the strong and weak wind; they cannot be uniform all the time.

There are two possible ways through which the sign of smoke can be experienced: first, the special skillful (Tantric) teachings through which the pranas are gathered into the Central Channel, as here instructed; second, the practice of the non-thought meditation through which the sign of smoke will also be experienced. The yogi should be extremely careful in discriminating between these two.

The signs experienced through the Tantric teachings are subject to the disturbance caused by the wicked earthly wind. The disturbance (or the retrogression of signs) can be differentiated in three degrees — the things of retrogression, the little retrogression, and the definite retrogression. The extreme outgoing winds from the different organs are being checked (by the practice) and turned inward. When a small portion of the outgoing winds is checked, the due portion of prana is reversed, and when this due portion of prana enters the Central Channel the appropriate sign will appear. From then on, the reversal (of prana) in the path and its unique signs will appear successively. There are a great many different signs to be experienced, but our concern is with the Life-Prana entering into the Central Channel, of which the complete process – from the phantasm stage to the clear sky of no-clouds – will take place.

When the earth element enters into the water element, the sign of the phantasm appears; when the water enters into the fire, the smoke sign appears; when the fire enters into the air, the fire spark appears; when the spark enters into the mind-prana – upon which the distracted thoughts ride – a steady lamp light burning in the air without any wind disturbance appears. By the power of these successively appearing signs, the yogi will attain the accomplishment of Mahamudra.

As to the kindling of Dumo, there are many different types, such as the kindling of Dumo in the Central Channel from the Navel Center and the Secret Center in the beginning stage; the kindling of Dumo outside of the Central Channel or the ordinary kindling. The manners of the kindling are also various, such as the kindling of the Dumo from the depth of the body; the kindling of Dumo in between the skin and the flesh, the intensive and weak kindling-warmness in the beginning stage; the kindling warmness going upward, blowing upward, and fleeing upward; and the strong and weak kindling. Of these kindlings, the former are better than the latter. The blisses produced by these varieties of kindling-warmness follow this pattern. In addition to these numerous experiences that arise successively, one should pay special attention to discriminate between the kindling of the unique Dumo, the kindling of the ordinary warmness, the bliss produced by prana and the bliss produced by prana and the bliss produced by the melting of elements.

If the unique Dumo is ever kindled, the appropriate Bodhi-Heart will melt. In this case the yogi will have no sickness caused by the unbalanced elements, while in the case of the ordinary kindling-warmness, the melting of the Bodhi-Heart is very uncertain; the gall secretion will increase; the feeling of bliss is always weak, and the pain induced by the warmness is great. If a qualified Dumo is kindled as it should be, the White Bodhi-Heart will melt and multiply the Red Bodhi-Heart. Dumo will also increase.

The melting of the Bodhi-Heart brings about the arising of the Four Blisses. The respective places wherein the down-coming Four Blisses arise are named in the *Tantra Rdo-rje-rin-wa*.

"At the Wheel of Great Bliss in the head,
The (first) bliss arises.
At the Wheel of Enjoyment [Throat],
The Superlative Bliss arises.
At the Wheel of Dharma [Heart],
The Beyond-Reach Bliss arises.
At the Wheel of Transformation [Navel]*,
The Innate Wisdom arises.

* There is an alternative order in which the Innate Bliss relates to and arises in the Dharmachakra or Heart Center. From prolonged study, theoretical and practical, we feel that that order is preferable. — *Ed.*

Thus, one shall experience these Blisses."

When the Bodhi-Heart coming down from the head reaches the throat, the first Bliss arises; from the throat coming down to the heart, the Superlative Bliss arises; from the heart coming to the navel the Beyond-Bliss arises; from the navel coming to the top of the precious organ the Innate-Bliss arises.

As to the up-going Blisses, the Tantra says:

"The up-going Blisses arise like this:

At the Wheel of Transformation arises the Bliss.

At the Wheel of Dharma arises the Superlative Bliss.

At the Wheel of Enjoyment arises the great Innate-Bliss,

This is the reverse of the process of bliss-arising."

These explanations are in accord with the *Great Symbol Thig-le*[72]. Each of the four down-coming and up-going Blisses can be divided into four, making the so-called sixteen portions of the Moon-Elements. Following the viewpoint of the Sun, each bliss can be divided into three, making the total of twelve.

The [above] Tantra says:

"The signs of hare and so forth

Are the Thig-le of sixteen-fold bliss.

They are the substance of the Ā-li [the vowels].

The four Wheels come in order.

Following these different sayings,

They can be understood as twelve Sun-Elements."

When the Bodhi-Heart goes upward or downward, the blood element always goes with it. As it reaches the four respective centers in each level of each center, a specific Bliss is experienced, making a total of sixteen. From the viewpoint of the intensiveness of the Bliss, the Bliss of each center can be divided into three – the Extreme Bliss, the Medium Bliss, and the Small Bliss — making a total of twelve. The experienced yogi should know the subtle differences between these.*

The four up-going Blisses should be much stronger than the down-coming Blisses. In the up-going process, until the reversed operation has become steady, the Bliss will not be steady at the Head Center. When the Head Center becomes steady, the Bliss will also be steady. Says the [same] Tantra [*ibid.*]:

"Upon the life is the mind;
Because of the reversal it flows,
Dwells in the center of the lotus's navel;
Thereafter, it will stabilize.
At that time the refuge will not go away.
As in a utensil without any hole,
The water in it will never be exhausted.
That is the time the bliss will become steady.
The Innate-Bliss (comes) from the stabilization,
Thus, the nerve-ending Buddha is accomplished
Through this way, the yogi attains his conviction."

The mind means the secretion (or drops). Reversal means reversing the process of the ordinary route. Stabilization means the head. These explanations are given in the *Mang-snag*, the intimate pith-instruction.

There are a great many pith-instructions. According to one of them when the warmness becomes stabilized, the

* In the light of the text quoted above, we see here a subtle astro-philosophical doctrine of an isomorphism between the Twelve Blisses and the twelve sectors of the earth's orbit (with the equinoctial and solsticial points as references) — "the twelve Sun-Elements." Such a doctrine of isomorphism is the key to the Samkhya Tattvic doctrine as it is employed in the Hindu (Dvaita) and Buddhist Tantras. — *Ed.*

Bodhi-Heart in the nerve begins to melt; because of the melting of Bodhi-Heart the Bliss arises. When the Bliss becomes steady, the Non-Discrimination (Wisdom) arises. This explanation is very general; it does not give the specific explanations on the up-going and the down-coming Blisses. Nor does it make clear the recognition of the great Innate Bliss. In view of this, I have given the explanations of the Four Blisses in two categories, as stated in the Tantras and instructed by the great accomplished yogis.

Generally speaking, there are two different kinds of Bliss – the Bliss produced through meditation, and the Bliss produced through ordinary ways. Through the dropping of the melted Bodhi-Heart to the Secret Center, one experiences the Bliss; however, even in this process the kindling of Dumo by which the Ti Le is melted is a necessary condition required in the production of such a Bliss. But though the Dumo is kindled and the Bodhi-Heart melted, this by no means implies the entering into the Central Channel. Therefore, it is understood that some individuals may experience the Bliss of Thig-le-Melting but not that of the Entering-into-the-Central-Channel, as experienced by those who pracrice the vital physical exercises, given in the pith-instructions.

As the Thig-le arrives at the top of the Vajra Jewel, there are great difficulties in holding it. In the beginning, the outer and inner methods are applied to let the Bodhi-Heart drop, but before it reaches the Jewel, it should be reversed with great force. However, if it is not properly spread over all the body, some sickness may arise. In view of this danger, one may try to spread the Ti Le with many different methods. However, he may not go far enough to differentiate between the Thig-le-Melting of the Entering-into-Central Channel and the Ti Le-Melting through the ordinary process. To sense the difficulty or the ease of Tholding the hig-le, to carefully weigh whether or not to apply a very forceful halting exercise, to discover whether the Thig-le is properly spread and the danger of sickness avoided – these are necessary safeguards.

The reason and purpose for melting the Thig-le by the Dumo fire through meditation practices is to bring to pass the Innate Wisdom. To produce the Innate Wisdom requires, in general, the standing of the melting Thig-le below the navel; in particular, the halting of it at the Jewel. If it cannot be held for some time, the real Innate Wisdom can hardly arise.

The arising of the Great Bliss of the Innate Wisdom of Perfecting Yoga requires that the prana enter into and remain in the Central Channel. In case of the Thig-le melting through the Entering-into-Central-Channel, the yogi should still hold the Thig-le at the Jewel and not release it until the Innate Wisdom is fully unfolded. The yogi should visualize the Bodhi-Heart waveringly coming down from center to center, as if swayed by the wind, until it reaches the Jewel. This is to safeguard the out-going prana which might expel the Th'g le. There are some who merely look for an easy way to produce the Melting Bliss without a fair command of the gathering of prana [into the Central Channel]. By doing this, the melting of the Bodhi-Heart may easily be experienced, but, if the Bodhi-Heart is not reversed to a higher level, it will be extremely difficult to reverse it when the Thig-le comes down too low, unless the melting is weak. Even if it is reversed, it must be reversed to a higher level and be spread well, otherwise certain illnesses will result.

In the case of the Entering-into-the-Central Channel as discussed before, none of these difficulties ever arise. Some may ask what steps one should take to reverse and spread the Thig-le when the disqualified Melting Bliss[73] arises. If the Melting Bliss is produced slowly and gradually, step-by-step, it will not be necessary to apply the forceful methods to reverse it to the Crown Center and spread it over all the Centers of the body. Thereby, should a great Bliss ever arise, the yogi will still be able to reverse and spread it. If a great Melting-Bliss is produced not through the gradual step-by-step process, but in a very quick and vehement manner, the following practices are advised.

Sit in a lotus position and visualize clearly the self-patron Buddha. Holding the two fists tight, cross them in front of the chest forcefully, staring upward with both eyes, contracting the toes, and fixing the mind on the *Ham* word at the Crown Center. Meanwhile, the yogi should utter a prolonged sound of *Hūm* twenty-one times, thinking that the Thig-le ascends to the Crown Center through the Central Channel that is close to the spine. Then the yogi should practice the mild Vase Breathing and gently carry out the bodily movements. He should also think for many time (repetitions), that all the Thig-le's are thoroughly spread over all the nerves in his body.

How to Practice the Innate Wisdom

If, at the time of down-coming, when the Bodhi-Heart reaches the Jewel, the yogi is able to hold it within, the Innate Bliss will arise. Meanwhile, he ahould apply his view (on Reality) as instructed before (in the chapter discussing the Middle Way Doctrine). His mind should rest

Folio 4 *recto* (Muses MS, vol. II) depicting the Fiery Water (contact with which in harmony is achieved through certain forms of yoga) that protects against both heat and cold.

on the View, and safeguard the Void-Bliss feeling. Even if he does not have a good understanding of the View, he should avoid all disturbing thoughts and put himself right in the blissful feeling until it becomes steady.

In the up-going process, when the Thig-le reaches the Crown from the Jewel, the up-going Innate Wisdom will arise. The yogi should try to recognize it. Thus the identity of the Void-Bliss will be realized. He should also try to safeguard the single Bliss of Non-Thought as long as possible, as instructed [in the previous paragraph].

This should be one's practice in the meditation state. The practice of the after-meditation-state is explained as follows:

Generally speaking, whenever the Innate-Bliss arises in the after-meditation-state, automatically and naturally all manifestations appear to be blissful. However, this experience alone is by no means enough. If the yogi reminds himself about the Blissful-Void experiences of the real-meditation-state and identifies this experience with whatever manifests, an extraordinary Great Bliss will arise and he should safeguard it. Although this pith-instruction is not given by others, the Rngog-Pa School of the Marpa Succession gives many instructions on this aspect. This is the instruction of the *Hevajra Tantra* and other Tantras, and it should be kept from falling into oblivion. Thus, with the visualization of Dumo, the practice of Real-Meditation-State and After-Meditation-State, and the practice of breathing exercises of the Four Blisses, experience will be augmented.

The Outer Practice of Karmayoga

The practice of depending on outer conditions is the Karmayoga practice. (Both self and the Mudra should be the utmost well-gifted sentient being.) They should receive the perfect and pure initiation; observe the main and secondary Tantric precepts in a perfect degree; be proficient in all Mandala practices and affairs, and practice four periods without intermission every day; be acquainted with all the sixty-four qualifications and forms of the condition as instructed in the Books of Bliss; possess the power of halting the Bodhi-Heart within; have a definite understanding on the principle of Voidness and the successive steps of the Four Blisses, and especially be extremely learned in the field of the arising of the Innate Wisdom. These qualifications and requirements are stated in the Tantras and by many accomplished yogis; and they should all be fulfilled without the slightest concession. As to those who claim to have the so-called "profound teachings" and yet carry out the practice unscrupulously, there is nothing else but falling into the miserable path for them. The *Tantra of Heruka (Mngong-abyung)* says:

> "(If one unscrupulously) practices the yoga which is not
>   yoga,
> And unconscientiously practices the Mudra,
> Or claims the wisdom which is not wisdom,
> There is not the slightest doubt that he will fall into
>   hell."

If the outer conditions are utilized without the fulfillment of all requirements and qualifications, the sin is extremely great. This is admonished (by all teachers) and should always be carefully remembered. If one has not attained the capability of practicing this Yoga, one may practice on the (visualized) Vajra Dakini or the Non-Ego Mother, following the teachings of the Wisdom Symbol (Ye-shes-pyag-rgya). If the visualization is clear and steady, through such practice the Four Blisses will arise. When the Innate-Bliss arises, if the yogi is capable of acting in the Bliss-Void, he should also apply his View-on-Reality and safeguard the oneness or Void-Bliss. If he cannot do so, through the power of the bliss, he may be able to attain a one-thought Samadhi.

CHAPTER SIX

THE PRACTICE OF THE ILLUSORY BODY
OR DREAM YOGA,
DEPENDING ON FOREGOING HEAT YOGA

This is to be explained in two parts. First, following the Heat Yoga, other Yogas are to be discussed in general. Second, each of these Yogas will be individually considered. Now, the first:

Of this school, the teaching on Entering-into-the-Central Channel through the practice of Dumo is very clear, but, the practices and instructions on the Illusory Body and Light are very obscure. These teachings are very difficult to understand; however, I shall reveal some unique pith-instructions that I have obtained.

These instructions on the Illusory Body and Light Yoga are obtained from the source of Gsan Adus given by Apags-pa, father and son. According to their teaching, before the process of entering, remaining, and dissolving into the Central Channel by the life-Prana, the three steps of the Manifestation, Augmentation, and Attainment of the Peaceful-Mind Samadhi[74] can never be attained.

The mind-prana that perfects the genuine wisdom of the Peaceful-Mind-State is also the means through which the genuine Illusory Body is practiced. These teachings are clearly given in the pith-instructions on the Gsan Adus and are also found in the teaching of the Five Steps of the Marpa School. Therefore, though the teaching of Light Yoga and Illusory Body are not clearly given in Naropa's Six Yogas, relying on the instructions of Apags-pa, the explanations are given here:

In the *Commentary of the Epitome of the Five Steps* of the Marpa School, the stanza says:

"At first, (the yogi will) see the mirage-like visions
With the five-coloured light shining.
The next vision he will see is a moon.
The third one is the flowing light of the sun.
Then the vision of the brink appears.
Through this process manifests the Illusory-Body
That is manifested by the mind-prana."

The vision of moonlight shining from a cloudless sky appears; this is a stage of Manifestation. Then the glowing light of the sun shines in the sky; this is the stage of Augmentation. Then the brink period that appears like the dark sky before dawn comes in sight; this is the stage of Attainment. After the emergence of these stages, the real Illusory Body-with-light that is produced by the Mind-Prana of the Peaceful-Mind Teaching (will come to pass); but this point is not clearly stated in the Six Yogas.

Among the numerous teachings of the Illusory Body, one is to meditate on the shadow-like nature of the self-body. First let someone praise and then insult you and observe the reactions of pleasure and resentment. Thus the crude form of the delusory thoughts[75] are subdued; this is the practice of the Impure Illusory Body. Another practice is called the Pure Illusory Body Yoga. That is to meditate on the illusory-like self-Buddha figure and let another person praise and insult you and observe the reaction of pleasure and displeasure, until an indifferent feeling toward both praise and insult arises. But this practice is not a special practice; it is the common practice of the highest Yoga and other general teachings.

Other teachings of the Illusory Body are the Three-

Steps Illusory Body, or the Secret Illusory Body; and the Two-in-One Illusory Body of the Five Steps. However, the discriminations and differences among these Illusory-Body teachings are not even briefly mentioned here. Nevertheless the teaching of Illusory Body (in the Six Yogas) is an uncommon teaching of the Perfecting Yoga of the Anuttara Tantra. The former one [the practice of The Impure Illusory Body. *Ed.*] does not, however, fulfill all the qualifications of the *real* Illusory Body; the second one [the Pure Illusory Body Yoga. *Ed.*] is also common because this teaching can also be found in the lower Tantras.

(Through the practice of the above teachings), the thoughts of anger and lust are subdued and the mind-state of unconcern is attained. Then combining the decisive understanding of the Voidness of the Middle Way with the Innate-Bliss and the essence of meditation practice, the yogi should carefully remember this state of mind. If he can practice well in such manner, immediately after the arising of the Yi-Dam figure (or the completion of the Arising Yoga period) through the power of Samadhi, all the manifestations appear to him as insubstantial and delusory like the mirage. With this teaching of identifying the manifestations with the Mandala, one does not have to meditate on the non-self nature of the divine manifestation purposely; such feeling will arise naturally without effort.

A teaching of the pith-instruction of the Marpa School is that the yogi should stare at a mirror ...and see whether his own image reflects from the mirror as the true Buddha's image. This teaching is designed for promoting the meditation of Arising Yoga. According to the pith-instructions given by gurus at the time of the bestowal of the Third

Initiation, the image of the Vajrasattva reflected from a mirror is shown to the disciple to point out the non-self aspect of the Illusory Body and to illustrate its mirage-like nature.

Following carefully the teaching of the Five Steps, the instructions are given [by the guru]. A comprehensive survey of the Apags-pa pith-instruction is thus afforded, and the incompleteness of the Illusory-Body teaching of the Marpa School is also discussed fully.

Again, there are instructions such as given here: the teaching of the Two-in-One-with-Learning, the teaching of the Two-in-One-without-Learning, the principle of the four steps: Manifestation, Augmentation, Attainment and Great Light. Especially, the instructions on the following steps are given: How the illusory body is transformed from the mind-prana; how one can enter into the Absolute Light after making the Illusory Body; in what manner the Manifestation, Augmentation, Voidness, etc., come in sight; how the Two-in-One-with-Learning[76] (Body) is transformed after the Absolute-Light is stabilized and how through it the Two-in-One-without-Learning Body can be established how, if the Yogi practices the Light-of-Sleep, he is able to make the prana enter into the Central Channel during the awakening state; then how the four Voids will successively appear as light through his capability of gathering the prana of Roma and Rkyang-ma in the Heart Center (after the light state); and how the Illusory Body of Buddha will appear in the dream — in this stage, even if the Illusory Body of Buddha does not appear in the dream, the yogi will have no doubt.

Through the power of the prana's entrance into the Central Channel, one is able to hold the light of sleep;

or, if one has attained the general Samadhis of Mahayana or Hinayana, one can also apply his Samadhi's power in the sleeping state. Thus, the deep-sleep-Samadhi state can be brought into the weaker-sleeping-state Samadhi. There is no clear explanation here on the differences of these various experiences though the various approaches. Therefore, one should carefully discriminate between the holding-of-dream through prana power and the holding-of-dream through desire; and between the coming of death-light and sleep-light through the prana power and through the power of the strong will. How the Sambhogakaya is manifested in the Bardo state should also be studied. If one wants to know this in detail, one may study the instructions of Apags-pa who provides much information.

In the practice of holding the Light-of-Sleep and the practice of holding the dream state, though the power of prana, the first step is to grasp the Light-of-Sleep and then manipulate the dream state.

If one is not able to gather the prana into the Central Channel, but with a very strong will or intention sets one's mind upon the recognizing of the dream state during the awakening time, throughout exertion of will power a Samadhi of sleeping state will arise. However, this cannot be called a decisive or actual Light-of-Sleep state.

If through both the inner and outer daytime practice, one is able to proceed with the entering, remaining, and dissolving process in the Central Channel, the well-known Four Blisses and Four Voids will arise. Then the identity of Bliss-Void during the emergence of the Innate-Born can be practised. Eventually the Illusory Body will arise. By means of this practice, one will be able to impress the Bliss-Void feeling on all manifestations at all times. Thus the (identity) of manifestation and Mandala (practice of Tantrism) is exercised.

What is the reason for relying on the remaining two Wheels to practice the Sleep-Light and Illusory-Dream? Because in sleep the pranas will naturally gather in the Heart Center, and with the power of gathering the prana in the Central Channel and through the mental concentration on the Central Channel Heart-Center, the prana of Ro-ma and Rkyang-ma will gather in the Central Channel-Heart Center, and its power will be very great. Consequently, the Four Voids, especially the All-Void, will appear. If one can guard this light of Samadhi for a long period, through its power in daytime, one will be able to gather a greater portion of prana in the Central Channel where it will become more steady than before.

If the light-of-sleep becomes steady, it will help the path greatly. With it, the power of meditation will increase, without it, the power will decrease. This is extremely important for those who have not attained the ultimate accomplishment in this life and expect to attain the ultimate enlightenment at the time of death. This practice is superior to the teaching of (merely) recognizing the Light-of Death.

After the emergence of the light-of-sleep, if one knows how to radiate or raise up the superb Illusory Dream-Body, through its power the daytime practice on the Illusory Body will become more powerful and steady. If one cannot attain the ultimate accomlishment in this life and puts his hope in the moment of death, he must have the ability of holding the light with prana and must practice this teaching of Illusory Body of Dream. Thus he will be able to identify the Illusory Body of Bardo. Without these practices it would be impossible to do so; therefore, these two instructions are unique and of great importance.

The instructions on the actual practice of the Illusory Body and the Light Yoga follow:

In addition to the teachings given in the last chapter – the Tantric teaching of the perfect Illusory Body, the teaching of the light-of-awakening-from sleep, the teachings for the time of the reversed processes, there are other ways of practice found in the commentaries of the great teachers, which I will now relate in this chapter. First the instruction on the Illusory Body practice; second, the instructions on the Light Yoga.

The teaching of the Illusory Body will be discussed in three steps: the Illusory Body practice on the manifestations; the Illusory Body practice on the dream state; and the Illusory Body practice on the Bardo state.

With a decisive understanding or View on Sūnyatā, the yogi associates this view with the Innate-Born Bliss in meditation. After the meditation period, through remembering the View and remembering that all manifestations are Buddahood, the yogi will naturally experience, in all daily activities, the feeling that all manifestations are immanently illusory. He will also see all manifestations illustrating themselves in the forms of Mandalas. For these (capable) yogis, of course, there is no need for any visualization practices.

But in order to benefit those who cannot do the same in their meditation, the following practice is advised: In the after-meditation period, the yogi should observe the non-self nature of all Dharmas – the sentient beings and the material world – and identify his body with his image reflected from the mirror. Through this practice, the common visions of sentient being and universe[77] will appear as mirage without any substance or self-nature. Il this experience can be stabilized, all manifestations wilf appear in the form of the two Mandalas[78]. With an under-standing of the mirage-like nature, or with the view of the identity of non-self-nature Voidness and manifestation, the yogi observes the pure Mandala. And then he looks into the mirror and identifies the godly image there with his own body. In this way, the mirage-like nature of Buddha's body is observed.

With such an understanding, the yogi observes the Buddha's body in the mirror and concentrates upon it. Then he should think that this image of Buddha projects itself and merges with him. Since the former practice is a complete process, its power is much greater than that of the latter.

As instructed in *The Five Steps*, the picture of an image of Vajrasattva is reflected in a mirror so that by looking at this reflection, the yogi may observe the nature of the Illusory Body. Following this instruction, the two gurus, Marpa and *A*gog Lodrawa, have established this teaching to benefit those disciples who cannot quite understand the illusory nature of beings merely through hearing it explained. For that reason, this seeing-practice is given. To practice this teaching in the Arising Yoga, a specially constructed house is required; many different drugs and other materials are also needed. After all the preparations are arranged, the yogi then proceeds to observe the reflection of the image in the mirror. These instructions are found in both Marpa's and *A*gog's teachings.

(Generally speaking) there are two different aspects of the illusory-like and dream-like nature of all Dharmas:[79] the existent-but-not-real aspect, and the manifesting-yet-void aspect.

Here, the latter aspect which refers to the Illusory Body is stressed.

The manifestation and the manifestation-void should also be distinguished; and two different kinds of voidness[80]: the voidness of the utter non-existent such as the never coming-into-being of the horn of the rabbit or the son of a barren woman; and the voidness of the manifesting-yet-empty. (If one has not realized the latter, one will not be able to understand the illusory nature of manifestations.)

The illusory nature of beings is illustrated through analogies. For example, the phantasm of horses and cattle conjured by the magicians does not exist in reality, but one cannot deny the apparent reality of these phenomena (as one sees them). The same holds true in the case of sentient beings (and objects, etc.) as people see them. Although there is no immanent actuality in the self-nature of beings, (through their illusory thoughts) people see manifestations as having real existence.

The manifestations considered (by ordinary beings) as things having Dharma-form (color, shape, sound, taste, etc.) have never existed. Nevertheless, the actor and the action, the hearer and the sound, the seer and the vision, etc., are continuously manifesting themselves freely. If one realizes the Two-in-One View of "existence in voidness and voidness in existence,"[81] there will be no danger of falling into the extreme Realistic or Nihilistic views. Since all Dharmas are immanently void in nature, realizing their nature as void is quite sufficient; there is no need for creating a voidness through one's mind-effort, or a voidness of day, month, or year (past, present, and future).

If one meditates on this principle, all attachments and clinging to the actuality of beings will be subdued. This

profound principle (of voidness) is by no means impercep-
tible or unobservable. During the practice of the meditation on Reality Śūnyatā, and during the contemplation
of the Right View, it (the Voidness) can definitely serve
as an object of observation. It is utterly erroneous to say
that the reality of Voidness cannot be seen or known, that
it can never be practiced in the path, and that nothing of
it can be understood, as claimed by some scholars of the
old schools of Tibet.

The origin of all the conceptions of skandhas, self-
natures, and symbols, is the very thought of *I am!* Therefore one should stress practicing the non-existence of the
self-nature of beings. As the yogi perceives the "becomings"
with his mind, he should appreciate the existence of manifestations in the mundane category. The existence of causations – the existence of the doer and receiver – should
be confirmed within own mind. Though these causations are devoid of self-nature, they still manifest freely
without any hindrances. Should a conflict between the
two – the voidness and existence – appear in his mind,
he should think on the principle of delusiveness, reflected
by the parables of shadow, dream, etc., and reconcile the
conflict.

We know that the reflection of the face in the mirror is
in reality void. We also know that the reflection is caused
by the conjunction of the face and mirror, and that the
withdrawal of either of them will end the reflection. But
the disappearance of the reflection does not mean the annihilation of the face and mirror themselves[82]. In the same
way, though there is not one atom existing in sentient beings, the Karma-doer, the Karma-receiver, and the ripen-
ing of Karma through one's previous deeds can still take

place. We should ponder on and practice this principle; when its understanding is stabilized one may proceed to work on the practice of the Beyond-Measure-Palace, outwardly, and the Yi-Dam image (in the Mandala). Then, he should contemplate the View of the Identity of the Bliss and Void.

Through these practices, the yogi will experience all manifestations as the Bodies of Buddha, will realize these Bodies as delusory, and will find this delusiveness absorbed in the Great Bliss. These realizations will take place succes sively as three steps. If the yogi attains the Great Bliss in his main-meditation stage, he should pay especial attention to the observation of Śūnyatā. Thus, by concentration on Śūnyatā-Bliss the non-discriminating Wisdom will arise.

The yogi should practice the main-meditation and after-meditation stages, alternatively.[83]

The instruction on the Dream-Illusory Body Practice falls into four divisions: (1) how to recognize the dream; (2) how to purify and develop the dream; (3) how to overcome the rambling type of dreams and recognize them as illusory manifestations; (4) how to practice on the real nature of dream.

(1) There are two different ways to recognize or to hold the dream. The first way is recognizing and holding the dream through the power of Prana. That is, through the power which is produced by the gathering and dissolving of Prana in the Central Channel during the waking stage, the Four Voidnesses will arise. At the outset, when the light of the dream stage is realized, the yogi will be able to recognize the Four Voidnesses clearly. Through this realization, he will automatically recognize the dream (as

such). In this case, there is no need for him to practice any teachings for recognizing the dream. The second way is recognizing the dream by intention. These teachings are provided for those who do not have the power over Prana, as mentioned before. This practice is carried out by creating, in the daytime, a strong intention for recognizing the dream and concentrating on the Throat Center, etc.

Of these two (methods), the former is the unique teaching of recognizing the dream given by Tantra. The latter practice, however, is a common and general one. Here, I want to mention the so-called teaching of Matsur, of recognising the dream through concentration on the Heart Center, and the teaching of Mestson of accomplishing the same purpose by concentration on the Throat Center. Some claim that concentration on the Heart Center is for the practice of Light Yoga and that concentration on the Throat Center is for the practice of Dream Yoga. However, I think that, through the arising of the Four Voidnesses of sleep, before the dream appears, the power of Prana — which is produced by concentration on the Heart Center — will enable one to recognize the dream. Therefore it is permissible to say that concentration on the Heart Center will enable one to recognize the dream. In the case of practice through intensive intention, the yogi is not able to see the Four Voidnesses before the dream appears; therefore, concentration on the Throat Center is the right method.

In this connection, one may ask: "Since concentrating on the Throat Center is the right teaching, should we stick to it and disregard the others?" A brief discussion on this point may be helpful. Consider the case of the yogi who is able to hold (the dream) through Prana power; if he concentrates on the Throat Center during the time just before falling into the stage of sleep, the Pranas will gather and dissolve in the Central Channel at the Throat Center. Though the yogi has raised the Four Voidnesses beforehand, (because of the diversified attention placed on the Throat Center) the Prana is neither concentrated (completely) in the Heart Center nor gathered at the Throat Center. Since the Four Voidnesses can never be revealed through practices other than meditation in the Heart Center, the yogi should concentrate on the Heart Center just on the verge of falling asleep.

However, there is an advantage in concentrating on the Throat Center. If one concentrates at the Throat Center or at the forehead, the gathering of Prana in the Heart Center will become lesser and weaker; consequently, the sleep will become very light and the awareness of mind will become clearer. If a dream is produced through meditating on the Throat Center during sleep, this dream will last longer than usual (or be more steady than the usual dream.) Furthermore, if the yogi raises a desire to have a longer dream in his sleeping state after a certain dream he has experienced, he will shortly be able, through the power derived from previous concentration on the Throat Center (during repose), to hold his mind (and produce) a dream wherein he is able to practice the meritorious (Dream Yoga) for a longer period. For these reasons, the instruction for concentrating on the Throat Center is given.

Generally speaking, if the yogi has a sound foundation of the practice of the path, his dream is clear and he is able to recognize it frequently. In this case, he does not have to depend on the infrequent clear dreams (as do those who practice with intention). If he has strong desires in the daytime, these will usually be (represented) in his dreams. Based on this principle, if he creates a strong desire during the day to recognize his dream, and repeatedly strengthens this desire while awake, he will, when asleep, be able to recognize the dream. This is not a very difficult practice.

If no dream whatsoever appears, there is then no way for the yogi to practice the Dream Yoga; therefore, he must use all methods to produce a dream as given in the Tantric instructions. If the dream takes place but is not clear, it will still be difficult for the yogi to practice Dream Yoga. Therefore, it is necessary to have a clear dream – clear to the point that the yogi can relate it when he awakes. To dwell in a solitary place helps to purify mind so that it will be as clear in the evening as in the morning. Then it is easy to recognize the dream. In short, this intentional practice requires a very strong desire directed toward recognizing the dream in the daytime, and only by such strong habitual thinking and awareness can the dream be recognized. Therefore, the practice in the daytime is important. Besides this, there are many teachings such as concentrating on the Throat Center, on the point between the eyebrows, visualizing certain objects and shapes, some special Prana practices, etc. Through these methods, the clearness and awareness of the mind is strengthened.

Thus, the yogi should follow these Pith-instructions of Dream Yoga, study them, and learn them well. He should rely on a guru who possesses the unmistakable experience of Dream Yoga; otherwise (if he follows the wrong instruction from the wrong guru), he may have some experiences in the beginning, but will have nothing but confusion in the end.

Once the dream is recognized, the yogi should visualize himself as his Patron Buddha, or practice the Guru Yoga together with offering-prayers. (In the dream state) the yogi should make an effort to create many clear, auspicious dreams at his own will, try to recognize them, expand them, and utilize them as an opportunity to practice various benevolent devotions. If any ominous dream occur the yogi should transform it into an auspicious one. He should pray to his Guru with great earnestness to grant him the ability to do so. In the dream state, the yogi should perform the ritual of offering the Gtormas to the Yi-Dam and protective deities, pray them to grant his wishes, etc. In his retreat-confinement,[84] the yogi should work hard on these practices.

Practice during the daytime should put emphasis mainly on dwelling upon or retaining the memory of the desire (to recognize the dream at night). The yogi should think that all manifestations he beholds and all that cross his way in the waking state are (actually) in the dream state. This he does by reminding himself, "This is a dream. I now recognize it. I know that I am dreaming." With great earnestness the yogi should strengthen his wish by enhancing the desire. Thus, eventually, when the dreams appear, he will be able to recognize them and also to utilize them as a basis to exercise (the Dream Yoga practices). The yogi should not only strengthen his intention by repeatedly reminding himself of the desire during the day, but also strengthen the desire just before sleep. This will greatly nicrease the chance of recognizing the dream.

The instructions on the intensive practice at night are given in three divisions: first, to visualize the word-symbols in the Throat Center. When the yogi feels that he is about to go to sleep, he should visualize that he becomes the Patron Buddha and also prays many times to his guru who is sitting upon his head. Then he should visualize a red *Ah* word or *Oṃ* word situated in the center of a red lotus with four leaves in the Central Channel of the Throat Center. This *Ah* or *Oṃ* word is the symbol of the essence of Buddha's expression upon which the yogi should concentrate without distraction. In such a manner, the yogi should enter into the state of sleep (keeping these visualizations in mind).

There is another instruction on performing this practice, i.e. to visualize five words – *Oṃ, Ah, Nu, Da, Ra* – in a successive order, in contrast to meditating on one red *Ah* word alone. This method is quite different. *The (Tantra) of the Non-Twofold Victorious Illusoriness* says, "Meditating on the four words – *Ah, Nu, Da, Ra* – in a successive order does not increase more power. It helps little; therefore, this practice may be dispensed with." To meditate on the *Oṃ* word at the central point is in accord with the saying of Sambhudra and other Tantras. However, visualizing a red *Ah* word is also acceptable. The extremely important point is to meditate on the word at the "central point"; i.e., to meditate on the word in the Throat Center in the Central Channel. Should he be unable to recognize the dream through this visualization, he must practice many, many times. If he still cannot hold the dream, he should visualize a *Thig-le* [here in the sense of bindu or seed of power] at the point between the eyebrows and hold on to it.

It is difficult to recognize the dream after midnight and before dawn, for this is a period in which sleep is very deep. In the time after daybreak into and through dawn, the sleep is usually light. During this period it is easy to recognize the dream. Then the yogi should pray to his guru, remind himself of the desire (to hold onto the dream),visualize a white glittering *Thig-le* at the central point between the eyebrows on his self-Yi-Dam body, and hold onto the visualization. He should also practice the Vase-Breathing exercise seven times; then he will fall asleep again. If he stresses visualizing the glittering *Thig-le* too much, he will not be able to sleep, or will be prone to awaken easily. In this case, he should visualize the *Thig-le* as a little darker in hue.

Some say that if he cannot fall into sleep because of meditating on the Throat Center, he should concentrate on the forehead, visualizing a white *Thig-le* there. This is very erroneous, because the forehead is a place that, if concentrated upon, causes dreams to arise, (puts consciousness in operation in opposition to the tendency to sleep). This foolish statement is akin to saying that concentration upon the Sleeping Center will make one awake. If he concentrates on the Throat Center at dawn and twilight for a long period and still cannot hold the dream, he must be a person who requires a sound, heavy sleep. For him, meditating on the Eyebrow Center will help. If by doing this, the sleep then becomes too light and he is liable to awake, or he can not fall into sleep at all, he should visualize a *Thig-le* within the reproductive organ and also repeatedly strengthen his desire for recognizing the dream during the daytime as mentioned before. Before sleep, he should visualize a black *Thig Le* in the center of the organ and practice the breathing exercise twenty-one times. Thus the destructive thoughts will be halted, and he can fall into sleep more easily. One should know that meditating on that organ is a cure for light sleep.

If through the practice [of meditating on the frontal sinus center] one still cannot subdue or overcome heavy sleep, one may follow such instructions as meditating on the month and year (visualizing the moon and sun). If by doing so, the yogi still cannot practice the Dream Yoga, he should know that only through the power of the (Wisdom)-Prana produced by the arising of the Innate Born Wisdom through the process of gathering, entering, and dissolving in the Central Channel of the Heat Yoga practice, one is able to hold a dream properly. Through the practice of intensive intention, no matter how hard one tries, he may still not be able to practice properly. Therefore, he should work hard on the superb Heat Yoga and try to lead the Pranas into the Central Channel. This is the primary practice, others being secondary.

(2) How to purify and develop the dream: There are two ways to develop the dream: the mundane way and the Buddhistic way. The principle of developing the dream is to create a dream or to transform it. The yogi may think in the dream stage that he rides on the rays of the sun and moon and journeys to the thirty-three heavens or to any place in this world. To enlarge his visions and experiences, he may conceive that he walks or flies in the sky. The Buddhistic way is to conceive that in the dream state one goes to the Pure Land of Amitabha or the heaven-land of Maitreya or the Aog-min Pure Land, etc., visiting the Buddhas and Bodhisattvas, rendering one's offerings, and hearing the Dharma from them. To be able to do this, one must have attained the mastery of Prana power. Only through the Prana power is one able to transform or create any dream state at one's own will. For those who have this mastery

these things are not difficult. For the ordinary person, however, a great deal of practice is required.

In both cases (through intensive intention and through the Prana power), the yogi sees the Buddha's Pure Land in his dream vision; however, these visions are merely the pictures the (reflections) of the Buddha's Pure Land and cannot be considered as real. In the latter case (through the exercise of Prana's power), one may receive some revelations or prophecies in dream that prove to be true. Most of them, however, are not reliable. In the former case (through intensive intention), the yogi should rely on the meritorious instructions together with some breathing exercises to practice the Dream Yoga.

The following instruction will improve the practice of Dream Yoga: When the yogi sees a man, an animal, a pillar, a vase or any other object in a dream, he should transform them by multiplying them from one to two, from two to four, to eight – up to hundreds and thousands.

(3) How to overcome the rambling type of dreams and recognize them as illusory manifestations: When the yogi one sees a fire or flood in a dream and becomes frightened, he should think to himself, recognizing the dream, "How can the fire and water of dream ever harm me?" Also, he should try to jump the fire and cross the flood. To learn the illusory nature of dream means to realize the non-existent nature of the vase, and other objects of dream-visions. This is accomplished by recognizing the dream. But one is not able, merely through the understanding, to realize the non-existence Śūnyatā of the self-nature of the dream. For instance, in the waking state, when he sees the reflection in a mirror, though he knows that the reflection

is illusory, he still cannot realize the Suchness of the reflection.

One's incapacity for recognizing the dream is like that of a child who believes the reflection of his face to be his true face; while in recognizing the dream, one is like an adult who knows the reflection is unreal although it appears to be his actual face. This example is an illustration of the underlying principle, and is a good one to express the principle of the Voidness-as-Reflection (literally the Voidness of the face-like reflection in the sense of the non-existence of the "true" face in the reflection). According to this principle, one should know that all Dharmas are Void in their self-nature — self-nature in the sense of real self-existence. One should also understand that all Dharmas are dream-like and have no substantiality whatsoever.

With this understanding definitely in mind, the yogi should acquaint himself with the nature, manner and characteristics of the Clinging-of-Existence, and also familariez himself with the reasons for the non-existence of this (illusory) Clinging. With such an understanding, the yogi learns that all the visions, objects, and subjects that he sees in the dream are identical with (Buddha) and the Two Mandalas; they are void in nature yet manifest (freely) as conjurations. Further, the yogi should understand that all these visions are absorbed in the bliss-void, as one has experienced during the daytime.

(4) The Practice on the real nature of dream: This is a teaching combining the Light Yoga with Dream Yoga. In the practice of this teaching, the yogi clearly visualizes (in the dream state) the self-body becoming his Yidam. From his heart, the *Hūṃ* word emanates rays of light that gath-

er all the visions in the dream and draw them back into the *Hūṃ* word. Then both the lower and upper part of his body melt and become absorbed into the *Hūṃ* word. Then the *Hūṃ* word also vanishes into the non-discriminating Light, upon which the yogi should concentrate his mind.

The perception-of-mind[86] of the dream state is much easier to absorb than the perception-of-mind of the waking state. In the dream state, when some portion of the very coarse kind of Prana dissolves itself and gathers at the Heart Center, the dream will vanish, and one will fall into the sleeping state. This is the time in which one may recognize the Voidness; if not, through repeated practices, one will definitely be able to see the Voidness of sleep clearly. If the absorbing process[87] and Void-holding become stable, this will greatly help meditation – Prana exercise, visualization, Mahamudra – in the daytime. If the yogi cannot recognize the Voidness-of-Sleep at the beginning stage when he first falls into sleep, he will be able through the power of recognizing the dream, to see the special Voidness.

CHAPTER SEVEN

ON THE BARDO REALM

Now the third instruction on the Illusoriness of Bardo:

This topic will be discussed in two aspects; a general introduction to the subject of the Bardo[88] state, and instructions on the successive practices.

The former: In the process of dying and in the process of the coming into Bardo at time of death, one's feeling is very changeable and fluctuating, like the scale and arrow. The sentient being of Bardo [hereafter termed "Bardoist"] has the body-form, with all limbs complete, of the Loka wherein the Bardoist is destined to have his birth. The Bardoist is endowed with supernatural power and is capable of performing miraculous feats such as passing through solid matter without difficulty or hindrances; he can travel to any places except the place wherein he will be reborn. The lifetime of the Bardoist usually lasts seven days; in some cases it is even shorter than this. After this period, if the Bardoist can not reincarnate (for some reason) he will return to the Bardo state again. This may happen as many as seven times, making forty-nine days, if conditions necessary for his new reincarnation are not ready.

Within this period, when the time for reincarnating ripens, the Bardoist, if so destined by Karma, will have his consciousness drawn into the place of the Metamorphosis-Born. If the Bardoist is to have a birth of Warmth-Born, his consciousness will merge with smell and taste and reincarnate in the place of the Warmth-Born. If the Bardoist is to have a birth of the Egg-Born or Womb-Born, his lust and hate will be inflamed when he beholds the scene of his parents having intercourse. If destined to be born male, he will hate his father and lust after his mother; if destined to be female, he will hate his mother and lust after his father (at first sight) [Here is penetrating pre-natal psychoanalysis long before the advent of Freud. *Ed.*] In some cases, the Bardoist dies and reincarnates in a place because of his aversion to. In other cases, the Bardoist who has committed many evil deeds (in his previous life) sees his surroundings as dark as the twilight sky, while the virtuous Bardoist sees his surroundings bright as moonlight or white as woolen cloth. The Hell-destined Bardoist sees the burning tree-stump. The Animal-destined Bardoist sees the smoke. The Hungry Ghost (Preta)-destined Bardoist sees a color like that of water. Both the Human-destined and Desire-Heaven-destined Bardoists behold the gold color. The one destined for the Heaven-of-Form sees the white womb and enters into it.

The sentient being of the Heaven of Non-Form also experiences Bardo if he is destined to fall down into the lower Kingdoms. If sentient beings in the two lower Kingdoms are destined to reincarnate in the Heaven-without-Form, they will not experience Bardo after their death. Instead, a body for them will come into being (made) of the Skandha of the Heaven-of-Non-Form.

Some declare that the Beings of Non-Intermission[89] both of lower and upper, will not experience Bardo at all. This kind of statement shows ignorance. The *Abhidharma-Ghosa* says:

"In the previous time, the reincarnate (beings)
Who possess the face of flesh, etc."

This stanza refers to the beings possessing the body-form of their existence previous to the Bardo stage... [Gap in text, probably copyists' errors, occur here.] to the time before their future death. Those who do not understand this point claim that the Bardoist has a body-form like that of his previous existence. Some say that all those in Bardo have the same body-form and face as their previous existence. Some say that their body-form, visions, and perceptions are like those of their companions in Bardo. Some put various conceptions together, saying: "The face and body are like that of the face and body that will be born." On this saying is based the claim that the Bardoist possesses both the face and body of his next existence and those of his companions in Bardo.

Some say that the Bardoist has both the body and form of his previous life and of his future life. Thus they claim that in the seven-day period — the lifetime of Bardo — the bodily face, form, and visions of the first three-and-a-half days are like those of the previous life, and that the face, form and visions of the next three-and-a half days are like those of the future life. Some state that the Bardoist dies at the expiration of the three-and-a-half days that the so-called "Bardo" refers to this time. These statements have no basis at all.

As for the meaning of the "Bardo," the *Abhidharma-Ghosa* says: "Died from here. Gone to be born. (Between these two stages) the Bardo." This stanza explains that "Bardo" means the stage between death and the next life. Besides the Sg'ye-she-bardo (Bardo of Death and Birth) there is no other Bardo. But this Sg'ye-she-bardo is the Sridb'a-bardo itself.

However, in the teaching of the Six Yogas the classification or arrangement is somewhat different. It states that the period from the time of birth till the time of death is called the Sg'ye-she-bardo. The period from the sleeping state to the waking state is called the Dream Bardo. The period from the time of death till the time of the next birth is called the Sridb'a-bardo. If people ask how I would explain these two conflicting views, I answer that this problem can be clarified through the study of Gsan *H*dus, according to the teaching of Gsan *H*dus given by the Paoba School, the successive emergence of the Four Emptinesses manifesting as light finds illustration in the process of dying. The illusory Sambhogakaya corresponds to the manifestation of Bardo. The subtle Sambhogakaya, which transforms the coarse Nirmanakayas, finds correspondence in the process of taking a new birth.

Those who do not have the pith-instructions mistakenly interpret the esoteric teachings as referring to the vulgar Sg'ye-she-bardo and the other two (Bardos). But the yogis who possess the pith-instructions understand the Trikaya at the end with a clear understanding of the corresponding nature of the two, knowing how and why names of the Trikaya of the Path and Fruit are used to denote the Three Dharmas of the Foundation. They understand that it is merely the names of the Trikaya and not the real Trikaya being used to explain the Three Dharmas of Foundation. This background is found in many other sources.

From this view, the so-called practice of the Illusory Body Bardo in the waking state is merely a name, not the real Bardo. Likewise the so-called Illusory Body Bardo of Dream which manifests in the period after the appearance of the Light-of-Sleep stage is also a name (for explaining the Bardo-like nature of the dream). The name of Bardo is also given to that period in which advanced yogis realize the Sambhogakaya after the emergence of the Death-Light. For the ordinary sentient beings, however, the same period is merely Bardo.

For these reasons the "so-called" three Bardos are avowed; however, such statements do not make much sense and are superfluous.[91] The basic principle is to interpret and associate the Three Dharmas of the Foundation with the Trikaya of the Path (in order) to establish a system. Only after this first consideration can the Birth-Death Bardo and the other two Bardos be considered acceptable. The yogi should acquaint himself with the fact that the three Illusory Body teachings — Illusory-Body of the Waking State, Illusory-Body of the Dream State, and the corresponding Illusory-Body of Bardo State — are all based on the fundamental principle of Bardo. He should also know that by means of the practice of Heat Yoga in the daytime, through the process of Prana entering, remaining, and dissolving in the Central Channel, the Four Blisses or Four Emptinesses will successively appear. He should know that this process is in correspondence with the principle of the (Subsiding) Process of Mind Prana at time of death, so that the Light of Death will also appear.

Likewise, he should know that the teaching and practice of the Light-of-Waking State, Light-of-Sleeping State, and Light of Death correspond to the principle of the (Subsiding) Process of Mind Prana at time of death; because in both cases the Four Emptinesses will appear. With this interpretation of the three (above) conformities in mind, the yogi should know that at the end of the emergence of the Illusory Body of Waking State the crude Nirmanakaya will be transformed (literal text: "...Nirmanakaya will be seized"). At the end of a dream, close to the waking state, the

Subtle Sambhogakaya appears by which the Nirmanakaya will be transformed (seized). At the end of the emergence of the Light of Death the corresponding Sambhogakaya of Bardo arises, by which the crude Nirmanakaya will be transformed (seized).

The yogi should be well-acquainted with this basic principle so that he will be clear from all doubt (in his mind) and acquire a definite understanding. If he grasps the foregoing principle, he will then understand the correspondence of the Dharmakaya with death, the Sambhogakaya with Bardo, and the Nirmanakaya with rebirth. These three correspondences can also be subdivided into nine; one should know that this is the highest teaching.

Some (scholars), however, made a different interpretation. They aligned the Lust with the Third Initiation, the Blindness with Light, and the Hate with the Illusory Body. Although in the performance of the Third Initiation some aspect of lust is involved, there is little reason to align the Lust Initiation in this connection, because in the case of the Third Initiation many preparations and practices are required. (Since both the preparatory practices and the Arising and Perfecting Yoga are not aligned with the Bardo, there is little sense in connecting the Lust with the Third Initiation).

In view of the fact that the Bardoist always experiences the Lust and Hate when entering into the womb of the mother, some scholars mistakenly aligned the Illusory Body with the Hate. This view is erroneous,[92] because it implied the abandonment of the practice of the Illusory Body of the Waking and Dream states. By holding these views they neglect the real basis of the Illusory Body teaching. Also they cannot possibly explain the fact of the emergence of the Light of Death and the manifestations of the Illusory Body of Bardo. Besides, a lust-desire will arise in the Bardoist when he sees the scene of his parents' intercourse; if so, the Illusory Body should not only be aligned with the Hate but also with the Lust; therefore, this arrangement is not very sound.

Some declare that because the lust of the sentient beings of the Sg'ye-she-bardo is very great, it should be aligned with the Lust; the blindness of the dream is great, thus the dream should be aligned with the Blindness; the hate of the Sridb'a-bardo is great, this the Sridb'a-bardo should be aligned with the Hate. This saying is also incorrect, as explained before; furthermore the Tantra says:

"In between the Sleep and Dream state

Is the Blindness, the nature of the Dharmakaya."

According to this irrefutable quotation, the time to realize the Light is in the sleeping state when the dream visions have not yet arisen; it is erroneous to align the Dream-state with Blindness (as it should be aligned with Sleeping-state and Light).

Some claim that Marpa said that the Lust should be aligned with the Non-Leakage (Zag-med), the Hate should be aligned with the Illusory Body, the Blindness with the Light. The two former statements are not a convincing theory at all.[92]

Some Lamas say that in correspondence with the Sg'ye-she-bardo certain aspects of the Two-Successive Step Practice (Arising Yoga and Perfecting Yoga) are taught and should be practiced: the Dream-Bardo, Light, and Blindness should be aligned together with the related aspects of the Two Yogas; the Sridb'a-bardo, the Hate, and the Dharma-essence should also be aligned together with the related aspects of the Two Yogas. This saying makes no sense at all.

The Three Bodies aligned with the three Bardos make together nine different groups and aligned with other arrangements make the system of fifteen groups, etc. Since this is easily understood, there is no need to detail them here.

The instructions on the successive practice include (1) the explanations of the different groups of Bardoists (i.e. Bardo dwellers) and (2) the manner in which these various classes of beings can apply the Bardo practice.

First, the explanations. All Bardo dwellers may be divided into three groups (or levels) — the most advanced beings, the fairly advanced beings, and the least advanced beings. Discussions of the advanced beings are found in the books of *Zal-lun*, *Spyod-bsdus* and *Sgron-gsal*.

At the end of the death process, the illusory [in the sense of a but transitory means that is nonetheless useful and even necessary under the Bardo conditions. This technical use of the word "illusory" will be noticed on several occasions.] Sambhogakaya will appear in the Bardo; rely on it and you will attain Buddhahood. In the past the scholars of Tibet regarded this teaching of attaining Buddhahood while in the Bardo state as "the lazy man's teaching."[93] However, there are some yogis who are not lazy but nevertheless lack certain necessary conditions which are required (for the attainment of Buddhahood in this life), so that they cannot reach Buddhahood in one lifetime. Therefore the appellation "lazy man's practice" is merely valid from one particular viewpoint.

Someone may ask how much realization and practice are required in one's lifetime to enable one even to attain the Buddhahood in Bardo. The answer is, a perfect accomplishment of the First Successive Step (the Arising Yoga), the entering, remaining, and dissolving in the Central Channel, together with the successive arising of the Four Emptiness-Wisdoms and the actual accomplishment of attaining the Illusory Body. This is the best preparation – that found in the case of the most advanced beings.

Required of the fairly advanced yogi is the arising of the Four Emptinesses through the prana's entering into the Central Channel, so that the yogi is able to merge himself with the Emptiness of Sleep – because merging with the Emptiness of Sleep is just like merging with the Light of Death through prana power. If one is able to merge with the Voidness in a state of deep sleep, this is the best method.

In the case of the least advanced, it is required that they obtain an initiation and strictly observe the Tantric disciplines, and also diligently practice the Arising Yoga and the Perfecting Yoga. Then at the time of death, when the subsidence of the earth, water, and other elements takes place, the yogi should notice the arising of the Light of Death and the successive emergence of the stages of Bardo. Thus he should now in this lifetime practise the pith-instructions of the Sleeping and Dream yogas. Since the sleeping and dream states are in many ways like the death and Bardo states, practising the Dream Yoga is a good preparation for death and the Bardo state. At the time of death, even if the yogi cannot hold the Light through the prana power, he will be able through these practices to recognize it.

One who has worked mainly on the Dhyana practice (but not the Tantric Path) and has accomplished Dhyana to a great extent is able to apply his Samadhi-power at the time when his death is approaching. By the Samadhi which he has stressed in his lifetime the yogi is able at time of death to bypass the death process and Bardo. However, one should know that this is merely a result depending on the ordinary Samadhi.

How do these yogis (the most advanced, fairly advanced, and least advanced) recognize the Bardo?

Those who attain Buddhahood in Bardo are those who are unable to attain Buddhahood in this lifetime; therefore, through the holding of the Light of Death, Buddhahood is attained.

The [sometimes heard] saying: "At the beginning stage of Bardo, one may attain Buddhahood," is erroneous. The teachings found in the recognized holy books, have never said any such thing — the attainment in Bardo may be accomplished *before* the completion of the death-birth process. Furthermore, the saying just quoted should be interpreted to mean the attainment of Buddhahood in the lifetime, not the actual Bardo stage. Also, the saying that, through holding the Light of Death, Buddhahood may be attained at that time, can never be found in any of the recognized holy books — it is erroneous. If not, how can one explain the fact that the body of a new procurer of Dharmakaya becomes a corpse without having the magnificent (thirty-two and eighty) signs of Buddha? (Lit.: "the body of either With-Learning or Without-Learning").

For these reasons, one should know that the Dharmakaya, with which there is the so-called merging of time of death, is by no means the real Dharmakaya but a similar one. Therefore, it is necessary to rely on a perfect body of Bardo after the emergence of the Light of Death. The perfect accomplishment cannot be attained without this body or through depending on another body.

In the case of the most advanced yogi, it is required for his accomplishment that he establish a Sambhogakaya of the Path through his mind-prana in the state of Bardo. This instruction is also found in some other sources. The fairly advanced or the least advanced yogi should alert his mind before death comes and offer all his belongings to the Fields of Merits, in complete abandonment, without the slightest attachment to any wordly belongings. He should also confess all his transgressions of the precepts made during his lifetime.

Through confession he will have peace of mind and no regret at time of death. A pith-instruction concerning the practice of death and Bardo is to take them as the favorable conditions to practice Dharma: "One should think that in dying one is going to one's beloved home." Then, he should visualize his body as the body of the Yidam, render his offerings, and pray to the gurus, Yidam, and deities in the Front Sky before him. With great earnestness, he should sincerely pray them to enable him to merge with the Light of Death and Illusory Body of Bardo.

The fairly advanced and the least advanced yogi should practice as much as possible the gathering of prana in the Central Channel, whatever method he uses, before the sign of death appears. He should also try to raise the Four Emptinesses and the (Three) Bodies of Buddha. In addition, he should try to hold the Light of Sleep and the Illusory Body of Dream. It is important to practice these teachings before death comes.

The Instruction on Recognizing the Signs of Death

One should know the explanations on the subsidence of the Crude Twenty Lights; that can be found in other books. In brief, the signs of death are as follows: When the earth-element subsides into the water-element, the outer phenomenon is that one cannot move or hold his body – as if the body is collapsing and sinking so that the dying person feels like exclaiming "Hold me up!" The inner phenomenon is the experience of seeing a mirage. When the water-element subsides into the fire-element, the outer phenomenon is that one feels thirst, a burning in the mouth and nose, and that the tongue shrivels; the inner phenomenon is seeing smoke. When the fire-element subsides into the air-element, the outer phenomenon is the experience of decrease in the warmness of the body; the bodily warmth will gather at the end of the body. The inner phenomenon is seeing a tiny light like that of a glow-worm.

When the subsidence of the delusory mind-prana takes place, the outer phenomenon is the long exhaling of the breath. The dying person feels his breath to be hard and rough, and finds it impossible to stop the exhalation even if he wills to do so. The inner phenomenon is the seeing of a steady (unwavering) lamplight. Thereupon, the so-called "First" Voidness or first perception appears, which is like seeing the moonlight shining in a cloudless sky. After the emergence of the "First" Voidness, comes the so-called "Second" Voidness or the Extreme Voidness. The dying one sees an augmenting Voidness, bright and glaring like the sunlight blazing from a clear sky; this is called the Stage of Augmentation. After the subsidence of this stage, comes the stage called the "Attainment," in which the dying one feels his consciousness becoming dim and sluggish; this experience is like seeing a dark sky. Then comes the complete cessation of all thoughts, and the dying one experiences complete darkness.

Thereafter, his consciousness awakes from darkness, and the "Universal Voidness" appears; this experience is like seeing a clear and unobscured sky under the radiant sunlight at dawn. This light is the real Fundamental Light.

In short, the successive emergence of the three Voidnesses and the Light are experienced as outer phenomenon through seeing the smoke, the light of the glow-worm, the lamplight, and the cloudless sky; as inner phenomena they are experienced through seeing the white, the red, the black, and the dawn-like visions. Although there are two different explanations – that of the With-Form-Action and that of the Without-Form-Action -- the latter one is better; for in many holy books is found the saying that the smoke, etc., precedes the emergence of the Four Emptinesses (Voidnesses), and that all the Four Emptinesses cannot be literally described as having color and form. The closest description of the appearance of the Voidness is to say it is like the clear and cloudless sky.

At the time of the emergence of the Death-Light, the Three Steps (Appearance, Augmentation, and Attainment) successively come to pass and subside, one after another. Eventually, all the pranas dissolve in the Heart Center; the white *Thig-le* drops down from the Head-Center, the red *Thig-le* rises up from the Navel Center, and they join together at the Heart Center.* In the case of the sentient beings

* This is an extremely significant point. Compare our observations on pages 176–178, 182 and 191. *Ed.*

who do not possess all the six elements, such as devas, etc., these Lights will still appear, but not in the same manner.

Since the yogi has experienced these signs of subsidence before in his lifetime, he is able to recognize them clearly. When the first sign appears, he should apply the particular method of gathering the prana into the Central Channel that he has mastered, is most skilled in, or has practised most in his lifetime, and watch for the emergence of the signs. With such mindfulness and recollection, he may grasp these opportunities and accomplish the realization. When the First Emptiness emerges, the yogi should meditate on the view and try to recognize it. When the Second Emptiness and (the Third Emptiness) the Attainment and the Light appear, the yogi should also concentrate as long as possible on the view and try to merge with the Lights.

At the time of death when the Light of Death emerges, the mind-pranas all gather in the Central Channel and dissolve into the Heart Center; the erroneous views and the dualistic conceptions of the crude form also subside. Thereupon, the "vision" of the cloudless sky will appear. Even if the yogi can concentrate upon this light, however, it will be of no avail if he has not practised and meditated on the Middle Way View in his lifetime and knows how to absorb his mind in that view. Otherwise, this yogi will not be able to see Reality. It is, therefore, necessary to have had the experiences of the deep contemplation on the Madhyamkia principle on one's lifetime and the practices of the Bliss-Void or the practice of Son-Light or Light of the Path. Said the Jetsün [*i. e.* venerated *Ed.*] Milarepa:

"The light of Death is the Dharmakaya, itself; one should understand this point and thus identify it. In order to recognize it, the 'Pointing-Out-on-Mind-Essence' practice should be given by one's guru. Thus one will understand the view of reality and the practice of the expressive Light of the Path."

These were his words:

The Light of Death is the primordial Mother-Light. In order to merge the Son-Light with the Mother-Light, one should practice in the waking state the gathering of the pranas into the Central Channel and the entering, remaining, and dissolving exercises. One should also contemplate the Four Emptinesses, especially the "All Emptiness" (or the Fourth Emptiness). Only if a yogi is able to merge with the Light, even in the deep-sleeping state, will he be able to merge the Son-Light with the Mother-Light through his prana power at time of death.

If he can recognize the Light of Death and merge with it, he will be able to recognize the subsequent emergence of Bardo. The recognition of the Light of Death and the capability of merging with it, is the only right way of "holding" the Bardo; there is no other way to hold or recognize Bardo. If he exercises during his lifetime on the practice of pretending to go through the successive stages by reminding himself "Now, death has come... This is the such and such vision of Bardo...," he may to some extent hold or recognize the Bardo, but his power to do so will be extremely weak.

Likewise, if he keeps exercising on the practice of imitating the successive stages of death, he may at the time of the emergence of the Light of Death, be absorbed in (his) Samadhi for a long period. Nevertheless, because of his

Samsaric Prana (literally, prana of this life) that never enables him to identify the Light of Death, it is very difficult to consider this kind of practice a practice of the unique Anuttara Tantra.

If he puts too much emphasis on this practice, it is like abandoning the basic teaching to put stress on the secondary teaching. Instead, he should practice the Heat Yoga and work hard on the gathering of pranas into the Central Channel. In his waking state, he should practice the entering, remaining, and dissolving process and the arising of the Four Emptinesses; if he is able to do so, he will be able to hold the Light of Sleep through his prana power.

If the yogi can raise the Illusory Body after the emergence the Light of Waking State and the Light of Sleep, only then will he be able to hold or recognize the Light of Death and Bardo. Then he will have attained a supreme and unprecedented confidence.

This is the reason that the practice of Heat Yoga is considered the peerless teaching. This one should always remember. From the state of recognizing and holding the Light of Death, the dying person comes to another stage, and, through his ability acquired from meditation in his lifetime, and through his understanding of the key-instructions and his faith toward Dharma, he is then able to raise the Buddha's Bodies in the delusory Bardo state. The Bardo Body, however, cannot be used as a qualified means to accomplish the Supreme Bodies of Buddha, though at the time of Bardo one should recognize the Bardo state and try to take up the perfect Buddha Bodies. Nevertheless, one still should visualize the self-Body becoming the Yidam's Body, contemplate on the View of Thatness, and identify all manifestations — cosmos and sentient beings —

as illusory, dreamlike, and magic in nature. If the yogi practises these teachings in Bardo, he will procure superb benefits; therefore, he should realize the significance of these pith instructions and practise them.

The yogi who practices the Teachings of Path may not be womb-born in his next life. Very possibly he may take any of the other three forms of Birth[94]. Therefore the Bardoist should try all the more to practise the teaching of manifestation-as-Yidam, Yidam-as-delusion, delusion-as-Voidness, as instructed before. He should also identity his future parents as the father and mother Guru or the father and mother Yidam.

One may also apply the teaching of choosing the place of birth in the Bardo state — to vow earnestly to be born in the Pure Land of Buddha — as given in another part of Marpa's teachings. These teachings include the recognizing of Bardo and the longing for a birth in the Pure Land according to the pith-instructions of *Apo-wa* (the teaching of Transforming One's Consciousness).

CHAPTER EIGHT

THE YOGA OF THE LIGHT

The instruction on Light Yoga is given in two parts: The practice of Light Yoga in the waking state, and the practice of Light Yoga in the sleeping state.

This Light Yoga practiced in the daytime refers to the general or common Light (in contrast to the unique Tantric Light practice), which is the fundamental Dharma-essence apart from the realistic and nihilistic extremes[95]. This is the (so-called) Light-of-Object; the understanding or realization of which is (called) the Light-of-Object (literally, the Light-of-Comprehending-the-Object). This teaching is found in both Hinayana and Mahayana, in the Paramita Vehicle as well as in Tantra, and in the three Lower Tantras as well as the Highest Division of Tantra. It is a teaching common to all Buddhist schools. Sometimes it is called the Absolute Light. The unique Light (as taught in Tantra) is no different in essence from the common Light-of-Object. The difference lies in the Light-of-Subject, which (in the Tantric teachings) is the realization of the Innate Great Bliss.

The unique teaching of the Anuttara Tantra for the realization of the Innate Born Great Bliss, requires mainly the entering, remaining, and dissolving of the prana in the Central Channel, or the Bliss-of-the-Perfecting-Yoga. This Innate Great Bliss is not, however, produced through the melting of *Thig-le*, nor through the concentration practice of ordinary meditation — the no-thought experience apart from drowsiness and distraction. Neither is it produced through the *taming of prana*. For the Bliss produced through the taming of prana is quite different from the Innate Great Bliss. Through the taming of prana, the experience of brightness, no-thought, and bliss may be produced, but this bliss is different from the Innate Great Bliss. It may also be a Bliss-of-Melting, but it is not the same Bliss of the Arising Yoga – the Melting-Bliss is not produced through the prana entering into the Central Channel, etc. One should carefully distinguish the different Blisses, and understand them well.

As explained before, in the Heat Yoga, the Innate Great Bliss of the Perfecting Yoga should be merged with the well-studied View of the Soleness – thus arises the Void-Bliss Wisdom, called the Light, or the Light of the Path. In the practice of Perfecting Yoga, to unfold this light is required before the Illusory Bodies come to pass. In addition to this, many other practices are required for the raising of the Illusory Bodies. Here, the special Light practice is emphasized. The entering of Light requires a dependence on either the actual Illusory Body or on any similar illusory body.

The subsiding process of the Light [is now discussed].

The explanations on this subject are not very clear in most of the pith-instructions. However, there is a very good one that describes the process as follows:

The yogi should visualize himself as the Father and Mother Yidam. At the Dharma Wheel of the Heart Center in the Central Channel stands a blue *Hūṃ* word on the Sun Disc.

From this *Hūṃ* word emanate beams of light shining upon all the cosmos and purifying them; then the beams enter and are absorbed into the bodies of all sentient beings.

Thereupon, all the sentient beings melt (and are absorbed) into the Mother Yidam. Then, in the downward absorbing process, the head of the Yidam vanishes, then the neck, the chest, etc., one by one, and are finally absorbed in the *Hūṃ* word. At the same time, in the upward-absorbing process the toes first vanish into the leg, then the leg into the thigh, thigh into hips, hips into belly, and finally all are absorbed into the *Hūṃ* word. Thereon, the lower part of the *Hūṃ* word, the vowel *ū*, vanishes into the *Ha*, and the *Ha* vanishes into the half-moon; the half-moon then vanishes into the *Thig-le* [here to be understood as *bindu Ed.*] and the *Thig-le* vanishes upward into the *Nada*. Since this Visualization of the absorbing process is concentrated upon the Heart Center in the Central Channel, if one can stabilize the Visualization, the pranas of the Ro-ma and Rkyang-ma will all enter, remain, and dissolve in the Heart Center in the Central Channel; the Four Voidnesses will successively arise; the Light of Path will augment. At this time, with blissful mind, one should unwaveringly meditate upon the Visualization.

As mentioned before, this commentary on the Illusory Body and Light Yoga is prepared on the pith-instructions of the Pao School. The instruction of the Light Yoga given above is based on the unique teaching of the Five Steps of Gsun-*a*dus and it was introduced here as a little adornment for the pith-instructions.

In the Heat Yoga practice, if one can raise (unfold) the Innate [Wisdom-Bliss] through the entering of prana into the Central Channel, he will easily be able to raise the Innate Light at the time of Light Yoga practice. At least, he will be able to unfold it through the practice of the absorbing process (without difficulty).

If the practice of the Light of the Sleeping State can be done through holding the Light of Sleeping State by prana, which is the prerequisite practice of Dream Yoga, it accords with the instructions of many gurus. For holding the dream through prana is itself a very good method of practising the Light. At first, one should eat well and abundantly, and dress in very warm clothes (or cover oneself with a warm quilt). Depending on the needs and time the yogi should abandon sleep for two or three days, or sleep as usual (literally, do not abandon sleep). If he abandons sleep for two to three days, he will become too sleepy, and it will be difficult for him to recognize the Light of Sleep. Therefore, for the beginners, it is preferable to practice the Light Yoga in a comparatively light sleeping state. For the advanced yogi, whose meditation has already become steady, it is not necessary to abandon sleep; however, in order to test one's ability to recognize the Light in very deep sleeping state, he may abandon sleep for some days.

In the practice of the Light Yoga, the yogi should render offerings and pray to the Precious Ones, present the Gtor-mas to the Guards, and pray them to assist him in recognizing the Light of Sleep and in subduing all hindrances. He should visualize the Yidam's body, practise the Guru Yoga, and pray earnestly many times that his guru assist him to recognize the Light. The yogi should also repeatedly remind himself not to fall into dreams but to recognize the Voidness-of-Sleep when sleep comes.

The sleeping-posture should be as follows: Lie down on the right side, with the head to the north, the feet pointing south; the back, east; and the mouth, toward the west. Place the left foot on the right foot. This position is called the Lion-Sleep-Posture. Then, the yogi should visualize the self-Yidam body and also visualize a blue *Hūṃ* word standing in the center of a lotus, with four green leaves extending in each direction, situated at the Heart Center in the Central Channel. On the four leaves there are four words – *Ah, Nu, Da, Ra*. (In some other instructions no word is visualized on the four leaves). The *Ah* word sits on the leaf in the east; the *Nu* word; in the south; the *Da*, in the west; the *Ra*, north. When one feels sleepy, he concentrates on the *Ah* word; when he feels very sleepy or insensible, he should concentrate on the *Nu* word; thus the First Voidness will appear. When the yogi concentrates on the *Da* word, the Second Voidness or the Extreme Voidness will emerge; when he concentrates on the *Ra* word, the Third Voidness or the Voidness of Attainment will emerge. Thereupon, when the yogi concentrates on the *Hūṃ* word in the center, the Fourth Voidness or the Universal Voidness will emerge.

It is said that successively visualizing these four words will cause the Four Voidnesses to emerge successively. However, this saying makes little sense, because some do not understand that in meditating on these words at the Heart Center in the Central Channel, the life prana will automatically gather; consequently, the Four Voidnesses will arise. Based on this reasoning, one should not misinterpret the text "visualizing the word of the center at the Heart." The essential thing is to visualize at the central point of the Heart Center in the Central Channel. Because the words of the instructions are not clear, it is wrongly said that concentrating on the three words on the three leaves will produce the Three Voidnesses. This opinion completely misses the essential point of the teaching. Therefore, we may dispense with this *Ah, Nu, Da, Ra* word-practice, which is difficult and results in little benefit.

The important thing is to concentrate on the *Hūṃ* word in the center.

There are two different kinds of meditator of the Sleeping Light: the yogi who has attained a stable Samadhi of the visualized object before (engaging in this practice), and the yogi who has not attained a stable Samadhi. In the latter case, the yogi will attain a Sleeping Samadhi immediately after he falls into sleep through holding his mind on the instructions given before, but this Sleeping Samadhi will last only a very short while. Therefore, relying merely on the mindfulness of recognizing the sleeping state, through desire will not give one a stable Samadhi even though great efforts are made. For if one cannot "hold" the Light through the prana power, the inhalation and exhalation will still take place. Though the breathing may be very subtle and calm, the breath cannot be completely stopped. Thus a counterpart of the Fourth Emptiness will emerge but not the real Fourth Emptiness. Consequently, the Sleeping Light cannot be (fully) recognized.

In the case of the yogi who has already attained a stable Samadhi and has mastered the Heat Yoga capable of gathering the Life Prana in the Central Channel and raising the Fourth Emptiness, he will have no difficulty in unfolding the Light-of-the Sleeping-State. If he follows the instructions as given before and visualizes the *Hūṃ* word in the Central Channel at bedtime, he will be able to unfold the Fourth Emptiness of the Sleeping State through the dissolving process of prana within two or three days.

If the yogi cannot unfold the Emptiness through the prana power in the daytime, but if he attains a stable Samadhi with the experience of bliss, brightness and non-thought, he may either follow the foregoing instructions or absorb himself in his Samadhi to reach the state of Sleeping Samadhi. Some people say that if one has attained a stable Samadhi of any general type it is not necessary for one to lead the prana entering into the Central Channel. This is not correct, for doing so will not bring about the actual Sleeping-Light of Anuttara Tantra. Nevertheless, if the yogi concentrates at the Heart-Center, through the power of the habitual thought produced by the practice he may well bring about the fruit. Though through the power of any general Dhyana one may induce a certain sleeping samadhi with the capability of contemplating on the Sole-ness and the Light of the general Paths (Hinayana and Ma-hayana Path), that is by no means the Light as taught by the teaching of Anuttara Tantra*.

Recognizing the Light through the prana power by con-centrating on the Heart Center will cause the Four Void-nesses to successively arise; the manner of their emergence is explained as follows:

Meditating upon a *Thig-le* in the Heart Center at the deep-sleeping state in the preparatory stage will cause a perfect Light-of-No-Thought to emerge. Even if it does not emerge and the yogi falls asleep, his prana will naturally gather in the Central Channel. As instructed before, if one

* It is clear that throughout the text Tsong Khapa is refer-ring to a practical yoga-type discipline, very different from the very philosophical and verbal context of the Anuttara Tantra as presented in most of the occidentally accessible texts, e. g. in the Vow of Mahamudra, for example. That practical teaching and the realization it brings is the true heart of the Anuttara Tantra. — *Ed.*

is able to gather the pranas in the Central Channel in the daytime practice and practises the concentration of the *Hūṃ* word at the Heart Center in the Central Channel before bedtime, the pranas will be gathered easily in the Central Channel. The experiences of the emergence of the Voidness are as follows: First, the yogi sees the water-reflection-like mirage, then it vanishes and becomes smoke. The yogi sees many sparkling lights like those of the glowworm, then they vanish again and become the stable light of a lamp. This light vanishes, and the yogi sees the manifestation as the lucid *Thig-le* like moonlight shining in the clear sky. The serene moonlight spreads over all the universe; this experience is called the "Voidness" or the "Emergence." Then the vision vanishes again, and the yogi experiences all his mental manifestations appearing to be a clear sky and sees the all-spreading glaring sunlight, its color not like the blazing fire-ball but sparkling and gleaming. This experience is called the "Extreme Emptiness" or the "Augmentation of Manifestation." Then the yogi experiences, as the sky extending over all the universe, his mental manifestations appearing to be the dark firmament at night, dark but not black. At this time, if the yogi concentrates on the upper part of the body, the vision will not disappear; if he concentrates on the lower part of the body, the mind will become dim and dull; however, this experience is not harmful. Keeping one's mind on the instruction, the yogi cultivates this experience of darkness and eventually a very stable "Light" will emerge. The emergence of this light is called the "Great Emptiness" or the "Manifestation of Attainment."

When the yogi arises from the darkness, a vision like the clear sky of dawn will emerge, which is neither exactly like the color or shape of the sky, nor like the sunlight, moonlight, or darkness. This stage is called the "Universal Voidness." He should try to absorb himself in this great voidness as long as possible.

In the teaching of Gsun-*a*dus of the Marpa School, one may find instructions for avoiding either the sudden awakening from sleep or the falling into dream state.

The Four Voidnesses are also called the Four Blisses. The Fourth Voidness is identified with the supreme Innate Bliss. The rapturous and non-thought aspects of this Innate Bliss are expediently called "bliss"; actually they are two characteristics among others of the Voidness which are seen as clearly (by the enlightened beings) as one sees his own palm.

The teaching of the identity of Bliss and Void of the Un-paralled-Vehicle[96] is to meditate on the View of the Soleness together with the produced Bliss, as mentioned before. Although this term, the Identity-of-Bliss-Void, is claimed by many, there are numerous incorrect and misleading explanations of the teaching. They are similar, [to the true teaching *Ed.*] but erroneous; one should examine them very carefully.

Although the pith-instructions of this school are many, in this connection there is no mentioning of the "Three Voidnesses." Some people avow the "Four Voidnesses principle," but it seems not befitting here. One may not be able to find this point in the pith-instructions of the Rngog-pa School; nevertheless, it is clearly stated in the book of *Spyod-bsdus (Collective Instructions on Performances* – commentary of Gsun-*a*dus), which says:

"The skhandas then enter into the subtle elements, the subtle elements into the consciousness, the consciousness into the subtle-consciousness (Sattva), the subtle-consciousness into the Blindness.* Following this proceeding and coordinating with it, the sleeping procedure is reversed. At the time the 'Entering-process' of consciousness, of subtle consciousness, and of the great Blindness takes place, in a split second the yogi forgets his meditation (or completely fails to keep his attention on the meditation-object). Later, when the forgetfulness is overcome, the Light — essence of the wisdom — will shine forth. If one can liberate himself from the forgetfulness, he will attain the 'essence' through the Prana (force). If any dream takes place during this time, the yogi should try to reverse the sleeping-procedure and concentrate as long as possible on the illuminating Light."

Having fully understood the secret meaning of the books of the accomplished one, I have given the explanations on the Four Voidnesses and the (practical) instructions on holding the Light. These instructions cannot be found anywhere else[97]; one should try to understand them properly and follow them.

In the above quotation, "the skhandas" means the crude visions; "the subtle elements" implies the time when the elements enter into the prana — that is, the time when the earth, water, and fire elements successively subside from one to another until the fire elements enter into prana. "Entering into the consciousness" means that the prana subsides into the consciousness; here, the consciousness means the First Voidness. The "Sattva" implies the stage of the Augmentation; "entering" implies the consciousness enters or (subsides) into this stage. "The Blindness"

* Here is the "entering process of the three consciousnesses" mentioned below. See note 98. *Ed.*

means the stage of Attainment. "Following this proceeding and coordinating with it" means the yogi should coordinate and combine himself with the Three Voidnesses at the time of sleep.

In short, this quotation from the "Collective Instruction on Performance" is the essence summarized from Ye-shes-rdo-rje. "This time" means the time of sleep. The "entering-process of the three consciousnesses[98]" means that former consciousnesses successively enter into the later consciousnesses, and at the time of the third stage of the third consciousness the mind becomes dim. "Later" implies the time after the attainment, or the "After-stage" of the Attainment. "When the forgetfulness is overcome" denotes the time when one awakes from the non-thought consciousness in the deeply slumbering state — the experience is like beholding the clear sky at dawn. During this time no other visions (or thoughts) come to pass. "If [there is] liberation [from forgetfulness *Ed.*], the prana *arouses* the essence[99]." Before the various dreams come in sight, one should try to concentrate on the Light as long as possible. Here, the "liberation" implies the Light Samadhi; if the Samadhi becomes dim or weakened and the yogi is forced to arise from it, through the force of the (moving) prana the flowing-thoughts will also be set in motion; whereupon the dreams also take place. In case no dream whatsoever arises (at this time) the yogi should meditate on the Light without distraction as long as possible.

If the yogi is able to bring forth the Samadhi of Sleep, but not to produce the "Light" through the prana-holding-practice, he may experience the transparency and clearness in the Samadhi of Sleep, but (since it follows not the way of Light Yoga) the Three Voidnesses preceding the sleeping-stage would never appear. Therefore, it by no means can be considered as having the qualifications and significance of the "Light of Sleep." Besides, in the Samadhi of Sleep, the qualified and plentiful experiences of the mirage, smoke, etc., preceding the First Voidness will never come into being, but only those resembling them.

One should acquaint oneself with the two different Lights of the Light of Sleep, i.e., the Light in Experience and the Light in Realization – also the thick and thin Light, or the bright and dim Light. Though many people declare that the thoughtless, lucid, and transparent Samadhi of Sleep is identical with the Light of Sleep, no sufficient reason is found for this claim.

This exposition, based upon the teaching of the "Holy Father and Son" [see last paragraph, Chapter Two *Ed.*], of the Light Yoga with both the instructions on the Light of Daytime and the Light of Sleep, is given here after careful studies and contemplations. Thus one should hold it dear as most valuable instruction.

If one has tried his best to remain in the Light, but, because of the drifting prana is unable to hold on, one may then resort to the special teaching on dream-arisings given in the pith-instruction of *Gsun-adus* of the Marpa School.

CHAPTER NINE

THE TRANSFORMATION YOGA

The ramifications or sub-instructions of the main path are given as follows:

1. The teaching of going above to the pure land – (instructions on the Transformation Yoga).
2. The teaching of entering into another's body (instruction on the Yoga of Entering Another's Body).

The teaching of transforming one's consciousness to the Pure Land, is a special teaching of the Unparalleled [i.e. Anuttara *Ed.*] Tantra. It is found in both the *Tantra of Bde-mchog's Teaching* and that of *Jerdo*, and their common *Tantra Sambhuda;* in the *Tantra of Vajra Dakini*, a special Tantra of Bde-mchog; in the *Two Tantras of Sdom-abyung* (Bde-mchog's teaching) and in the *Admonishment of the Holy Mañjuśri*, etc. If one intends to get well acquainted with the pith-instructions of the Transformation Yoga, one may study these Tantras and their special commentaries. The instructions given here are all based upon these sources, with careful arrangement.

The merit of this practice is stated in the *Tantra of Vajra Dakini:*

"If one has committed the sin of killing a kinsman,
Of slaughtering the Brahmins;
Or has committed the Five Paramount Crimes[100],
Or has stolen or robbed from others for pleasure
All these sins can be cleansed
By practicing this superb teaching.
No evils or sins can ever defile it,

It stays aloof and far apart from all wickednesses of
Saṃsara."

Its advantages are also claimed by the *Tantra of G'a-
sbyor and Gdan-bzhi*. Therefore, this yoga is of utmost
importance and should receive greater attention. These
sources say that this teaching can liberate one from falling
into the miserable path, cleanse one's sins, and bring one
to the happy land.

The time to apply this yoga is instructed by the *Tantra of
Vajra-Dakini* as follows:

"When the time (of death) comes,
This teaching is applied.
If the time (of death) is not near when anyone applies
    the teaching,
He is committing the crime of slaughtering Buddha;
He will certainly fall into hell and be scourged.
Therefore, one should carefully and diligently study the
    signs of death."

This point is also stressed by the *Gdan-bzhi* and the *G'a-
sbyor* – if the yogi uses this teaching at the wrong time, he has
thus murdered the Buddha-like self body. If he has taken
the precepts of Tantra, he is then violating the eighth rule
of the basic precepts of Tantra, and he is exposed to the
danger of falling into hell. Therefore, he should clearly
understand the time factor, and industriously study the
signs of death to forsee the coming of death. When the
signs appear, he should try to prevent it by all possible
means. If everything is done but to no avail, he should
know that it is the right time to apply this teaching. According to the commentary on Gdan-bzhi, *Bhaba Bhadras*,
he should practise this teaching, or make his preparations
six months before the time of death. For this reason one

should carefully study the lines in the books concerning the signs of death.

Furthermore the *Tantra of Gdan-bzhi* says:

"The best condition under which one transforms (his soul)
Is without disease or other illness."

The Transformation Yoga is applied under condition that one has not caught any disease. If the practitioner is caught by disease, he cannot perform the transformation in a perfect way, though he may have tried his utmost.

In the case of an old, miserable man with great sufferings who foresees the coming of his death and intends to leave this world by means of the Transformation Yoga before the time of death comes, it is still forbidden. It is also forbidden in the case of one who suffers from an unbearable sickness. Some ignorant people say that in the former case, the old man is allowed to use the Transformation Yoga (before his time comes).*

The main instruction on the Transformation Yoga consists of two practices. The *Tantra of Vajra* says:

"The foundation of all (feelings) should be purified.
After the purification the transformation from existence
is applied;
Otherwise it will be futile."

"The foundation of all (feelings)" implies that the human body is the foundation or base of all agreeable or disagreeable feelings. (Purification means that through the practice of Heat Yoga the body and mind are purified.) Without purifying the body through practicing the Heat

* To use Transformation yoga to try to circumvent karma is forbidden; it would be absurd to try to do so, for the "escaped" karma would only return in aggravated form later. *Ed.*

Yoga it will be useless and futile to perform the Transformation Yoga. This is said in *Bhaba Bhadras,* because the Tumo practice is the very foundation of Transformation Yoga. The *Tantra of Vajra Dakini* also says:

"By means of the Vase Breathing the door is bound (opened).

Thus, the hole of the door is purified."

The *Tantra of Gdan-bzhi* as well as the *Tantra of Sambhuda* says the same thing. They stress the necessity of having a (tamed) prana for practicing the (Transformation Yoga), only because through practicing the Vase Breathing can the pranas, which run wild toward all organs and gates in the body, be fairly gathered (or tamed). Some people say that, if one reaches the lowest stage of Vase-Breathing practice, one is qualified to perform the Transformation Yoga. This shows their ignorance of the teaching of Tantra.

In performing the Transformation Yoga, all the nine gates of the body[101] except the Golden Gate on [top of the] the head should first be closed to prevent the excape of the consciousness through these gates. The consciousness should be allowed to exit only from the Golden Gate. According to Tantras, these conditions are required to meet the qual ifications of a perfect ground upon which the qualified Tantric yogis may perform the Yoga of Transformation.

Furthermore, a perfect visualization on the exit of consciousness described by the Tantras is required. The procedure of the visualization is profusely described in the *Fourth Book of Transformation Yoga* as well as in the *Book of Transformation Yoga* of the Rngog School. However, the instructions I give here are mostly based upon the verbal instruction from the gurus who primarily follow the teaching of this school.

One may ask, "Upon which deity's body should one practice the Transformation Yoga?" According to the gurus, one may depend on any patron Buddha of his own choosing. Though the *Tantra of G'a-shyor* and *Gdan-bzhi* have pointed out some particular deity for Transformation Yoga together with the instructions on their practices, I shall not introduce them here; for it would take excessive space to explain them.

The Practice of the Transformation Yoga.

First, the yogi visualizes the self-body become the body of the patron Buddha; then visualizes a red *Ah* word at the reproductive center or at the navel center, a dark blue *Hūṃ* word at the Heart Center, a white *Kha* word at the Gate of Purity[102]. Then he should pull up the lower prana (from the reproductive center) to the navel center; thus the *Ah* word is pushed up to the place of the *Hūṃ* word (in the Heart Center); again the *Hūṃ* word is pushed to the *Kha* word. Some say the *Hūṃ* word and *Ah* word should come down and return to their own places once, then rise up again; but I think the first way is simpler and more convenient. One should repeatedly practice this until the signs or symptoms appear. The signs are the feeling of itching, throbbing, etc., at the top of the head.

Thereupon, the yogi may proceed to practice the formal or real Transformation Yoga as follows: Sitting in a crouching posture, grasp the two knees with hands clasped, recite the prayer of Taking Refuge and the prayer of Raising the Bodhi Heart. Then visualize your body become the body of one's patron Buddha; also think that the patron Buddha whose essence is identical with that of your guru, sits in the sky in front of and above your head at a distance of one to six feet. With great earnestness and faith the yogi should pray to him. Then, with a clear visualization of the *Ah* word at the Navel Center, the *Hūṃ* word at the Heart Center, and the *Kha* word at the Pure-Gate Center, the yogi pulls the lower prana to drive up the *Ah* word into the *Hūṃ* word through the Central Channel, and thus the two words are fused in one. Meantime, he should pull up all his strength and say loudly "Ah-hi-ga" many times, until he feels that the *Ah* word has been actually driven into the *Hūṃ* word. Then he says again "Ah-hi-ga" loudly twenty times, and the *Hūṃ* word thus rises to the Throat Center. At this time the yogi should visualize clearly the *Kha* word standing at the Gate of Purity; the gate is open and through it can be seen clearly the firmament as one sees the bright sky through an open window. Then the yogi pulls all his strength together and shouts "Ah-hi-ga" five times; through this force the *Hūṃ* word is ejected (with great speed) from the Gate of Purity and hits right into the Heart Center of the patron Buddha [above your head]. Thereupon, the yogi concentrates his mind in the realm of Non-Thought.

Based on the *Tantra of Gdan-bzhi* as well as the verbal instructions given by gurus is this brief instruction on the Transformation Yoga.

Furthermore, according to the teaching of Tantras and their commentaries, the yogi will gain great profit if he understands the way of meditating on the crown of two sounded letters, of visualizing the two words with the heads of the letters seeing upward and downward; the way of "calling-with-prana" during the upgoing and down-coming performance; and other special superb instructions.

Generally speaking, the teaching of transforming one's consciousness to a felicitous plane, (such as the thirty-three Heavens and the Heavens of Forms in Saṃsara) is of great importance and value; especially, the Tantric Transformation Yoga designed for the qualified Tantric Yogis. With the power of the unique Samadhi, the Tantric yogi is able to close all eight gates and make the consciousness exit through the Golden Gate. If he can keep the (horse-like) prana, upon which the consciousness rides, from running through the eight gates, he can automatically stop the consciousness from escaping through the eight gates. The yogi should know how to use the words to close the gates and control the consciousness, and he should be able to control the prana at the different gates through the Vase Breathing [practice].

It is difficult to find a clear instruction in the books concerning what kind of words should be used to close the gates. However, according to the *Tantra of Sambhoda* and *Man-snye*, only the red *Ah* word like that of the *Ah* at the Navel Center should be used. Some say the best teaching is to use a red *Hūṃ* word instead of *Ah* to close each gate. This saying proves ignorance of the meaning of the Tantra and of the clear instructions about using the word to close all the nine gates, in the *Tantra of Gdan-bzhi* and others.

The instruction of Grong-hjug (House Entering) is also called the instruction in the Yoga of Entering Another's Body. Grong (literally, *city* or *house*), here implies the physical organs of eye, ear, etc., (for they are like houses wherein the consciousnesses dwell). Says the *Sutra of the Paramita Vehicle:* "One's consciousness entering into the not-yet-decomposed corpse of another is called Grong-hjug – Entering into Another's House." This teaching is the unique teaching of the Unparalleled Tantra. It frequently appears in the Mother Tantra, and sometimes in the Father Tantra.*

What is the purpose of practicing this yoga, or what is this teaching for? Who is qualified to practice it? How is the teaching of this Yoga exercised?

The person who practices this teaching, as well as those who practice the Transformation Yoga, must have well obtained the initiation and observed the Tantric precepts in a perfect manner, etc., as required in the practice of the Arising Yoga.

According to Tantra there are three different teachings of the Transformation practices: the special Transformation Yoga; the Teaching of the self-mind (or soul) entering into another's corpse; and the teaching of expelling another's soul from his body so that one's consciousness may enter this body. All these three Transformation practices require, first, the capability of closing the nine gates by words; second, the mastery of Vase Breathing, by means of which all the pranas of different organs are gathered and entered into the Central Channel; third, the mastery of Tumo, whereby the small *Ah*-word of the red-element in the navel center is able to attract and hold the wisdom *Hūṃ* word (which is the rider of the subtle prana) at the Heart Center. This is said in the *Tantras of Vajra Dakini* and of *Gdan-bzhi* and in their common commentary *Bhaba Bhad-ras;* and in the *Tantra of G'a-shyor* and its commentary, the Fruit-Bearing Pith-Instruction.

* Comparable to the Kali and Śiva Agamas respectively of Hindu Tantra. See note 60 and also the discussion of śakta-śakti vs. upāya-prajña in the editorial introduction. — *Ed.*

I believe that in both cases, whether the self-consciousness enters into the corpse or into another's living body, a special prana performance is required in addition to the requirements and qualifications mentioned before [103]. The details may be found in some other sources.

It would be difficult to benefit sentient beings on a great scale with a low-born human body; therefore, it is desirable to have a human body of high class to accomplish the undertaking. Because the possession of a sick, aged, crippled body would handicap self-improvement as well as altruistic deeds, one resorts to the Yoga of Entering Another's Body to procure a fair and healthy body.

According to gurus there are three requirements for practicing this Yoga: first, the person who intends to practice this yoga must have an *infinite compassion* for all sentient beings; he must be absolutely sure that great benefits and boons for sentient beings will be achieved if he performs this yoga; he also must have mastered both prana and mind. A yogi who meets these requirements and conditions may then proceed to a very secluded, sheltered place. He should dispense with all distracted thoughts, keep away from all wordly activities, prepare the offerings, and establish the altar for the patron Buddha. With all these arrangements made, he should then engage himself in meditation under strict Confinement of Contemplation [104].

Then he should prepare a Mandala painted black as the supporting-platform and put a human skull on it. In the center of the human skull a *Hūṃ* word should be clearly written with a white stone (chalk). Visualizing himself become the Patron-Buddha, he then recites and meditates on the prayer of Seven Wishes of Bodhisattva Samantabhadra. Then the yogi visualizes a *Hūṃ* word in the center of the heart, and, when the exhalation goes through the right nostril, he should think the *Hūṃ* word comes out along with the exalted air and enters into and is identified with the *Hūṃ* word in the skull. Meantime the yogi should hold the air outside as long as possible. When he cannot hold it any longer, he slowly takes the air in. Then he exhales and visualizes as before. Continuing this practice for a while, the yogi will see the skull shake, jump and move – these are the signs that will appear.

The yogi may now proceed to the actual transformation of soul. First, he should procure a fresh corpse with no signs of decomposing, not being dead from any injuries or disease; or he may procure a clean and fresh corpse of cattle or any livestock. Then he washes the corpse with clean water, decorates it with pleasing ornaments, and places it well on the Mandala in a sitting position. Then, the yogi visualizes the *Hūṃ* word which symbolizes the mind, both in his own heart and that of the corpse. He then arouses his prana to drive the *Hūṃ* word out through his right nostril and through the corpse's left nostril into the *Hūṃ* word at the Heart Center. If the yogi practices this again and again, the corpse will start to breathe and to regain its senses. When these signs take place, the yogi should know his performance is effective and should (temporarily) stop the practice.

When the yogi is ready to carry out the real performance, he should release himself from the Confinement and go out to find a qualified and fresh corpse, bring it back, and place it on the Mandala facing him. Having decorated the corpse, the yogi then visualizes the self-Yidam-body and lays aside the attachment to the vulgar human body. He then reminds himself that all Dharmas in the cosmos are magic-like and illusory. Now it is time for him to cut off all vulgar, fallacious thought, as well as delusory habitual thinking, and render his body as an offering to the gurus and guards.

With great earnestness, he should pray them to protect him from all evil hindrances and influences. Then the yogi should clearly visualize both himself and the corpse transformed into Patron Buddha and vividly visualize the *Hūṃ* word in the Heart Center of both. Then the yogi contacts the air-gate of the corpse and actuates his prana to drive the *Hūṃ* word in his Heart Center out through his right nostril and into the *Hūṃ* word of the corpse through its left nostril. At this time the yogi should pull up all his strength to aim at the *Hūṃ* word of the corpse with his prana-mind. By means of this exercise, the corpse will begin to breathe and jerk, etc. Whereupon, the yogi's friendly companions should take care of him, foster him with proper food for half a month in a solitary place. Until the yogi can stably live with the new body, he should not appear before people. In order to express his gratitude to the deceased one, the yogi should perform the Offering Rituals, such as the Ritual of Tsa Tsa and the Ritual of Burning Performances. With this new human body, the yogi should devote himself to the welfare of sentient beings on a great and broad scale.

These instructions were given by gurus. Thus, the instruction on the Yoga of Entering Other's body which are based on the genuine contents of (several) Tantras and their commentaries has now been given here without wavering ambiguity.

(Now the important question concerning the rightfulness of performing this yoga will naturally arise in people's minds); [105] if it is sinful to transform one's consciousness to some other consciousness to some other place before the coming of death as admonished in the Instruction on Transformation Yoga, is it not also sinful to perform this Yoga? Though no clear statement answering this question can be found in Tantras, I consider the problem in the light of the following: first, since the performance of this yoga excludes itself from the category of normal death, it cannot be considered a crime of committing suicide, for it does not meet the qualifications of normal death and rebirth; it belongs to none of the regular Four Births of Saṃsara. Though there is a (tiny) intermediate stage between the time the consciousness leaves the body and the time it enters into the other's body, this cannot be considered a qualified Bardo-stage. Besides, in the case of a right performance of this yoga, the yogi has a pure and altruistic wish, and, since his mind aims at Dharma, he cannot be regarded as committing the crime of suicide. If one wants to know more about this topic, one may study the pith-instructions on the Illusory Body in the *Tantra of Gsun-adus*.

Though both the instruction of the Self-Transforming Yoga and the Yoga of Transforming into Others were available in the past, the latter was not given to gurus; therefore, it is not explained here.

CHAPTER TEN

HOW TO IMPROVE THE PRACTICE
IN THE PATH

If one intends to attain the Highest Accomplishment (Buddhahood) in one's lifetime, one should practice both the Arising Yoga and the Perfecting Yoga. Each of them has three different practices: the With-Form-Practice, the Without-Form-Practice, and the Extremely-Without-Form Practice. This is said in the Book of Sgron-gsal *(The Light of the Lamp)*. Here, some explanation of the term "Practice" is needed. The so-called "Practice" [with and without form] means the practice of enjoying all pleasures with a spirit absorbed in the realization of the Dharma-essence [the very heart of Tantric practice, whether Hindu, Taoist, or Buddhist. – *Ed.*]; especially it implies the enjoyment of the negative embodiment. Through this practice on the (excessive) enjoyments, the Enlightenment on the Soleness will be elevated to consummation. The Extremely-Without Form Practice denotes the practice of the Wisdom-Yoga, which is a practice of enjoying the blisses of the negative embodiment*. The other practices imply the Karma Yoga. [Only the Extremely-Without-Form is karma-free.]

These practices can be performed in three different ways: the elaborate way, which is the joyful performance including dancing and singing, etc.; the modest way; and the simplest way. These practices are applied at the beginning

* We feel that "Body of Non-Form" better expresses the meaning here, which points to the Without-Form Practice of the Anuttara Tantra. – *Ed.*

stage of the Illusory Body Yoga practice, and at the time when one wants to attain the Without-Learning-Two-In-One Position from the With-Learning-Two-In-One Position. These are the three times one may carry out the practices. It is for the purpose of planting the Dharma-seed in the mind of sincere disciples that I have mentioned these practices and given all the essential instruction in full. For fear of involving too many words, the foregoing instructions are not given in detail. If one wants them elaborated, one may study and search in the works of the Collective Pith-Instructions (of Gsun-*a*dus).

What happens when the Final Accomplishment comes into being?

Having attained the position of the With-Learning-Two-in-One, one furthers the meditation on the Light Yoga; thus, in time, the dualistic thoughts and manifestations are purified and the absolute Dharmakaya is fully unfolded. The Two-in-One-Illusory Body of the With-Learning is transformed into the Two-in-One-Body of the Without-Learning. As long as the Saṃsara exists, this body will not change or vanish; (for the welfare of sentient beings) this pure body of Buddha will remain.

Here, the two-Hindrances-Free Objective-Light is the immutable Dharmakaya itself. The Subjective-Light is the Wisdom Dharmakaya itself; it is also called the Body of Great Bliss. Coexistent with it is the Body-of-Form, or the Sambhogakaya, which is the (consummated) transformation of the Mind-Prana. These two Bodies are one in essence and two in aspect. This Body-of-Form is identical with the Not-Two-Wisdom-Body [better: "Non-Twofold Wisdom Body" *Ed.*]; this is frequently mentioned by the gurus. Some people say that the Body-of-Form cannot beascribed to (or do not exist in) the realm of Buddha, but only appears through the Karma of sentient beings 'or, more accurately speaking' this Body-of-Form only appears as a reflection from the mind-mirror-of-Karma of sentient beings. They also claim that this Body-of-Form is in essence insensible and non-conscious. Some even say that in the Absolute Accomplishment (or Enlightenment) there is no wisdom whatsoever. One should know that all these sayings are false!

From this Unparalleled Two-in-One Body emanates the supreme Nirmanakaya, and from it are conjured numerous Transformation-Forms.

CHAPTER ELEVEN

TSONG KHOPA'S SUMMARY OF SOURCES

Some say that this teaching (Six Yogas) appears in the first part of the general-contents section of the Book; some that it is in the last part of the Book[106]. The former claim apparently has two mistakes. According to those who avow the latter, there is a commentary as well as a book called *Collective Instructions* written by Marpa; but this seems neither reliable nor convincing. It is also said that there is a book by Marpa containing the instructions of the Six Yogas in both stanza style and prose style. And there is a book called the *Six Yogas of the Diamond Song*. But this is merely an introductory book; it only serves the purpose of sowing the seeds of Pith-Instructions; it cannot bestow great power (to the followers).

The worst sources are those so-called "Six Yogas" texts discovered in the *Dharma of Treasury;* though they are numerous, I can have no confidence whatsoever in them[107].

Marpa (the founder of the Kagyupa school) imparted this teaching to Rngog-ston, Mds'ur-ston, and Milarepa; that made three lineages in the school. Then Milarepa imparted the teaching to the Holy Gambopa and Rechung. From Gambopa this School branched out into many sects, their teachings and practices quite different from one another. This book is written after a thorough study of the different pith-instructions from these sects. The instruction of Heat Yoga is based on the fundamental teachings and the (special) instructions bestowed upon Tilopa [the teacher of Marpa's guru Nāropā *Ed.*] by the Master Tsarayawa, the Black Practitioner.

The Light Yoga is mainly based on the pith-instructions and the available commentary *Wisdom Essence*. In addition to these sources, writungs of the "Holy Father and Son" [two revered and learned lamas who were father and son, with family name of A pags-pa *Ed.*] have been relied upon. The Transformation Yoga and the Yoga of Entering into Another's Body are based not only on the *Tantra of Gdan-bzhi* as mentioned before, but also on the *Tantra Sambhoda* and the *Tantra Vajra Dakini*. Therefore, these instructions are trustworthy, and one may have full confidence in them.

"O, the peerless teachings of Buddha Shakyamuni
That were preached for the good of sentient beings!
Among them, the unparalleled is the Tantra of
    Highest Division,
Including the Mother Tantras and Father Tantras.
Based (mainly) upon the Mother Tantra
The instruction on the Dumo Yoga
With the essential practice of Small *Ah* and Life-Prana
    are given.
It is the path, the teaching that
Leads to the unfoldment of the original Innate Wisdom.
From the skillfully instructed main teaching (of Dumo
    Yoga)
Come the Illusory Body and the Light Yoga of Gsun-
    *a*dus.
Derived from it and based upon it
Are also the Transformation and Entering-Body Yoga
    of Vajra Gdan-bzhi.
These are the famous Six Yogas,
The supreme teachings of the great Masters Tilopa and
    Naropa.
In the Country of Snow this teaching is widespread;
It is practiced by all gifted ones in Tibet:
It is the quintessence of Tantra,
The teaching of profundity, the happiness-bestower!
Urging me to write a book on Six Yogas is Lord Canopy
    of Fame —
He whose crown is adorned with the Three Precious
    Ones;

Through the power of his great merits in the past lives
He now becomes the dominant master of the broad
　　kingdoms.
Because of his sincere request, this book is written.
Also petitioning me to comment on Six Yogas
Is the Reverend Dharma-Brother, Canopy of Merit.
He is the one who has perfectly mastered the Holy
　　scriptures
And absorbed the deep intuitive meditations.
Because of his sincere request, this book is written.
They offered me grains of fine gold and the precious
　　Mandala,
And said to me,
'There are many disciples who yearn for this supreme
　　teaching;
Pray, for their sake, write a book of Six Yogas!'
Thus, with diligence and effort I wrote this book.
It contains the clear instructions and explanations
On all practices and visualizations.
It is trustworthy,
For it is based on the holy writings.
It is a special book, the Book of Three Confidences.
Oh, difficult indeed it is to understand the profound
　　teaching!
And human dispositions vary greatly!
If anyone misunderstands this teaching and finds faults,
I beg the guards and Dakinis
Grant their mercy and pardon him;
Through the merits of this well-spoken instruction,
May all the sentient beings enter into the Unparalleled
　　Vehicle!
Let this teaching spread afar!

Let the supreme path increasingly expand!"

This book is called "The Six Yogas of Naropa, with the Successive Instructions Leading to the Profound Path – the Book with Three Confidences" [i.e. The Book of Threefold Faith – see Note 1 *Ed.*].

Because of repeated requests from the Lord Canopy of Fame (Mi-Dong-grogs-b'a-rgyal-mds'an) and the Reverend Canopy of Merit (Chos-rje-bsod-nams-rgyal-mds'an) I wrote this book. It includes the well arranged instructions on the practice of Heat Yoga, etc., and some explanations on the common teachings, together with the elaborate expositions on each of the special practices (of the Tantric Yogas). This book was written with a pure wish of spreading the Dharma of this school [Gelugpa], low School), which is thriving in this region to a great extent; however, it has not yet reached the full-flourishing state. In consideration of the welfare of many of those who have faith in and admiration for the teaching of this school, this book was written at the Victorious Place Dge-ldan on the Great Hill of the Pasture Land by me, the well-learned Buddhist monk, the renouncer, Good Mind Fame Tsong Khapa of the East [of Eastern Tibet].

May goodness and prosperity thrive!

1 *Three Faiths:* The enumerative terminology of Buddhism becomes very complicated, so that unless one belongs to a particular school it is not always possible to say with certainty what terms like "The Three Faiths" and "The Four Hindrances" refer to. Here it may be presumed, however, that the Three Faiths refer to the disciple's progress in Buddhism through three stages: Veneration (respect for Buddha and practice of the precepts); Understanding (reached by studying Buddhist philosophy); and Realization (highest personal attainment through practice of meditation and other Yogic practices. Likewise in understanding the Six Yogas, the disciple who hears of them, venerates them. Next, he gains the faith of understanding by studying them. Third, he achieves the faith of realization by practicing them. Hence, the relevance of calling the Six Yogas also *The Book of the Three Faiths* [or *The Book of Threefold Faith Ed.*].

2 *Vajra Dhara:* (Rdor-rje-chang, in Tibetan) lit. "Thunderbolt Holder." This is the Buddha from whom all Tantric teachings originated, according to tradition.

3 *Supreme Vehicle:* Tantric teachings, the Diamond Vehicle (Vajrayana). The term "Tantricism" is not used in Buddhist countries, instead the terms Hinayana, Mahayana, and for the esoteric teachings, *Vajrayana*, are used.

4 *Paramita Vehicle:* the Bodhisattva's Path; the esoteric teaching of the practice of Mahayana Buddhism.

5 *True Word Vehicle:* Vajravana (Buddhist Tantricism); the esoteric teaching. [Literally "Thunderbolt Vehicle", associated with doctrines of sudden enlightenment and the Short Path to liberation for those who take the Kingdom by storm. The cognate Tibetan term rDo-rje connotes "Diamond," i.e. pure and irresistible. – *Ed.*]

6 *Lama Rngog-pa:* One of the chief disciples of Marpa (See Biography of Milarepa).

7 *Tantra of Two Forms* (Tibetan Stags-gnyis): The main Tantra of Hevajra.

8 The implication of this quotation is that the student should advance step by step from the practices of a novice serving

his guru until he understands the Doctrine of the Middle Way (Madhyamika).

9 *Goddess: Lit.* the Sky-traveling-lady (Dakini), female angelic deity.

10 *Three Gradual Paths of Lam Rim:* Lam Rim (Steps to Buddhahood) was Tsong Kapa's great contribution to Buddhist literature, in which he pointed out the necessity for a *gradual* progress of the disciple, beginning with the Lower Path (observation of ethics); through the Middle Path (understanding of the Four Noble Truths); to the Highest Path (observation of the Bodhisattva's Vow and Precepts).

11 *Adisha* (A. D. 980–1052): Famous Indian Buddhist who journeyed to Tibet and founded the Bgha-gdams-b'a School.

12 According to Buddhist belief, the human embodiment is the best in which to work for liberation, since the heaven-body is too blissful, whereas lower births or embodiments are too full of suffering.

13 *Dhayana:* Buddhist term for a special psychic state of absolute concentration.

14 Terms referring to the illusory, non-real, and void nature of Samsaric existence.

15 The chief aim of Mahayana Buddhism, to develop the Heart-for-Bodhi, includes two aspects: (1) the wish or pure desire for this state, called "Wish-for-Heart-of-Bodhi"; and (2) the vow to practice to achieve this aim. "Practice-for-Heart-of-Bodhi."

16 *Eight Non-Freedoms:* Conditions in which it is impossible to practice Buddhism, such as falling into the realms of hell, hungry ghosts, or animals; being born at a time when there is no Buddha, or before a Buddha begins preaching, or in a country where there is no Buddhist teaching; lacking the intelligence to understand Buddhism; becoming absorbed in the Samadhi of non-form.

17 *Habitual-Thinking:* The clinging of ego and the kleśas, is the cause of all sufferings and Samsara, and has its roots in the peculiarly human ceaseless, and automatic type of thinking (mentation).

18 *Mes-sdon and Ngo-sdon:* Two chief disciples of Milarepa. Ngo-sdon is mentioned in Milarepa's biography.

19 *Arising Yoga:* The first stage of Yoga; Perfect Yoga is the final or complete stage. The purpose of the Arising Yoga is to bring the mind and body to perfect control and to set the mind upon the practice of *visionary* concentration. The Perfect Yoga emphasizes the transformation of the body and mind. It is a final psycho-physical practice.

20 *Pith-Instructions:* The essential practical key directions for Yogic practice communicated privately from Guru to disciple.

21 *Hevajra and Bde-mchog:* names of two important Tantric Buddhas.

22 *Buddha's Sons:* The Bodhisattvas.

23 *The Fundamental Precepts:* Contain Fourteen Rules; the Secondary Precepts are the so-called Eight Transgressions.

24 According to the philosophy of reincarnation, in endless cycles of rebirths every sentient being is related as parent to child.

25 The incantation of Vajrasattva, which comprises one hundred words.

26 *The Two Acts:* Offering self to Buddha, and offering self for the liberation of sentient beings.

27 *Four Mighty Ways:* (1) Public confession of one's past wrong-doings; (2) Taking an oath never to repeat these wrong acts; (3) Performance of meritorious deeds; (4) Meditation on *Śūnyatā*.

28 The sin, sinner, and act of sin are likened to wheels turning about and keeping the world of Saṃsara in manifestation.

29 Offerings are more than acts of reverence. According to the law of Cause and Effect, one reaps merits through sowing offerings. The more enlightened the recipient, the greater the blessing; hence, the Buddhas and Gurus are the best Fields of Merits for the disciples.

30 *Six Buddhas:* In most Tantric mandalas these are deities of the four directions and of the center, together with the all-en compassing primordial Buddha Rdo-rje-chang, making six in all.

31 The translator does not agree with Tsong Kapa's reasoning here, since it implies that a Buddha may refuse to accept a sincere offering. This would mean that the Buddha could be less than all-compassionate, an impossibility. [The sense of the text, however, rather appears to be not that the Buddha would refuse to accept any offering, but that there is no necessity that the Buddha will or should make a special miraculous appearance in a personal nirmanakāya (body of transformation) to do so, when the yogi's guru, who is already personally accessible, can act as just such a vehicle or channel. – *Ed.*]

32 *Mandal:* a bowl-like utensil, symbol of the universe, which is offered to Buddha. The treasure in it are symbols of the most perfect wealth and gifts of heaven and earth.

33 *The Inner Offerings and Secret Offerings:* The Inner Offerings are the bliss and enlightenment produced in the Tantric meditation – the meditation with breathing and physical exercises. The Secret Offerings are the highest bliss and ecstasy produced by the Third Initiation.

34 *The Three Vajras:* The perfecting of body, speech, and mind. *Vajra* may be translated as *Diamond*, meaning the strongest most precious; here, it means the highest perfection.

35 *All the Gates:* all the pores of the body, in addition to the nine chief gates – two eyes, two ears, two nostrils, the mouth, the anus, and the sex organ.

36 *Subtle defilements:* According to Mahayana Buddhism these are the subtle, or fine, *Clinging of Dharma*, only to be destroyed in the Eight, Ninth and Tenth *Bhumis* in the advanced stage of the Bodhisattva's path. (See *Avatansaga Sutra and Yogacara Bhumi.*)

37 These names are the title of the sub-schools or branches of Kagyutpa (the White School, or the School of Marpa.)

38 This quotation from the *Tantra of G'ye-rdo-rje* is incomplete, being only a part or the original stanza. It therefore can be given many different interpretations.

39 *The Tantric Yogi:* The original text is *Brtul-zugs-chans,* meaning literally "the one with oath."

40 *The Yoga of Forms and Non-Forms:* This is not a perfect but
an expressive translation. The Tibetan term *Spros-pa* means
"Nonsense" or "Play-Words" which implies that all the conceptions and patterns of human thought are relative and
illusory; they are "play-words" when applied to reality.
For convenience, the translator has used the term "Yoga of
Forms," because in the practice of Arising Yoga one cannot
free oneself from conceptualism and symbolism. All visualizations, recitations, and prayers practiced in the Arising
Yoga have form, while Mahamudra or the Yoga of Non-
Forms transcends all these practices.

The reader may consider "The Yoga of Away-From-the
Play-Words" and "The Yoga with Play-Words" as alternative translations.

41 *Four Castes:* the four castes of India.

42 *Four Periods:* Morning, noon, afternoon, and evening. Here
Tsong Kapa's commentary is not explicit. The translator
presumes that he means that the Yogi meditates on a different part of the body (corresponding to the Five Buddhas
and their adornments) during each of the four periods.

43 *"Sketchy Visualization":* a general, non particularized mind-
picture of the tutelary deity.

44 *Tutelary Pride:* to cure the Saṃsaric Pride-of-Ego, Tantricism teaches the yogi to expand instead of abandon, as
Hinayana Buddhism taught, this pride to a cosmic scale — to
the identification of one's self with Buddha, this being the
highest pride of all.

45 *Superb Visions:* When the Yogi reaches this stage he no
longer views the world and its objects in the ordinary,
common, Saṃsaric way but sees the outer world as the
Palace-Beyond-Measure and himself as the tutelary Buddha.

46 *Bodhi-heart* means in this case, the male life-force or semen.
Pad symbolizes the stability and the union of the two forces
(male and female).*

* [The translator here, we feel, is imposing a very restricted
interpretation on the text, which may apply just as well to

274

47 *Mind-Functions:* Buddhism distinguishes between the mind and its activity. Mind is that which acts, but the functions are the different ways in which this mind manifests. According to Yogacara, the mind or the No. 6 Consciousness has 51 mind functions.

48 *The eighteen dhatus* (groups): The six outer-objects, the six sense-organs, and the six consciousnesses.

49 *Ayatanas:* The six places where the consciousnesses abide and the six objects observed.

50 *Medrepa:* The Guru of Marpa, an accomplished Indian Yogi.

51 The philosophies of these schools are very complicated. Because of the limitation of space, the translator cannot explain all their differences here.

52 This is Tson Kapa's view and does not reflect that of Tibetan scholars in general.

53 *Innate Wisdom:* The perfect wisdom of Buddhahood, which is not made by humans but is inborn in every sentient being.

54 This complicated conception is unique in Tsong Khapa's philosophy. Tsong Khapa's definition of the self-nature is very peculiar; his philosophy of Middle-way is greatly different from those of the old schools and is refuted [rather, "opposed," for the Middle Way doctrine's meaning is really not different from Mahamudra] by many outstanding scholars of these schools. Since it takes a great deal of careful thought and study to understand Tsong Khapa's philosophy and how it differs from that of the old schools, the translator believes that it is not wise to explain the different views here briefly, for that would definitely lead to misunderstanding. It is the wish of the translator to write an essay on this topic at some later date.

a female yogi, who also has Bodhi Heart. This term actually refers to the inner love-power which is released or "melted" by "the taming of prana." It is by no means simply to be conceived in any naive physical sense, which would succeed only in mis-defining it as a false limitation. The same is to be said of *Pad. — Ed.*]

55 Here is shown Tsong Khapa's "timidness" on Śūnyatā, and his materialistic view is clearly reflected*.

56 *Rtsa* in Tibetan, *Nadi* in Sanskrit. All the tubular structures of the human body, including the nerves, capable of transforming the fluids and energies of the body. In the text this term is translated usually as *nerve* or *nerves*. [See also Part I, Ch. VII, Note 13. *Ed.*]

57 Literal translation would be "enables me to become Buddha in eight lives in the future."

58 Naropa held a professorship in an Indian college-monastery that had four doors. He held the office of guardian of the North Door.

59 Lacking Marpa's original text, it is felt that the meaning of the Tibetan is substantially conveyed by the three English terms given (barring any esoteric meaning they might have carried and that is now lost).

60 The Father Tantra is one division of the highest, or Annutara Tantra, in which emphasis is on the Skill [*upāya* in the sense of perfect Love's boundless means to aid. *Ed.*] Teachings. The other division, called the Mother Tantra by Tibetan scholars, is that which emphasizes the Wisdom [*prajñā*, in the sense of transcendental wisdom. *Ed.*] Teachings.

61 "Light" is the term used to symbolize the transparent nature of the pure consciousness. This consciousness has, however, many degrees, hence many terms are used to describe these gradations and manifestations of consciousness, such as the Original or Mother Light, the Light-of-Sleep, Light-of-Death, and Light-of-Bardo.

* We cannot agree with the translator here. Tsong Khapa at this point is simply referring to the error of the Nihilistic Extreme (see note 95). The *Anuttara Tantra* (which Tsong Khapa follows, thus being on no account a materialist, as the very next paragraph in the text also confirms) very explicitly states that to reduce all things to non-existence is as wrong as to affirm naively the ultimate reality of their phenomenal existence. The Śūnyatā is not in question at all here. – *Ed.*

62 Roma and Rg'yng-ma: the Right and Left Channels.

62a *gTum-mo:* Tibetan name for the Heat-Yoga. *Ed.*

63 Tantrism provides two types of teachings. The Skill
   Teachings instruct in those methods used to carry the yogi
   beyond the habitual patterns of human thought so that he
   may grasp that real beyond thought, the Pure Consciousness. The Wisdom Teachings begin with the mind to penetrate beyond it to the Realm of Pure Consciousness. [Such
   skill is technically called *thabs. Ed.*]

64 Here, Tsong *Khapa* wishes to emphasize the differences between the blisses produced by the experiences of ordinary
   meditation and those produced by Tantric meditation.

65 *Brave Ones (Dpao Wo* in Tibetan): The male heavenly beings who practice Tantricism.

66 In tantric meditation, the yogi visualizes himself as becoming the Patron Buddha or yidam; he is no longer of human
   form.

67 The special belt wrapped around the body to keep it in the
   right posture for meditation.

68 This is Tsong Kapa's own view which is refuted by Gamaba
   VIII of the White School.

69 *Two pranas:* the up-going air and the down-going air; one
   negative and the other positive.

70 There are a great number of pranas in the body of many
   different natures and functions. In the past, thousands of
   different pranas were named and classified. Today there still
   exists well-defined knowledge of fifty or sixty pranas, but
   most of the traditional prana-knowledge has been lost.

71 *Two lower gates:* the anus and urethra.

71a *Tur Sel Prana:* The down-going Prana.

72 *Great Symbol Thig-le:* A commentary on a Tantric book.

73 There are various degrees of the Melting Bliss. Here, "disqualified" refers to a lower, more mundane, bliss, rather
   than the highest actual Melting Bliss.

74 *Peaceful-Mind:* This refers to a special system of Tantric
   teahing given by the *Gsan Adus Tantra.* "Peaceful-Mind" is
   an expedient translation of a Tibetan term (Sems Dben)
   which can be translated variously.

75 There are various levels of delusory thoughts to which sentient beings are subject. The crude delusory thoughts such as resentment, anger, and pleasure are easily recognized and felt by all conscious beings as well as by those seeking enlightment. However, Buddhism says that freedom from these gross illusory thoughts does not result in enlightenment, since there are deeper, more subtle illusory thoughts in sentient beings of which they are ordinarily unaware but which are the source of bondage. These must be struggled with and eliminated before enlightenment is obtained.

76 *Two-in-One-with-Learning* refers to all these teachings provided for the instruction and enlightenment of those who have progressed up to the stage just before Buddhahood. *Two-in-One-without-Learning* refers to the stage of final enlightenment, Buddhahood, in which nothing remains to be learned.

77 The Tibetan words *Snod* and *Bjud* [pronounced "nu" and "ju". *Ed.*] mean not only the "Sentient beings" and the "Universe" but also "the supporter" and "that which is supported" — implying the idea of the subjective and the objective.

78 *Two Mandalas:* Here, Tsonkapa does not clearly state which Mandalas he refers to. Perhaps he means the Samaya Mandala and Wisdom Mandala. See footnote 6 of Chapter IV (Initiation of Hayagriva) on the "Samaya and Wisdom Buddhas."

79 The original text uses the term Dharma, which has the several meanings of existence, objects, beings, becomings, Perceptions, etc.

80 and 81. These statements reflect the typical thought of Tsogn Khapa's own philosophy, according to which there is a Voidness to be realized and a (Reality) Voidness to be observed and contemplated, even from the viewpoint of the Absolute Realm (the final transcendental truth). The Old Schools declare that while in the Mundane Category it is permissible to say that there is a giver and a receiver, a Voidness to meditate upon, and one who meditates, etc.,

from the viewpoint of the Absolute Realm there is no Voidness to be realized, nor anyone to realize this Voidness. As stated in the Diamond Sutra by Gotama Buddha, himself:

> "If anyone says, 'I see Buddha',
> If anyone says, 'I hear the preaching of Buddha',
> He treads a vicious path and will never behold Buddha."

Also in the same Sutra:

> "Because there is no Wisdom to be attained, [i.e., because the Buddha knew this *Ed.*]
> Buddha said, 'I attained Wisdom'."

82 This statement reflects Tsong Khapa's philosophy of Voidness to the effect that, briefly, "all conceptions are Void (Empty)" but that beings, themselves, exist.

83 Main-meditation Stage: The period in meditation when the yogi is concerned only with the central object of his meditation-practice in contrast to the After-meditation Stage when he is engaged in daily activities while, nevertheless, keeping his meditation experience in mind.

84 The meaning of this sentence is not entirely clear. The translator presumes that a solitary, isolated place is recommended as being most conducive to the success of this yogic practice.

85 Tantra: This term may refer to a Tantra, a commentary on a Tantra, or to some other book.

86 Perception-of-Mind: (Tib. Snang-wa). Tibetan terms have many meanings; this the reader should keep in mind. In this case, not only 'perceptions' are meant but any subjects, objects, or visions created or apprehended by the mind.

87 The absorbing process: The sinking of the different consciousnesses into one fundamental consciousness during the process of death, enlightenment, the Main-Meditation Stage, etc.

88 Bardo: The intermediate stage between life and death.

89 *Beings of Non-Intermission:* This refers to the most virtuous beings and the most sinful beings. Both classes, because of their very strong Karma, are said to have no Bardo experience but, instead, reincarnate immediately.

90 Since Tsong Kapa's commentary was designed for Tibetan scholars, the quotations are often incomplete, for it was presumed that the readers were familiar with the various Tantric texts, or had access to the texts. At the time of this translation, these texts were not available to the translator; therefore, it has proved most difficult to translate and comment upon these scattered, fragmentary stanzas.

91, 92 These statements reflect the typical polemic and pedantic characteristics of Tsong Kapa and many other Tibetan scholars who have been busily engaging in controversial argumentations on trifles and matters of secondary importance in the past few centuries. Except for Mahgi (the great woman philosopher of Tibet) and a handful of scholars, few of them had a creative mind capable of producing a new philosophy like the glorious teaching of Hwayan and Zen Buddhism of China. [We do not feel Tsong Khapa's explanations here so useless as the translator alleges and suspect that a bit of understandable partisanship of his own has colored his views here. See too p. 244 note. – *Ed.*]

93 *"Lazy man's teaching"*: In comparison with other teachings, the Bardo Yoga is much easier and faster for attaining Buddhahood; hence the nickname.

94 *The four births of Saṃsara:* (1) the metamorphosis-born; (2) the egg-born; (3) the womb-born; (4) the wet-born.

95 *Realistic and nihilistic extremes* (or the Realistic and Nihilistic Views): According to Buddhism most of the philosophies and religious beliefs in the world are either "realistic" or "nihilistic." Realistic Views are those philosophies and beliefs that assert the absolute existence of beings, god, retribution, etc. Nihilistic Views are those philosophies that do not accept the existence of soul, reason, causation, and the like. Both of these extremes are erroneous, says Buddhism; as a matter of fact, these two *clingings* are basic causes of Saṃsara. The right view is the view that transcends both extremes; namely, the Middle Way Doctrine.

96 *Unparalleled Vehicle:* The Highest Division of Tantra, Anuttara Tantra. [This appellation is a term used by the Madhyamika apologists themselves. Many would disagree. See the

discourse on the *Gotra* concept in the Introduction as well as the previous footnote in the text.] *Ed.*

97 A little bit presumptuous in the translator's opinion.

98 This paragraph is very confusing. Either Tsong Khapa himself made the mistake by quoting this sentence that does not appear in the preceding paragraph, or the negligence of the Tibetan book printer caused the mistake. [The sentence *is* mentioned and here we have straightforward commentary. See our footnote on page 247.] *Ed.*

99 Here is another incongruous statement about the quotation. The sentence that appeared in the foregoing paragraph was "Yaṅ grol ba na rluṅ gis raṅ bzin rnyeg de." But here Tsong Kapa quotes it as "Yaṅ grol ba rluṅ gis raṅ bzin gyos te." The meaning and implications of these two sentences are completely different. Since the original text of the quoted matter is not available at present, the translator has no sure way to correct this mistake. [See editor's note to note 88 and text. We disagree with the translator that there is any essential difficulty here, the reference to the quotation existing and being uniquely determinable.]

100 *Five Paramount Crimes:* (1) matricide; (2) patricide; (3) killing an Arhat (Buddhist saint); (4) causing disunion or division among the priesthood; (5) malignantly causing Buddha to bleed.

101 *Nine gates of the body:* two eyes, two nostrils, two ears, rectum, urethra, top of head.

102 *Gate of Purity:* another name for the Golden Gate or the gate of the head.

103 According to Tibetan lamas, the essential teachings of the Yoga of Entering Another's Body was lost in Tibet. It was lost after the death of Dharmadorje, son of Marpa. See the biography of Marpa. [See Tsong Khapa's own statement in the last paragraph of Chapter 9.]

104 *Confinement of Contemplation:* Any Buddhist who wants to practice meditation in a serious manner must retreat to solitude or strictly confine himself in hermitage for his devotion; he makes a vow not to go beyond the boundary

of his room, hermitage, or the like for a certain period of time in confinement to practice meditation.

105 The translator feels that it is necessary to add this sentence to make the text understandable.

106 This sentence is not clear, nor did the writer clearly state which book he referred to. [The *Book of the Collected Pith-Instructions* appears to be meant. See in the text five paragraphs above, p. 263. *Ed.*]

107 Here Tsong Khapa discredits the authenticity of the scriptures of the Nyingmapa. In the translator's opinion Tsong Khapa fails to remember that the entire Mahayana Buddhism, both Paramitayana and Vajrayana — the teaching that he himself follows — was based on the very Sutras and Tantras that have an accountable historical origin, so to speak; for most of the Sutras and Tantras of Mahayana were "brought out" through divine revelations. This is exactly the Nyingmapa way — receiving the teaching from the Heavenly Treasures. According to the Nyingmapa Lamas, the teachings from the visible human lineage are by no means better or more reliabie than the teachings received from revelation. As a matter of fact, the latter are much superior, for they are closer, clearer, "warmer," and more direct. Besides, there are less human prejudice and dogmatic hocus-pocus involved.

APPENDIX

THE VOW OF MAHĀMUDRĀ

Buddhism seldom positively asserts what is the Truth.*
Rather, it teaches the truth-seekers to understand and to
explore their own minds, for in the quest of Reality nothing is more important or befitting for the seeker than to
know *what the mind actually is* rather than to know only *what
mind knows of* – the so-called knowledge and objects known
by the mind. Reality is the object known, but the first step
is to understand the knower of this Reality.** Whatever
one's beliefs, opinions, and thoughts, all these depend on
the mind and come through the mind, for there is no
possibility for one to escape from the sphere of mind in
thinking or knowing.

After waking from sleep, each day of our lives begins
with an awareness of 'I'. Decartes observed, "I think,
therefore I am" – which seems logical to common sense
since it feels the necessity for a knower in order for anything to be known. But whether or not this 'I' really exists
and is substantial is debatable, says Buddism. Although
Buddhism denies the reality of the ego, it does not absolutely deny the reality of the "awareness," or thinking-pro-
cess (at least in Mahayana Buddhism). Therefore, it is of
the utmost importance to know what this "awareness"
or "mind" is.

* The translator must here be restricting himself to the
skeptical method of Nagārjuna and some schools of Zen, for
there exist very explicit Buddhist cosmological and psycholo-
gical texts, both in Hinayana and Mahayana. – *Ed.*

** The translator overlooks here the ancient Upaniṣadic dic-
tum, which became part of the essence of the much later Zen:
O Maitreya, the knower cannot be known! *Ed.*

Buddhist schools employ two different approaches in the study of mind. The Vaibhasika and Yogacara may be said to use the "horizontal" approach, i.e. studying the mind analytically by mapping its divisions, characteristics, functions, etc.. including the 8 Consciousnesses and mental functions of the different stages of Samadhis. The Tantric [Buddhist] schools and Zen,* however, employ what may be called a "vertical" approach – urging the student to disregard the analysis of functions and peripheral knowledge of mind and instead to penetrate directly and deeply to the very foundation of mind-essence.

To clarify for the readers the Buddhist view of these two approaches in studying the mind, the translator will explain them through applying what may be called the "three-dimension system" to the mind: The first dimension – function; the second dimension – the form; the third dimension – the essence-of-mind.

The first dimension (Chinese "*Yung*"; Tibetan "*Rtsl*") means "activity" or "function"; the second dimension, (Chinese *Shang;* Tibetan *Rnam Pa*) refers to the "form" or "characteristics." The third dimension (Chinese *Ti;* Tibetan *Ngo wo*) points to the essence or real nature of mind. The manifestations in the first dimension of mind – the peripheral or outer realm of mind – are comparatively easy to comprehend. The second dimension, the form and characteristics, is not easily understood without a certain kind of study or investigation. The third dimension denotes the transcendental aspect of mind or the Dimension of Beyond.

The function of mind refers to the capability of the

* Growing out of more of a Mādhyamika emphasis. *Ed.*

mind to know or to be "aware" of the Five Objects (of sight, sound, touch, taste, feeling, smell), of Dharma (all objects, existences, and ideas, etc.), and if we include the two obscure consciousnesses (No. 7 and No. 8) their functions are to become aware of the illusory ego (in the case of No. 7) and the "form of all Dharmas" (in the case of No. 8). Also, the function of mind refers to the emotional manifestations of mind in being able to express love,* hate, anger, joy, etc. This realm, of the functioning-aspect-of-mind or the first dimension of mind, is very obvious and immediately known by all. Now, the second dimension — the form or characteristics of the mind — refers to the awareness** of the mind, or more clearly, the "awaring-aspect-of-the-mind". This "awaring-aspect-of-mind" is found in all the Eight Consciousnesses, though some consciousnesses (such as No. 8, the Alaya) are not as sharply aware as the mind-consciousness or the eye-consciousness.

Although this "awareness' continually takes place in the mind of every individual, seldom is the individual conscious of the "awareness" itself but is rather primarily conscious of the objects of the awareness. To become "aware" of the "awareness" requires some study and effort. Holding onto the "awareness" for long periods during meditation will in

---

*Not the correct word here, merely "affection" being meant; (see our note to stanza 15) the word "mind" in the same line could also be bettered by "consciousness", "mind" having too intellectualistic a connotation. *Ed.*

** The editor here assumes responsibility for this term throughout, having suggested it to the translator, in several discussions preceding the writing of this essay, as a better one in this context than "consciousness," quoting to him the editor's definition of *mind* as "that which orders awareness." The awareness is thus more primal than the ordering. — *Ed.*

time produce a change in the function and pattern of the 8 Consciousnesses and a *relative* transcendental accomplishment will be achieved. According to Buddhism, the final transcendental accomplishment – the perfect Buddhahood – will only be reached through the realization of the Void-nature of the "awareness." The frequently used terms in Mahamudra – "brightness" and "light" – refer to the "evolved-awareness" of the mind, while the "Void," "non-existent," and "non-creating" refer to the "root-nature" of awareness. This realm of the "Void-bright" is the essence of mind, here – the third dimension of the mind. In short, the essence of mind, as taught in Mahamudra, is the "void-bright" or "awareness without subject-object".

Thus the teaching of Mahamudra disregards the first dimension of mind and even does not concern itself much with "awareness" but strives to cut through the Saṃsaric "awareness" which stems from the subject-object pattern of thought.

To completely realize the essence-of-mind is by no means an easy task. It requires years and *lives* of study and effort. One may ask, Why is it so difficult if the Buddha-nature is inherent in one's mind? What prevents this realization is the *force* of our "habitual thinking." On a small scale this bondage may be likened to that of some childhood habit or obsession which, although we know it is illusory and irrational, nevertheless grips us and influences our thinking and behavior because of early, deep-set conditioning. It is much the same in the case of our "endeavor for enlightenment"; though the Void-nature of mind is somewhat glimpsed or even realized, this does not permanently eliminate habitual thoughts which have been operating through immeasurable lifetimes in the past.

Therefore, Mahamudra and Zen can never be considered merely philosophy or art, for they are actually the most serious teachings of the Buddhist religion. They are teachings of liberation* and should not be abused, as Zen ha- recently been in the Occident, by being made a subject of vain talk or subtle speculations as though they were only a game of the mind.

The reader will discover that the opening stanzas of *The Vow* express the religious and spiritual tradition of Mahamudra. The first five stanzas present the fundamental principles and the necessary "wishes" of the Buddhists. The author of *The Vow* is Garmapa III (1284–1339) a very great authority and accomplished yogi whose numerous writings include *The Profound Inner Meaning Of Tantrism*, considered by Tibetan scholars the greatest work on the subject. *The Vow* is recited by the White School as a daily prayer.

Although this Vow is comparatively short, ilt contains the majority of the essential teachings of Mahamudra. In Tibet, there exists quite a body of books and commentaries explaining this Vow. At present these works are not available; therefore translator has supplied a short commentary to accompany the stanzas; also. Also, since the original text was not available, the present translation was made from the Chinese text that the translator had previously made from the Tibetan.

The translator is confident that this *Vow of Mahamudra* is one of the highest teachings of Tibetan Buddhism and

* They become such only when linked to a definite practice of tantric yoga type. See also our remarks in the footnotes on pages 244 and 296. — *Ed.*

firmly believes it will contribute much to the search by psychologists and religionists for a deeper understanding of man's essential nature.

EDITOR'S NOTE

Mahāmudrā (Tib. p'yag-rgya-chen-po) means literally "the great attitude or symbolic gesture". The term derives from the Hindu Tantra (as *śri* or *mahāyantra*) and the subsequent Buddhist Tantra of North India. One writer of that school, Advayavajra, in his *Čaturmudrā*, refers to Mahāmudrā in very much the same way that Śakti – as ultimate Divinity as *Goddess* – is referred to in higher treatises of the Hindu Tantra: "She is not an object subject to time... she combines saṃsāra and nirvāṇa; her substance is universal Love; she is the unique essence of the Innate Transcendent Bliss."

THE VOW OF MAHĀMUDRĀ

By Garmapa Rinchen Dorje

With Commentary (in smaller type)
by the translator and
notes by the editor

1

I pray to the Guru, to the Yidam, and to those holy be-
  ings in the Mandala,
I pray to the Buddhas and to their Sons (Bodhisattvas)
  in the Three Times and in the Ten Directions,
Remember me, have compassion and pity on me,
Bless with accomplishment my wishes.

First, according to the traditions of Buddhist Tantric ritual,
a supplication is offered to one's teacher (who is considered
more important than the Buddhas), next to one's patron Buddha, then to the Darginis, Guardians, and other beings of the
Mandala who grant protection and certain powers to the yogi.
This supplication to the esoteric or Tantric lineage is followed
by one to the esoteric lineage of the Buddhas and Bodhisattvas
in the past, present, and future, and in all directions of space.

2

The pure action of my body and my mind
My virtuous deeds and those of all sentient beings
Are like clear streams flowing from the Snow Mountain
  — devoid of the defilements of the Three Circles
May they flow freely into the great ocean —
  the ocean of the Buddha's Four Bodies.

The pure action of body and mind and the virtuous deeds of sentient beings exist (pure in essence) only if one realizes that the action, the doer, and the receiver (The Three Circles) are alike empty and void. The unimpeded realization of this enables one to merge with (obtain) the Four Bodies of Buddha, or the three-in-one — the Dharmakaya, the Sambhogakaya, the Nirmanakaya, in the all-encompassing (Tantric) Body of Universal Essence.

3

Until I attain the Four Bodies of Buddha,
May even the name of Samsaric miseries ans sins
Be unheard in all my future lives
While I enkoy the happy Dharma-Oceans.

It is a long journey from sentient being to Buddhahood. Even a diligent and well-gifted person, after strenuous efforts, may not attain Buddhahood in one lifetime, even though he depends on Mahamudra which is considered an "Abrupt" or "Sudden Enlightenment" teaching like that of Zen. Therefore, in Buddhist countries, people are made mindful of this and taught to pray for auspicious conditions and favorable environments in their future incarnations.

4

May faith, intelligence, diligence and leisure,
Good Gurus and the essential teachings come to me,
May I practice rightly without stumbling and hin-
    drances —
The blessings of Dharma filling my future lives.

Mahamudra is not just philosophical. Without faith, intelligence, diligence, favorable environment, and skilled teachers there would be no base for its study and practice and no result for sentient beings still existing in the realm of causation.

5

The Holy and Wisdom reckonings liberate me from
  ignorance
The pith-instructions destroy my dark doubts forever
Through the light from meditation, vividly and unmis-
  takenly, I behold Reality
Increase, O Light of the Three Wisdoms!

Buddha taught that to judge rightly one should rely on the
admonishments of the Sutras and on one's own innate reason
(the Holy and Wisdom reckonings). By not leaning blindly on
just one or the other, one is less likely to err.

Some doubts can be dispelled through intellectual reasoning,
but more subtle and deeply intrenched doubts cannot be eliminated through reasoning or study of the Sutras. These can only
be destroyed by the "pith-instructions" – the clear, precise,
practical instructions given by one's own Guru.

The real nature of mind can best be compared to the transparent brightness of physical light. Here, however, the word
"light" is also used in a symbolic aspect to refer to the experience of the Three Wisdoms of the Foundation (the undevel-
oped Buddha-nature in every sentient being), of the Path (the
partially realized Buddha-nature from meditation practice), and
of the Fruit (or full enlightenment).

6

The Root-Principle is the Two Truths – the absence of
  the concrete and the null views
The superb Path is the Provisions – without either the
  exaggerating or minimizing views
The Fruit is the Two Benefits of neither Nirvana or
  Samsara
In future life, may I meet such right teachings.

These three terms – Root or Foundation, Path, and Fruit – are frequently used terms to explain the complete philosophy and procedure of Buddhism, though in Hinayana, general Mahayana, and Tantric Buddhism the terms Root, Path, and Fruit are applied differently. Here, the author points out that the basis or "Root" of Mahamudra is the view which transcends Yes and No, which goes beyond the truth of either existence or non-existence. The Path of Mahamudra is knowing the mind in its essence without either adding or deducting anything to its original nature. The Fruit is Buddhahood, the realization which transcends the concepts of both Nirvana and Sansara. This Fruit is expressed in the Two Benefits – blessings accruing to oneself and blessings bestowed on others.

7

The Essence of Mind is the Two-in-One – the void and
    radiant original source,
Mahamudra, the Diamond-Practice, is the Purifier
The Purified are the flickering and insubstantial Blind-
    ness and Defilements
May I attain the immaculate Dharmakaya, the purified
    Fruit.

Mahamudra is called the "Diamond-Practice" because it is held to be the *strongest* antidote for delusory thoughts and worldly desires. To the sentient beings the Blindness (ignorance) and Defilements (desires) appear real and substantial, but the enlightened being knows them as insubstantial and non-existent.

8

The View of Mahamudra lies in neither adding nor de-
    ducting from the nature of mind
Being mindful of this, (the View) without distraction,
    is the root-action of Mahamudra
Of all meditations, this is the highest practice

294

Let me always find this right teaching of the View,
    Action, and Practice.

To understand the nature of mind is easy if one can recognize
it without making any mental effort, and *grasp it instantaneously
as it is at this very moment*. The practice of Mahamudra lies in the
constant awareness of this view. Other teachings using visualization, mantras, and bodily and prana exercises must all employ
effort and are With Form. Compared to them, the practice of
Mahamudra, effortless and Without Form, is superb.

9

All Dharmas (manifestations) are the expression of mind
The mind is of no-mind — void in essence
Void, yet not extinct, it manifest all
Let me observe this essence, and retain this immutable
    view.

Dharma: In Buddhism "Dharma" has two meanings. It
means "Doctrine" and is also a general term to include all
"objects, manifestations, and existences".

10

In our confusion, we consider the self-manifestation
    (which never came into being) apparent in outer ob-
    jects
In our blindness, we hold the self-awareness to be the
    real ego
Because of the Two Clingings, sentient beings wander
    in Samsara
May I cut this root of Confusion and Blindness.

Two Clingings: 1) The Clinging of Ego — clinging to the
individual conditioned and continuously changing conscious-

ness as the ego. 2) The Clinging of Dharma — clinging to objects and minifestations as real.

II

"Nothing really exists!" Buddha, himself, sees no existence
"All is not empty!" since the causes of Nirvana and Samsara exist
This, is the Middle Path of the Two-in-One, neither agreeing nor contradicting.
May I realize the discrimination-free Mind-essence.

One trying to understand Buddhism is often puzzled by its apparently contradictory statements such as, "Everything exists," "Nothing exists," "There is an ego," "There is no ego," "Meritorious deeds are beneficial," "Meritorious deeds do not exist." Such statements can be understood only if one learns to think from the standpoint of different categories of truth. For instance, in the Mundane category (or point-of-view) everything exists; but from the standpoint of Transcendental truth, nothing exists.* This distinction in Buddhist philosophy between the Mundane and Transcendental views must be kept in mind.

* We most strongly disagree with the translation of the idea that there is nothing that is not Śūnyatā as "there is nothing that exists." Śūnyatā is by no means non-existence (see our comments on notes 55 and 96). Until this is clearly understood, Zen and Mahamudra will remain word-play, only sparkling but unenlightening. Without experienced knowledge of the nature of Śūnyatā no treatise on Mahamudra is very helpful, and with such experiences, such treatises are unneccessary except as confirmation. The transcendental view is not that "nothing exists," but rather that it is not true to say either "nothing exists" or "everything exists." The view that there is nothig that exists is the "Nihilistic Extreme" criticized in Tsong-kha-pa's text of Nāropā. See note 95 and the text of page 238. *Ed.*

296

12

No one can describe *that* by saying, "This is it!"
No one can deny *that* by saying, "This is not it!"
Such is the Non-created nature of Being which trans-
cends the realm of Consciousness
May I attain, decisively, this uttermost truth.

Because "the Non-created nature of Being — Mind-essence"
lies beyond the realm of words and thoughts, it is indescribable;
therefore, it can neither be affirmed nor negated. Furthermore,
this Mind-essence though beyond words and thought is, nevertheless, all-pervading. Since it embraces all, no one can deny it
by saying of anything, "This is not the Mind-essence".

13

Ignorant of this, we drift in the ocean of Samsara
If one realizes this essence, there is no other Buddha
In the final truth, there is neither Yes nor No
May I realize the Dharma-nature — the principle of
Alaya!

The cause of Samsara is the Blindness — the subject-object
pattern of thought which does not exist in the dualistic-free
Mind-essence. Enlightenment or the attainment of Buddhahood
is nothing but the complete realization of this Mind-essence.
The experience of the final realm of truth lies beyond the opposites and thoughts of Yes and No.

14

The manifestation is mind, the Voidness is also mind
The enlightenment is mind, and the Blindness is also
mind

The springing of things is mind, and their extinction is
   also mind
May I understand that all Increasing and Decreasing
   inhere in mind.

All activities, existences, experiences, Sangsaric or Nirvanic,
all stem from the mind. If one understands and realizes the
mind, he understands and realizes all.
   'Increasing' and 'Decreasing' here means the two opposites:
the purity and defilement, the merits and sins, the enlightenment
and blindness etc.

15

Unsullied by intentional practice or meditation-with-
   effort
Away from the Worldly-Wind of distraction
With no effort and correction, I rest comfortably on
   the natural state of mind
May I find the adroit and subtle teaching of Mind Practice.

The difference between Mahamudra and other types of meditation is that in Mahamudra no meditation-effort and no correction is employed; but in most other types of meditations
such as visualizing a subject, holding the breath, meditating on
love and divine mercy a mental effort is always required*,

* Here the translator is repeating, and we fear incorrectly, a
conversation between himself and the editor, who pointed out
to him that in the true meditation of love (*not* "on" love, as it
is a meditation without seed) there is a spontaneous awakening
and melting of Bodhi Heart, distinctively characterized by the
fact that no mental effort is required. The translator, in saying
here that mental effort is required in the love-meditation,
evinces that he did not apprehend either the editor's meaning

298

concentration – choosing one and rejecting the other – is always stressed, whereas in the practice of Mahamudra, no effort whatsoever is required. After one has realized the essence of mind, concentration or non-concentration, distracted thoughts and Samadhi all become Mahamudra itself. Though for the beginners of Mahamudra, the distractions are obstacles for their meditation, they still should not '*intentionally* practice Mahamudra' or *meditate Mahamudra with effort*. Because any effort or intentional practice helps not but impedes the realization of Mind-Essence. Hence, to comfortably rest on "the awareness of mind" and observe it is the key-instruction of Mahamudra.

16

The waves of Thought-Flow – strong and weak, clear
    and dim – subside
Without disturbance the River-of-Consciousness flows
    naturally
Far from the mud of drowsiness and distraction
Let the steady and immutable Ocean of Samadhi, absorb
    me!

The chief difficulty for the meditator arises from the habitual flow-of-thought common to everyone and which, according to Buddhism, has had this characteristic *flowing* nature from the very no-beginning. Besides this uncontrollable and habitual thinking the two chief obstacles hindering the meditator are drowsiness and distraction. Only through the attaining of a steady Samadhi can these obstacles be overcome.

or that meditation. Long before the Buddhist Mahāmudra sect, the Hindu Tantra and the higher yoga practice of Patanjali taught the effortless meditation – become part and parcel of spontaneous living – "without seed" or partaking of the nature of the unconditioned.

17

Repeatedly contemplating the incontemplatable mind,
Clearly discerning the indiscernable meaning,
I forever eliminate the doubts of Yes and No
Let me surely behold my original face.

"Original face" — A symbolic term denotes the original Buddha-nature innate in every sentient being from the very no-beginning. It is interesting to note that this term, "Original face", is widely used in Chinese Zen as well as being found in the Mahamudra teaching of Tibet. [Here we have a fleeting reference to the all-important *gotra* concept. See our introduction. *Ed.*]

18

When I observe the (outer) objects, I find nothing but
    my own mind
When I observe my mind, I find nothing but the Void-
    ness
Observing both mind and objects, free am I from the
    Two Clingings
Let me realize the true nature of the illuminating Mind-
    essence.

In the first step of Mahamudra practice, the yogi is taught to observe the outer objects and to keep on observing them. Continuing in this, he will come to the actual realization (not merely through belief or intellectual reasoning) that all objects are the phenomenal reflections of mind. Then he is taught to observe the mind, itself. From this continual observance, the yogi finally arrives at the realization that mind, itself, is merely voidness. When the yogi observes both mind and objects he is liberated from the Two Clingings — the Clinging of Ego which is the subjective-illusory conception of mind, and the Clinging of Dharma, which is the objective-delusory conception of mind. When one realizes the illuminating Mind-essence, one finds

300

that neither ego nor objects exists. [The two-fold egolessness —
of persons and of things — taught also in the Lankavatara
Sutra, one of the texts basic to Mahamudra and Zen. *Ed.*]

19

Because *that* transcends the mind, it is called the Great
　Symbol
Because *that* frees from the extremes, it is called the
　Great Middle Way
Because *that* encompasses all and embrace all, it is called
　the Great Perfection
Let me understand that knowing one is knowing all.

The Great Symbol (Tib. Pyag Rgya Chen Po) literally means
"The Great Hand-Seal," referring to the custom of ancient
times when the Emperor signed imperial edicts with the print
of his hand. Mahamudra is like the imperial law which was supreme in its own realm and came to be called "The Great Symbol," being acknowledged as the teaching which could not be
violated and which surpassed all others.

Since Mind-essence is intrinsically apart from the subject-
object pattern of thought, the teaching of realizing the Mind-
essence is in this respect called the teaching of the Great Middle
Way (Tib. Dwu Ma Chen Po). Since Mind-essence intrinsically
encompasses all and its teaching is the consumation of all teachings, it is called the Great Perfection (Tib. Rdzogs Pa Chen
Po). If one succeeds in practicing one teaching, no matter by
what name it is called, he succeeds in realizing all.

20

With Clingings absent, the great bliss continuously
　arises
With no form to cling to, the radiant light outshines the
　dark hindrances

May I constantly practice the practice of no-effort –
    transcending mind
The natural and spontaneous Non-Discerning.

The sufferings and miseries of sentient beings are the result
of 'tensions' which are originated from the 'fundamental tension'.
Buddhism denominates this fundamental tension as 'clinging'
(Tib. *atsin Pa*). If one can eliminate, or even subdue this Clinging to some extent, a great bliss or Nirvanic ecstasy will arise.

Hindrances cannot exist without being embodied in forms;
therefore, if the yogi can realize in his Mahamudra meditation
that no forms whatsoever exist at all, he automatically over-
comes all hindrances.

Any effort, or intentional practice in Mahamudra meditation
is redundant, useless, and even harmful since the Mind-Essence
is ever-present and has always existed. The closest description
one can give of the experience of the enlightenment mind is the
feeling of a natural and spontaneous non-discriminating, sub-
ject-object-free awareness.

21

The craving for ecstasy and *good experience* in meditation
    naturally dissolves
The evil thoughts and blindness rest innately pure in
    Dharma-dhatu
In the "ordinary mind" there is no loss or gain, no claim
    or disclaim.
Away from words, let me realize the truth of Dharma
    Essence.

It is common for the yogi to cling to the rapture, brightness,
and pleasant visions and feelings experienced during meditation-practice. Buddha, however, has warned that those who
continue to crave such experiences cannot liberate themseves.
In practicing Mahamudra rightly, the yogi will find his craving
for such ecstasies diminish and finally dissolve.

Dharma-dhatu may be translated as "the Universal Whole" in which evil thoughts and virtues, blindness and enlightenment are innately identical*.

There is a famous Zen story that once a monk asked the Zen master Chow Chu, "What is Tao (reality or path)?" The master answered, "The ordinary mind is Tao." This "ordinary mind" can be easily misunderstood as referring to the ignorant and illusory mind of the ordinary person. However, it really means the Mind-essence which the enlightened being sees and which *is not a new mind* or something which is different in essence from the common mind. The enlightened see mind as it is — natural, common, and intrinsic. In this sense, Mahamudra denotes the Mind-essence as "the ordinary mind" wherein one finds no loss or gain, no claim or disclaim, since it excludes all discriminations and includes all differentiations.

Before actually and directly realized the Mind-essence, whatever philosophy or theories he holds ("Reality is one," "Reality is two," "Truth is this or that") are nonsense like 'Playwords' of children. When one directly and actually realizes the Mind-essence, he reaches the word-beyond or the state called here "Away From Playwords."

* Here we strongly disagree; Dharma-dhātu may *not* so be translated; defilements and the buddha-nature are not at all identical in the context of Dharma-dhātu, much less innately so. If the were, and hence if blindness and enlightenment were innately identical, there would be no point in either the translator's translation or comments, nor indeed in the existence of this or ony other book. The expression of the matter by the translator tends to confusion. We would rather see it put that the essential Buddha-nature is the self-nature of all things, and constitutes the ultimate reality stripped of all manifestation, and even the ultimate substance of those manifestations we call evil or defilements. It is important to point out, however, that in the samsara, what is evil uses the innate nature parasitically, while what is good tends to increase the explicit manifestation (nirmaṇakāya forms) of the Buddha-nature. — *Ed.*

22

Not knowing their natures are identical with Buddha's
Sentient beings wander endlessly in Sangsara
To those misery-bound who have undergone endless
  sufferings
May I forever pity ["Succour" would be a better translation then the condescending "pity," we feel. *Ed.*]
  them with the unbearable great compassion!
May I forever pity them with the unbearable great compassion!

23

Right in that moment when the Great Compassion arises
Emerges nakedly and vividly the Great Voidness.
Let me always find this unmistakable Two-in-One Path
And practice it day and night.

The teaching of Buddhism on Great Voidness and Great
Compassion is not rightly understood by most people. These
two are, actually, one entity manifestated in two aspects. But
to the Sangsaric beings, these two are seemingly irreconcilable
since in many characteristics they seem opposed, the wisdom
seems 'cold' while the compassion is 'warm'; the Voidness has
no object while the Compassion demands an object, etc. Only
the Buddha and enlightened beings can merge the two, or,
more accurately speaking, realize and unfold the identicalness
and simultaneous-existing-nature of the two. Here the author
points out that the unmistakable sign of the experience of the
enlightened being is that during the moment of enlightenment,
when the great Voidness is seen, the Great Compassion automatically arises, or, in some cases, a great and unbearable compassion, should it ever arise, will automatically bring forth the
emergence of the Great Voidness.

[In this stanza is expressed the essence of the Buddhist
Tantra: that the Śunya (or prajñā) and active Love (or vajra)

must be and are forever joined at the heart of reality. Here is the true inner meaning of the profound Yab-Yum symbolism of the phrase "the jewel (or diamond, *i.e.* upāya, vajra) is in the lotus (padma, śunya, prajñā)." In the terms of the Hindu Tantra, with its emphasis on the formative center and energy, Śakta and Śakti are forever united in a not indistinct, but rather in a dynamic polar union. *Ed.*]

24

With meditation-produced clairvoyance and other mi-
    raculous powers
May I ripen all the sentient beings and adorn Buddha's
    Pure Land
May I fulfill the compassionate vows of all Buddhas
And eventually achieve the highest enlightenment and
    perfections.

25

The power of the compassion of Buddha
The power of the loving Bodhisattvas
The power of all virtues and good deeds
May I bind these powers into one great force
By which the pure vow of mine
And the benevolent wishes of others may be readily
    fulfilled!

ERRATA
(+ = from top of page; – = from bottom)

Page	Line	Instead of	Read
17	+12, 13	Shri	Śri
17	+14, 15	Sambhogyakaya, Dharmakaya, and Nirmanakaya	Sambhogakaya, Dharmakaya, and Nirmanakaya
49	+12, 13	Śhri	Śri
93	+16		omit entire line
106	+9		insert: (see note, Folios 26-41, p. 115)
121	–8		omit "declares that"
167	–11	Whon	When
178	–10, 19*		**
179	–15	holy,	holy
182	+1	sesence	essence
194	–3, +15,	Ti Le	Thig-le
195	+1, 3	Ti Le-, hig-le	Thig-le
234	–3	Madhyamkia principle on	Mādhyamika principle in
247	–12	skhandas	skandhas
257	–12	prajña	prajñā
257	–3	Agamas	Āgamas
266	–6	A pags-pa	A̱pags-pa
274	note 42 etal.	Tsong Kapa	Tsong Khapa
278	–7	Tsogn	Tsong
288	+7, +12, +14	Māhamudrā	Māhamudrā (Reader, make this correction throughout chapter.)
289	+4	ha-	has
289	–14	ilt contains	it contains
289	–9	delete ";also"	
294	+11	Sansara	Samsāra (Reader, make this correction throughout.)
296	–3	nothig	nothing
303	+17	he	one
303	+20	word-beyond	world-beyond
303	–12	the	they